Financial Management
of Financial Institutions

PRENTICE-HALL FOUNDATIONS OF FINANCE SERIES

Herbert E. Dougall

Capital Markets and Institutions

Edwin J. Elton and Martin J. Gruber

Finance as a Dynamic Process

Jack Clark Francis and Stephen H. Archer

Portfolio Analysis

George H. Hempel and Jess B. Yawitz

Financial Management of Financial Institutions

Robert K. Jaedicke and Robert T. Sprouse

Accounting Flows: Income, Funds, and Cash

Baruch Lev

Financial Statement Analysis: A New Approach

Dileep R. Mehta

Working Capital Management

James T. S. Porterfield

Investment Decisons and Capital Costs

Alexander A. Robichek and Stewart C. Myers

Optimal Financing Decisions

James C. Van Horne

Function and Analysis of Capital Market Rates

J. Fred Weston

The Scope and Methodology of Finance

PRENTICE-HALL FOUNDATIONS OF FINANCE SERIES

Ezra Solomon, *Editor*

Financial Management of Financial Institutions

George H. Hempel

Professor of Finance
Washington University

Jess B. Yawitz

Associate Professor of Finance
and Business Economics
Washington University

PRENTICE-HALL, INC., Englewood Cliffs, New Jersey 07632

Library of Congress Cataloging in Publication Data

HEMPEL, GEORGE H.
  Financial management of financial institutions.

  (Prentice-Hall foundations of finance series)
  Bibliography: p.
  Includes index.
  1. Financial institutions — United States —
Investments — Management. I. Yawitz, Jess B.,
1946–   joint author. II. Title.
HG181.H35   658.1'5933   76-40921
ISBN 0-13-315978-7
ISBN 0-13-315960-4 pbk.

Printed in the United States of America

10 9 8 7 6 5 4 3 2 1

PRENTICE-HALL INTERNATIONAL, INC., *London*
PRENTICE-HALL OF AUSTRALIA PTY. LIMITED, *Sydney*
PRENTICE-HALL OF CANADA, LTD., *Toronto*
PRENTICE-HALL OF INDIA PRIVATE LIMITED. *New Delhi*
PRENTICE-HALL OF JAPAN, INC., *Tokyo*
PRENTICE-HALL OF SOUTHEAST ASIA PTE. LTD., *Singapore*
WHITEHALL BOOKS LIMITED, *Wellington, New Zealand*

TO

Elaine and Alice

Contents

Figures

Tables

Editor's Note

The subject matter of financial management is in the process of rapid change. A growing analytical content, virtually nonexistent ten years ago, has displaced the earlier descriptive treatment as the center of emphasis in the field.

These developments have created problems for both teachers and students. On the one hand, recent and current thinking, which is addressed to basic questions that cut across traditional divisions of the subject matter, do not fit neatly into the older structure of academic courses and texts in corporate finance. On the other hand, the new developments have not yet stabilized and as a result have not yet reached the degree of certainty, lucidity, and freedom from controversy that would permit all of them to be captured within a single, straightforward treatment at the textbook level. Indeed, given the present rate of change, it will be years before such a development can be expected.

One solution to the problem, which the present Foundations of Finance Series tries to provide, is to cover the major components of the subject through short independent studies. These individual essays provide a vehicle through which the writer can concentrate on a single sequence of ideas and thus communicate some of the excitement of current thinking and controversy. For the teacher and student, the separate self-contained books provide a flexible up-to-date survey of current thinking on each subarea covered and at the same time permit maximum flexibility in course and curriculum design.

EZRA SOLOMON

Preface

The purpose of this book is to demonstrate modern financial management techniques for financial institutions. Financial institutions are business organizations, the majority of whose assets and liabilities are financial. In this book we emphasize management of the financial resources, both assets and liabilities, of the major financial institutions in the United States. The book is written to be understandable to advanced level undergraduate students and to master's degree level graduate students. While a few symbols and elementary mathematical expressions are embodied in the text, most of this type of material is in footnotes or the appendices.

The book is organized into three basic sections. The first section contains a concise discussion of the economic role of financial institutions and the necessity that they continue to fill this role. We present a general conceptual model for the financial management of any financial institution in Chapter 2. This model abstracts from real-world constraints, such as past practices and regulatory limitations. We demonstrate that, with wealth-maximization as the primary objective, this model can be subdivided for practical financial decisions and linear programming can be used in solving many problems. In Chapter 3 we identify the basic types of assets and liabilities used by financial institutions, indicate how the returns (costs) of these securities can be measured, and integrate the conventional techniques of portfolio analysis into the institution's management decisions. These conceptual financial management ideas are followed by a discussion of the historical patterns of development of our existing financial institutions and the current regulatory environment faced by these institutions.

The second section is organized around the major types of financial institutions: commercial banks, thrift institutions (savings and loan associations, mutual savings banks, and credit unions), insurance companies, and other financial institutions (investment companies, public and private retirement funds, and finance companies). Each chapter discusses the existing asset, liability, and capital (reserve) positions of the financial institutions in light of their historical development and regulatory environment. Each chapter then demonstrates how the general conceptual model can be adapted and applied in the financial management of the discussed institution in the current environment. We also show how linear programming can be applied as a mathematical model for wealth-maximization in several of these institutions.

In the final section, we demonstrate that the environment in which financial institutions must operate is not static but dynamic. We present some of our forecasts as to how this environment may change in the next few years. While we conclude that financial institutions in tomorrow's environment will be considerably different from today's financial institutions, we strongly believe our general wealth-maximization model will remain the appropriate criteria for financial management decisions in future environments.

Numerous organizations and individuals provided essential data and helpful comments during the preparation of this book. Organizations that provided special assistance include the American Bankers Association, the Federal Deposit Insurance Corporation, the U.S. League of Savings Associations, the National Association of Savings Banks, the Credit Union National Association, the Institute of Life Insurance, the Securities and Exchange Commission, the National Consumer Finance Association, and Alfred M. Best Company, Incorporated. Individuals who gave helpful guidance or comments during the course of preparing the manuscript include Professor Alexander A. Robichek of Stanford University, Dr. George Hanc of the National Association of Savings Banks, Professor William S. Townsend of Southern Methodist University, Professor E. James Pilcher of the University of Michigan, Dr. Kenneth J. Thygerson of the U.S. Savings League, Professor Keith B. Johnson of the University of Connecticut, Professor Lyn D. Pankoff of Washington University, Professor David W. Cole of Ohio State University, Professor David Kidwell of Purdue University, and Professor Richard McEnally of the University of North Carolina. Professor Ezra Solomon of Stanford University provided general guidance as head of Prentice-Hall's Foundation of Finance series. Three graduate students at Washington University, William Marshall, Maurry Tamarkin, and John White, provided assistance in gathering information and with the linear programming examples. Mrs. Dee Goodman typed and retyped the manuscript more than either she or we would like to remember. Finally, the Graduate School of Business Administration at Washington University provided cooperation and support to allow us to complete this book. While the assistance received was essential, we hold ourselves responsible for any remaining errors and for any opinions presented unless so indicated in the text.

GEORGE H. HEMPEL
JESS B. YAWITZ

Financial Management
of Financial Institutions

The Economic Role
of Financial Institutions

SERVICES provided by financial institutions have become so commonplace
in the United States that we sometimes forget just how recent their development is in our economy and that they are absent in many areas of the world
today. In this chapter we establish the relative size of the financial institutions discussed in this book and consider their role in a market economy.
The economic role of financial institutions is emphasized not only because
of their importance as an ingredient in economic growth, but, also because
an understanding of this role is essential for their proper financial management.

Financial Institutions: Definition and Types

Financial institutions are firms that supply financial services to the
economic community. Their assets are almost exclusively financial in
nature. These assets consist primarily of money owed them by nonfinancial economic units such as households, businesses, and governments;
secondarily, of money owed them by other financial institutions; and, corporate stock. The composition of their assets distinguishes them from
other productive units of the economy whose assets are composed of tangi-
ble assets such as land, plant, equipment, and inventory. Most financial
institutions issue contractual obligations in order to obtain the funds to
purchase these financial assets. The institution's net worth (or reserve)
position, which results from the sale of stock or the accumulation of re-

1

tained earnings, represents a relatively minor source of funds. Indeed, it can be argued that financial institutions with the mutual or trusteed forms of organization, as opposed to the corporate form, have only obligations and no net worth.

We have limited the financial institutions discussed in this book to major financial institutions whose primary objectives are (or probably should be) to maximize the wealth of their shareholders. In this way, we are able to analyze the financial institution's objective function with the same basic framework that has proven to be valid for the typical nonfinancial firm. The shareholders may be holders of common stock in the corporate form or organization, deposit or policyholders in the mutual form, or beneficiaries in the trusteed form. (We discuss why we believe wealth-maximization is appropriate for each of these forms of organization in Chapter 2.) Financial institutions whose primary objectives are public policy (even though some are partially privately owned) are not specifically discussed, but some of the management strategies proposed should prove useful in their management. Financial institutions not specifically covered include: mortgage banks, investment banks, dealers and brokers, the Federal Reserve System, the federal land banks, and federal lending agencies such as the Federal National Mortgage Association, the Export-Import Bank, the Commodity Credit Corporation, the Federal Home Loan Banks, and the Rural Electrification Administration. The number and the asset size of the financial institutions in the United States in 1974 appear in Table 1-1. We relate these figures to aggregate economic measures after the discussion of the economic role of financial institutions.

The Role of Financial Instituions

The primary role of financial institutions can be stated very simply — to fill the diverse needs of both ultimate borrowers and ultimate lenders in our economy. Perhaps the best way to understand this important function is to first consider an economy without financial institutions. The simplest such economy is one in which goods and services are exchanged in a barter system; by definition, there is neither money nor other financial assets or liabilities. There are, therefore, no financial institutions. The exchange of economic goods and services takes place in kind. In such an economy any increase in real capital (net investment) would have to be accompanied by simultaneous savings decisions by the investing unit. All economic units would be required to have balanced budgets at all times. External financing is, therefore, absent in a barter economy. A typical exchange in a barter economy involves two economic units and two goods or services. With such an inefficient means of exchange, one would expect the level of capital formation and income would be quite low. Capital formation would be tied rigidly to the distribution of current income and would not be responsive to the profitability criterion.

A more advanced, though still rudimentary, economy might be one in which there exists sufficient money to facilitate transactions but in which

TABLE 1-1   Size of Financial Institutions, December 31, 1974

Type of Institution	Number of Institutions (in thousands)	Assets (in $ billions)
Commercial banks	14.5[a]	$ 916.3
Savings and loan associations	5.1[b]	295.6
Mutual savings banks	0.5[c]	109.6
Credit unions	23.0	32.0
Life insurance companies	1.8	263.3
Property insurance companies	3.0	81.3
Investment companies	0.7	62.7
Private pension funds	170.0	133.7
Public pension funds	2.1	178.5
Finance companies	3.5	93.4
Investment bankers, dealers, and brokers	0.8	16.8
Others[d]	3.3	593.1
All financial institutions	228.3	$2,776.3

Sources: Federal Reserve Bulletins; 1975 Savings and Loan Fact Book; 1975 National Fact Book of Mutual Savings Banking; CUNA 1975 Yearbook; 1975 Life Insurance Fact Book; Best's Aggregates and Averages, Property-Liability, 1975; Wiesenberger's Investment Companies for 1975; SEC Statistical Bulletins; 1975 Finance Facts Yearbook; Social Security Bulletins; Treasury Bulletins; and Governmental Finance.

[a] The total number of banking offices, including branches, was 42,891.

[b] The total number of association offices, including branches, was 13,922.

[c] The total number of savings bank offices, including branches, was 2,121.

[d] Includes the Federal Reserve System, government lending institutions, trusts, postal savings, and mortgage companies which are not covered in detail.

no other types of financial instruments are available. In such an economy, every unit—household, business enterprise, and government—would still spend roughly as much as it receives and there would be no need for financial intermediaries. In this situation, no economic unit would have external financing—its receipts and any cash balances would have to suffice to finance not only current consumption but also capital expenditures on plant, equipment, housing, and inventory. Enterprise would be severely restrained since economic units with productive ideas and/or a willingness to take greater risks in the ownership of real assets would be unable to expand their holdings of real assets beyond their own net worth. Accumulation would also be constrained because economic units desirous of holding their net worth (accumulated savings) in assets of relatively stable value could only apply their savings to a limited menu of assets—money or perhaps some types of physical capital. While there might be some division of labor in the separation of household and business activities, such an economy would tend to be relatively inefficient in allocating resources and would tend, therefore, to have a low rate of economic growth.[1]

The role of financial liabilities (contractual obligations) in the saving-investment process can be demonstrated quite simply. Two cases are con-

[1]For a more thorough discussion of the inefficiencies and low growth in an economy without financial claims, see James C. Van Horne, Functions and Analysis of Capital Market Rates (Englewood Cliffs, N.J.: Prentice-Hall, 1970), pp. 2–11.

sidered: with financial institutions and without financial institutions. In the simplified economy there are two sectors, households and businesses. Households receive in income ($100 of money) an amount equal to the total value of the goods and services produced in the business sector. This income can be from wages, profits, rents, or interest. Figure 1-1 portrays the initial position of the household and business sectors after production has taken place. The first intersectoral flow involves an exchange of money ($80) for consumer goods. (Figure 1-2) After the consumption decision, households desire to save $20 while business desires to invest $20. In an economy without financial liabilities there would be no means whereby the ultimate savers could be matched with ultimate investors. An economy with primary financial liabilities allows for such a matching of interests. Figure 1-3 portrays the transfer of $20 in purchasing power (money) from the household sector to a $20 financial liability on the business sector. After this exchange the business sector has sufficient purchasing power to undertake the desired $20 investment expenditure. The relevant portions of the household and business balance sheets are present in Figure 1-4.

Figure 1-1. Initial Allocation of Purchasing Power and Product

Figure 1-2. Households Purchase Product From Business for Consumption

Figure 1-3. Households Purchase Primary Securities from Business to Allow for Investment

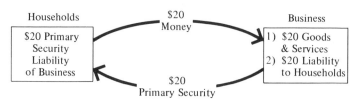

Figure 1-4. Household and Business Sector Balance Sheets
Without Financial Intermediaries

Households			Business	
Assets	Liabilities		Assets	Liabilities
$20 Primary Security			$20 Goods & Services (Real Capital)	$20 Primary Security

The existence of primary liabilities in the economy would be expected to stimulate capital accumulation by facilitating both saving and investment. Savers are not forced to hold net worth solely in the form of real assets since they can purchase more liquid financial assets that carry a claim on the earnings from business sector assets. This broadening of the available menu of assets to savers would be expected to increase saving for any given level of income. Similarly, the possibility of external financing allows the business sector to undertake profitable investment opportunities which could not be financed out of retained earnings. In this way, overall investment is expanding since the system of funds transfer allocates purchasing power to the most efficient users. As such, the ability of both sectors to exchange a contractual security for purchasing power effectively expands the budget constraint facing each economic unit.

There are two basic forms of *primary direct liabilities* that allow deficit units to obtain funds from surplus units—borrowings and equity. *Borrowings* typically represent a series of fixed cash flow commitments with a lump sum payment at maturity. Borrowings allow deficit units to finance the holding of real assets in excess of their net worth and to provide an alternative lower-risk form of wealth for savers to store purchasing power. *Equities,* on the other hand, represent a limited pro-rata ownership in business deficit units. These securities have neither a maturation date nor a specified cash flow commitment. Furthermore, the equity claim on assets and income is secondary to all borrowings. Equities do, however, represent a marketable property right entitling the owner to a share of any dividend declared, a share in assets less borrowings if the unit is dissolved, and a pro-rata vote in selecting management.

While the ability to emit primary liabilities to finance investment would result in a greater rate of capital accumulation in the economy, there would still be a need for financial institutions. When deficit units are unable to fund projects with financial instruments at acceptable financial terms, their desired expenditures will be limited. Similarly, surplus units unable to find suitable assets might curtail saving in favor of current consumption. Differences between surplus and deficit units' desired terms of financing would also tend to depress both the saving-investment flow and the growth rate in the economy. Such differences might include size, maturity, legal character, marketability, liquidity, divisibility, redeemability, and risk.

The next (and, at this time, final) step toward a fully developed financial system is the creation of institutions whose primary purpose is to satisfy the desires of surplus and deficit units. Two basic institutions have been developed. The first involves *brokers* or *agents* who serve as go-betweens and receive commissions for their services. This service helps match deficit and surplus units but does not overcome the differences that may exist between them. The second institution involves middlemen, called *intermediaries,* who facilitate the flow of funds between surplus and deficit units. In so doing, the financial intermediary creates two separate markets. The financial intermediary purchases primary securities from the deficit units and emits a *secondary indirect liability* to surplus units. In this way, the financial intermediary is able to tailor its asset and liability structure so as to satisfy the desires of both the ultimate borrowers and ultimate lenders in the economy. Financial intermediaries simply substitute their own more desirable (to the surplus units) financial liabilities for the financial liabilities of the deficit unit. Deficit units are assisted in finding funds in the desirable amount and form.

The effect of financial institutions on the flow of funds is simply to add an additional stage in the exchange of purchasing power between households and businesses. In Figure 1-5, the financial institution first emits a secondary liability on itself by accepting the $20 in money held by households. This purchasing power is then transferred to the business sector for a primary liability on the business sector. The business sector then has the ability to finance its desired investment expenditure. The relevant portions of the household, financial institution, and business sectors'

Figure 1-5. The Role of Financial Intermediaries
in the Saving-Investment Process

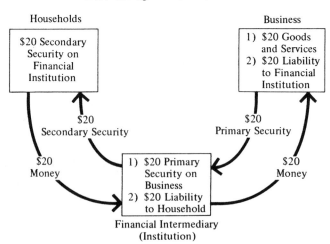

balance sheets are illustrated in Figure 1-6. Note that the form of financial asset held by the household sector has changed from a direct claim on the business sector to a claim on the financial institution.

Figure 1–6. Household, Business, and Financial Institution
Balance Sheets

Households		Financial Institutions		Business	
Assets	Liabilities	Assets	Liabilities	Assets	Liabilities
$20 Secondary Security		$20 Primary Security	$20 Secondary Security	$20 Goods and Services (Real Capital)	$20 Primary Security

In a fully developed financial system, potential surplus units can choose among a wide variety of alternative financial assets — including primary securities of deficit units and the numerous liability forms offered by financial intermediaries. Deficit units, often assisted by a broker or agent, can generally acquire purchasing power in a desirable form, either directly from surplus units or, more commonly, from a financial intermediary. Liquidity and marketability of the securities created in the direct or indirect flows between surplus and deficit units are vastly improved by the existence of a secondary market (the New York Stock Exchange is an example) in which such securities may be traded. Such a setting encourages economic efficiency since the allocation of financing is based on a unit's ability to pay and profitability rather than on the form of financing. This greater efficiency in financing would be expected to stimulate both capital accumulation and growth in the economy.

The economic role of financial institutions (and the financing instruments they create) can now be summarized. Some financial institutions aid the saving-investment process by serving as brokers or agents. Most financial institutions aid economic growth much more with their efforts to intermediate the saving-investment function. *Intermediation* affects this process in several ways. First, it facilitates the separation of the saving decision from the investment decision. Each unit is not required to spend exactly what it earns in each period. In this way the budget constraint is expanded. Spending units can escape the straitjacket of balanced budgets so as to allocate their spending more efficiently. Second, intermediation encourages saving by providing a varied menu of financial assets particularly suited to the needs and/or desires of surplus units. Third, intermediation encourages investment by providing a variety of available sources of funds to the deficit units. Fourth, by making borrowing and lending more attractive, the full-employment saving and investment rate and, therefore, the growth rate of capital and income, are increased over that which would exist without financial intermediation.

The intermediation process of financial institutions also contributes to economic growth in several more subtle but also important ways. Intermediation assists in the separation of administration and ownership of wealth. Specialization of activities increases productivity. Financial institutions also tend to reduce risks to both surplus and deficit units. The uncertainties associated with direct relationships between surplus and deficit units become predictable within reasonable limits when financial institutions work with portfolios of assets and liabilities. By pooling their assets (primarily liabilities of deficit units), financial institutions reduce the risks of default (on the institutions' liabilities) to surplus units. The institutions can also increase liquidity, marketability, and divisibility of their liabilities because the combination of outflow demands of numerous holders is more predictable than the demand by one or a few holders. Deficit units have a greater availability of funds in a form better suited to their payment capability. Thus, financial institutions contribute to the real productivity of the economy and to the overall standard of living since they are able to satisfy, simultaneously, the needs and preferences of both surplus and deficit units.

It may be argued further that specialization of labor and efficiency of size and scale allow financial institutions to act in a cost-reducing role, with surplus units receiving a higher net return and deficit units paying less for their funds than would be possible in the absence of the intermediary role of financial institutions. One could also argue that financial institutions save on the required search cost for both borrowers and lenders. In such a system the task of asset selection for portfolio management is delegated to a professional specialist. Financial institutions with large asset holdings and contiguous operations possess a trading advantage in lower per unit transaction costs over smaller, nonfinancial units. Deficit units are not required to hire specialists for their generally irregular borrowing (or equity-raising) pattern but can rely on specialists hired by financial institutions.

To make Figure 1-5 even more representative of the actual financial flows of the United States, we would have to add five additional financial considerations which further enhance the role of financial intermediaries. Two previously mentioned phenomena are the existence of secondary markets and changes in a unit's desired monetary balance. First, the existence of secondary markets makes the asset holdings of financial institutions and surplus units more marketable and more liquid. Both institutions and surplus units now have an expanded list of options from which to choose when establishing their portfolios. Second, deficit units will be more likely to receive funds in a highly usable form since institutions and surplus units can adjust their portfolios fairly easily. Changes in the monetary balances desired by economic units have a minor impact on flows into financial institutions and on the desires of surplus and deficit units.

A third advantage of financial intermediaries is that the monetary policies of the Federal Reserve are often implemented through at least one of our financial institutions — commercial banks — and these policies strongly affect most of the other insitutions. An increase in bank reserves brought about by the Federal Reserve may stimulate growth because deficit units are able to borrow funds in excess of what surplus units make available. In this way, financial institutions have a key role in the transmission of monetary policy to the real sector. Such policies have a marked impact on the interest rates available to surplus and deficit units, as well as to financial institutions.

Fourth, fiscal and debt management policies of the federal government have an impact on the size and composition of the national debt. The taxation aspect of fiscal policy has an additional multiplier effect on the level of disposable income which, in turn, tends to affect the flow of funds to financial institutions from financial intermediaries.

Finally, financial flows into and out of the United States from foreign countries have both a direct and an indirect effect on financial institutions. The direct effect occurs when foreign units invest directly in U. S. economic units or deposit or withdraw funds from U. S. financial institutions. Overall foreign prosperity in trade has an indirect impact on our economy and its financial institutions. In the short run the direct and indirect flows often exert a significant effect on the economy and on financial institutions.

Measuring the Size and Impact of Financial Intermediation

We now present some summary data which indicates the size and impact of financial intermediation. Table 1-2 contains data on the financial assets and liabilities for the private nonfinancial sectors of our economy and for our various financial institutions as of December 31, 1973. The data in the top half of Table 1-2 demonstrate that household units have been the only surplus nonfinancial sector. Households have provided the majority of the funds for the deficit sectors — business, state and local governments, and the federal government — through financial intermediaries rather than through financial liabilities for these deficit units. As expected, over 80 percent of all financial liabilities for the nonfinancial sector are owned by financial intermediaries rather than by nonfinancial units. The bottom portion of Table 1-2 presents the primary financial assets and liabilities for our principal private, nonbank financial institutions. These data indicate the types of claims employed in order to attract funds from the various financial sectors and the forms of financial assets employed to finance the nonfinancial sectors.

Figure 1-7 provides a graphical presentation of the relative size of the primary private financial institutions in 1900, 1929, 1964, and 1974. Particularly noteworthy is the decline in relative importance of commercial banks (from 66 percent to 41 percent of total assets of all institutions from 1900 to 1964, then recovering slightly to 42 percent by 1974); the decline in

TABLE 1-2 Financial Assets and Liabilities, December 31, 1973
(Amounts outstanding in billions of dollars)
(A) All sectors

Line	Transaction Category	Households A	Households L	Business A	Business L	State & Local Govts A	State & Local Govts L	P.D.N.F. Total A	P.D.N.F. Total L	Rest of World A	Rest of World L	U.S. Govt A	U.S. Govt L	Fin. Total A	Fin. Total L	Fed. Spons. Credit Agencies A	Fed. Spons. Credit Agencies L	Monetary Authority A	Monetary Authority L	Commercial Banks A	Commercial Banks L	Private Nonbank Finance A	Private Nonbank Finance L	Table[1] A	Table[1] L	Discrepancies A	Discrepancies L
1	Total assets	2302.3		528.0		98.5		2928.8		200.8		102.9		2041.8		79.0		105.5		755.2		1102.0		5274.2		26.2	
2	Total liabilities		661.1		925.1		202.4		1788.6		194.2		408.6		1926.5		77.5		105.7		714.5		1028.8		4317.3		
3	Gold													11.6				11.6									
4	Official foreign exchange									47.3		2.3		*				*						61.1	*		
5	IMF position										.6	.6												.6	.6		
6	Treasury currency												7.4	9.1				9.1						9.1	7.4		
7	Demand dep. and currency	170.2		55.4		14.7		240.3		10.6		12.6		19.4	298.5	.3			65.0	1.0	233.5	18.2		283.0	298.5	-1.7	
8	Private domestic	170.2		55.4		14.7		240.3						19.4	275.1	.3			61.8	1.0	213.3	18.2		259.8	275.1	15.4	
9	U.S. Government											12.6			12.7				2.9		9.9			12.6	12.7		
10	Foreign									10.6					10.6				.3		10.3			10.6	10.6	.1	
11	Time and savings accounts	635.6		21.5		44.4		701.5		12.8		.4		1.2	715.9						367.7	1.2	348.2	715.9	715.9		
12	At commercial banks	287.8		21.5		44.4		353.7		12.8		.4		.8	367.7						367.7	.8		367.7	367.7		
13	At savings institutions	347.8						347.8						.4	348.2							.4	348.2	348.2	348.2		
14	Life insurance reserves	150.3						150.3					7.6		142.7								142.7	150.3	150.3		
15	Pension fund reserves	307.8						370.8					35.4		272.4								272.4	307.8	307.8		
16	Interbank claims													57.1	57.1			4.4	37.8	52.8	19.4			57.1	57.1		
17	Corporate shares	744.4						744.4		24.8				198.7	46.5					.7		198.0	46.5	968.0	46.5		
18	Other credit mkt. instr.	256.4	634.8	74.5	679.2	35.7	195.5	366.5	1507.5	61.5	68.5	65.2	354.4	1646.3	209.1	75.9	68.9	80.6		653.5	23.8	836.4	116.4	2139.6	2139.6		
19	U.S. Govt. securities	105.3		5.4		31.0		141.7		54.8		*	353.1	225.6	68.9	4.0	68.9	80.5		88.8		52.4		422.1	422.1		
20	State & local govt. oblig.	50.5		4.0	2.4	2.5	187.6	57.1	190.0					132.9						95.7		37.3		190.0	190.0		
21	Corp. & fgn. bonds	56.8			207.5			56.8	207.5	2.3	16.6	3.9		204.9	39.9					6.2	4.1	198.7	35.8	264.0	264.0		
22	Home mortgages	10.1	379.0		5.3			12.3	384.4			4.8		374.1	4.7	31.6				68.0		274.6	4.7	390.3	390.3		
23	Other mortgages	28.0	24.5	31.9	223.4	2.2		28.0	247.9				1.3	216.5	1.5	15.4				51.1		150.0	1.5	249.3	249.3		
24	Consumer credit		180.5	31.9				31.9	180.5		13.0			148.6						81.2		67.4		180.5	180.5		
25	Bank loans n.e.c.		24.7		180.5				205.2					255.9	37.6					255.9	8.0		29.6	255.9	255.9		
26	Other loans	5.7	26.1	33.1	60.1		5.9	38.8	92.0	4.4	38.9	56.5		87.7	56.5	24.9		.1		6.7	11.7	56.0	44.8	187.4	187.4		
27	Security credit	4.8	13.1					4.8	13.1	.3	.2			24.2	16.0					15.1		9.1		29.3	29.3		
28	To brokers and dealers	4.8						4.8		.3				10.8	16.0					10.8				16.0	16.0		
29	To others		13.1						13.1		.2			13.4						4.3		9.1		13.4	13.4		
30	Taxes payable				15.6			3.7	15.6			11.9		*	3.0						.8		1.8	15.6	18.5	2.9	
31	Trade credit	6.8		240.9	212.6	8.7	8.9	240.9	228.3	8.3	9.0	4.3	9.5	6.5										260.0	240.9		-19.1
32	Miscellaneous	32.8	6.4	135.8	17.7			168.6	24.1	35.1	115.8	5.4	.3	67.7	165.3	2.8	8.6	.1	2.7	32.2	69.3	32.7	84.7	276.9	305.5	28.6	

*Less than $.05 billion

Footnotes on following page.

Financial Assets and Liabilities, December 31, 1973—Continued
(Amounts outstanding in billions of dollars)
(B) Private nonbank financial institution

Transaction Category	Total		Savings and Loan Asns.		Mutual Savings Banks		Credit Unions		Life Insurance Cos.		Private Pension Funds		State and Local Govt. Retirement Funds		Other Insurance Cos.		Finance Cos.		Real Estate Investment Trusts		Open-end Investment Cos.		Security Brokers and Dealers		
	A	L	A	L	A	L	A	L	A	L	A	L	A	L	A	L	A	L	A	L	A	L	A	L	
1 Total assets¹	1102.0		272.4		106.6		24.6		244.6		133.3		81.6		68.8		88.4		17.0		46.5		18.4		1
2 Total liabilities¹		1028.8		255.3		99.0		24.6		231.5		133.3		81.6		46.1		80.4		14.4		46.5		16.1	2
3 Demand deposits and currency	18.2		3.4						2.1		2.3		1.0		1.5		3.5				1.2		1.1		3
4 Time and savings accounts	1.2	348.2			1.2	96.3	1.0	24.6																	4
5 At commercial banks	.8				.8		.4																		5
6 At savings institutions	.4	348.2		227.3	.8	96.3	.4	24.6																	6
7 Life insurance reserves		142.7								142.7															7
8 Pension fund reserves		272.4								57.5		133.3		81.6											8
9 Corporate shares²	198.0	46.5	22.0		4.0				25.9		89.2		18.6		19.6						38.3	46.5	2.4		9
10 Other credit mkt. instr.	836.4	116.4	257.5	22.8	98.2		23.2		204.6		36.8		62.1		41.1		84.9		15.1		7.0		5.8		10
11 U.S. Govt. securities³	52.4				7.1		2.6		4.4		4.3		4.6		3.4						1.2		2.0		11
12 State & local govt. secs.	37.3				.9				3.4				1.4		30.4								1.1		12
13 Corp. and fgn. bonds	198.7	35.8			13.1				92.5		29.8		49.4		7.2			33.9		1.9	4.2		2.6		13
14 Home mortgages	274.6	4.7	188.1	4.7	44.2		1.0		22.0								12.5		4.1						14
15 Other mortgages	150.0	1.5	44.1		29.0				59.2		2.7		6.7		.2				11.0	1.5					15
16 Consumer credit	67.4		2.6		1.7		19.6										43.4								16
17 Bank loans n.e.c.		29.6																20.5		7.0					17
18 Other loans	56.0	44.8		2.1	2.1				23.2								20.0	25.7		4.0	1.6				18
19 Security credit	9.1	16.0		15.1																			9.1	16.0	19
20 To brokers and dealers		16.0																						16.0	20
21 Other	9.1																						9.1		21
22 Taxes payable		1.8	.2							.8						.3		.4							22
23 Trade credit⁴	6.5														6.5										23
24 Miscellaneous	32.7	84.7	11.5	5.8	2.5	2.6			12.0	30.5	4.9				45.8				1.9				.2	.2	24

Source: Federal Reserve Bulletin, October 1974 (Washington, D.C.: Board of Governors of Federal Reserve, 1974).

¹Excess of total assets over liabilities consists of gold (row 3) and corporate shares (row 17) other than investment co. shares less total discrepancies (row 1), which are not included in sector assets.

²Assets shown at market value; nonbank finance liability is redemption value of shares of open-end investment companies. No specific liability is attributed to issuers of stocks other than open-end investment companies for amounts outstanding.

³Includes savings bonds, other nonmarketable debt held by the public, issues by agencies in the budget (CCC, Export-Import Bank, GNMA, TVA, FHA) and by sponsored credit agencies in financial sectors, and loan participation certificates. Postal saving system deposits are included in line 32.

⁴Business asset is corporate only. Noncorporate trade credit is deducted in liability total to conform to quarterly flow tables.

Figure 1-7. Assets of Selected Financial Institutions,
1900, 1929, 1964, and 1974

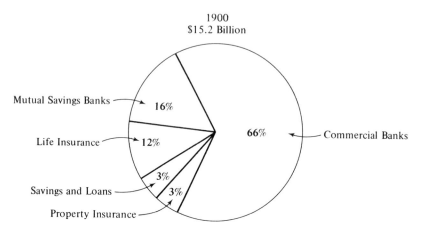

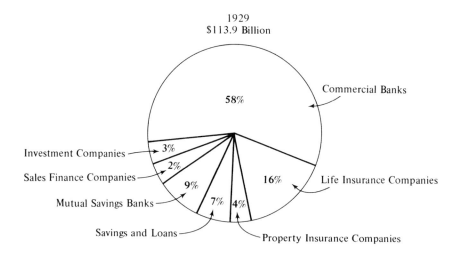

relative importance of mutual savings banks; and the increase in the relative share of pension funds and savings and loan associations. Greater detail will be provided on the growth of individual institutions in the chapters dealing with specific institutions.

Table 1-3 presents a summary statement of estimated net sources and uses of funds in the financial markets in 1974. Notice the degree to which financial institutions provided funds to the users—73.4 percent of all sources were institution-generated in 1974, a year purported to have substantial disintermediation.[2] This figure also illustrates the relative im-

---

[2]Earlier editions of Bankers Trust Company's *The Investment Outlook* indicated financial institutions provided over 90 percent of total use of funds in eight of the preceding ten years.

Figure 1-7 (Continued). Assets of Selected Financial Institutions,
1900, 1929, 1964, and 1974

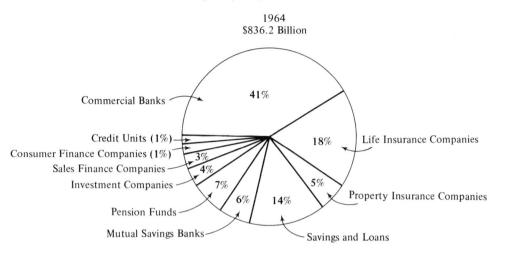

1964
$836.2 Billion

Commercial Banks

41%

Credit Units (1%)
Consumer Finance Companies (1%)
Sales Finance Companies
Investment Companies

3%
4%
7%

18%   Life Insurance Companies

5%

6%   14%

Property Insurance Companies

Pension Funds

Mutual Savings Banks

Savings and Loans

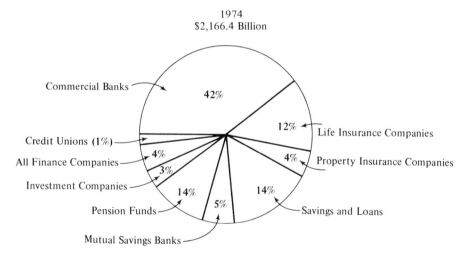

1974
$2,166.4 Billion

Commercial Banks

42%

12%   Life Insurance Companies

Credit Unions (1%)
All Finance Companies
Investment Companies

4%
3%

4%   Property Insurance Companies

14%

14%

Pension Funds

5%

Savings and Loans

Mutual Savings Banks

Sources: Federal Reserve Bulletins; 1975 Savings and Loan Fact Book; 1975 National Fact Book of Mutual Savings Banking; CUNA 1975 Yearbook; 1975 Life Insurance Fact Book; Best's Aggregates and Averages, Property-Liability, 1975; Wiesenberger's *Investment Companies* for 1975; *SEC Statistical Bulletins; 1975 Finance Facts Yearbook; Social Security Bulletins; Treasury Bulletins;* and, *Governmental Finance.*

portance of the various financial institutions and the markets into which the funds are channeled. The reader should note that the data in Table 1-3 are computed on a net basis; that is, only the net changes in assets and liabilities are taken into account. Thus, for example, the amount of gross

Table 1-3 Projected Sources and Uses of Funds, 1976
(Amounts in $ billions)

Sources of Funds (Net)	Predicted Amount	Percent of Total	Uses of Funds (Net)	Predicted Amount	Percent of Total
Life insurance companies	$ 18.6	8.5	Corporate bonds	$ 18.0	8.2
Private noninsured pension funds	14.0	6.4	Term loans by banks	6.1	2.8
State and local government retirement funds	10.4	4.7	Short-term loans by banks	7.5	3.4
Fire and casualty insurance companies	6.5	3.0	Net trade credit of non-financial corporations	7.5	3.4
			Finance company loans to business	2.5	1.1
Savings and loan associations	38.4	17.5	Total business debt	$ 41.6	18.9
Mutual savings banks	8.6	3.9	Corporate stocks	11.0	5.0
Finance companies	6.0	2.7	Open market paper	2.0	0.9
Investment companies	5.4	2.5	Consumer credit	15.7	7.1
Real estate investment trusts	− 2.7	− 1.2	State and local government securities	13.2	6.0
Credit unions	4.8	2.2			
Commercial banks	55.5	25.2			
Total — Financial institutions	$165.5	75.3	U.S. government securities	66.5	30.2
			Real estate mortgages	61.8	28.1
Nonfinancial corporations	17.9	8.1	All other	8.1	3.7
All other	36.5	16.6			
Total	$219.9	100.0	Total	$219.9	100.0

Source: Credit and Capital Markets 1976 (New York: Bankers Trust Company, February 1976).

mortgage credit extended is considerably in excess of the $56.5 billion shown in the table.

Figure 1-8 illustrates the general correlation between the growth of total debt (including equities), the financial assets of financial institutions, and the value of the nation's production of goods and services as measured by gross national product (GNP). Although these aggregates have moved roughly together since the turn of the century, they have not grown steadily. While all three have experienced major upsurgings in wartime, the only period in which assets of financial intermediaries declined was in the early 1930s. The growth of debt, financial intermediation, and economic activity has been most stable from 1950 through the mid-1970s. In spite of some differences, it seems apparent that the growth of financial intermediation, the increase in direct and indirect debt (arising from intermediation) and the growth of the economy are closely associated.

Conclusions

This chapter presented an overview of the topics to be discussed in the remainder of the text. We have presented a conceptual discussion of the important role of financial institutions in our economy and presented some evidence to support the interrelationship between financial institutions and economic growth. It is important to remember that financial institutions are service organizations. As such, they are unable to add directly to the wealth of the economy. Therefore, they must seek their justification in the value of the services they render. Only by supplying a desired economic function can the financial management of a financial institution be successful. In Chapter 2 we demonstrate how an individual financial institution can perform its economic role and carry out its financial management in a way that satisfies its objective function, that is, maximize the wealth of its shareholders.

Chapter 1

Review Questions

1. What are the two major differences between financial intermediaries and other firms?
2. What is the primary role of financial intermediaries? Given this role, how do financial intermediaries affect the saving-investment process?
3. Debts, or financial liabilities, are common in our economy today. What specific advantages do financial instruments afford, and how do they foster economic growth? Answer this by comparing an economy which has financial liabilities to one which lacks financial liabilities.
4. There are two general types of financial liabilities — primary (direct) liabilities and secondary (indirect) liabilities. Distinguish between the two types of liabilities in a funds-flow context. What are the two basic types of primary liabilities? Distinguish between the two.

Figure 1-8. Growth of Total Debt, Financial Institution Assets,
and Economic Activity

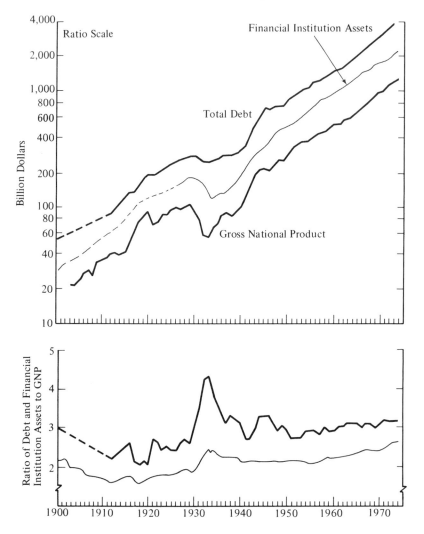

5. Financial liabilities stimulate capital formulation, saving, and economic growth. What, then, are the advantages of having financial intermediaries in the economic system as opposed to just having financial liabilities and no intermediaries?
6. What are the five factors affecting the funds flows of financial institutions? Which factors do you believe will become more important in the future?

Selected References

The First Boston Corporation. *Handbook of Securities of the U. S. Government and Federal Agencies,* 26th ed. New York: The First Boston Corporation, 1974.

Gurley, John and Shaw, Edward. "Financial Intermediaries and the Savings-Investment Process." *The Journal of Finance,* May 1956, pp. 257–276.

————· "Financial Aspects of Economic Development." *American Economic Review,* September 1955, pp. 515–538.

Hamburger, M. J. "Household Demand for Financial Assets." *Econometrica,* January 1968, pp. 97–118.

Henning, C. N., et al. *Financial Markets and the Economy.* Englewood Cliffs, N. J.: Prentice-Hall, 1969.

Ludtke, J. *The American Financial System: Markets and Institutions.* 2d ed. Boston: Allyn & Bacon, 1967.

Pyle, D. H. "On the Theory of Financial Intermediation." *The Journal of Finance,* June 1971, pp. 737–747.

Robinson, Roland I. and Wrightman, D. *Financial Markets: The Accumulation and Allocation of Wealth.* New York: McGraw-Hill, 1974.

Smith, Paul F. *Economics of Financial Institutions and Markets.* Homewood, Ill: Irwin, 1971.

Van Horne, James C. *Function and Analysis of Capital Market Rates.* Englewood Cliffs, N. J.: Prentice-Hall, 1970.

Woodworth, Walter G. *The Money Market and Monetary Management,* 2d ed. New York: Harper & Row, 1972.

A General Financial Management Model
for Financial Institutions

Introduction

THE basic purpose of this chapter is to provide a general conceptual model for the financial management of any financial institution. This material is somewhat abstract since we demonstrate how a financial institution should be managed, without regard to historical precedent or regulatory limitations. The concepts presented, however, should prove useful for the actual management decisions of financial institutions which are, of course, subject to real-world constraints. We also demonstrate how the technique of linear programming can be successfully employed to model actual decisions facing managers of financial institutions. The application of these management concepts to the decisions made for specific financial institutions appears in Chapters 5 through 8.

The Importance of Providing Needed Economic Services

It is important that the manager of any financial institution keep in mind that in order to exist the institution must provide needed economic services. While such a statement might seem trivial, it cannot be over-emphasized. As we discussed in the preceding chapter, every financial institution serves two markets, one for surplus units supplying funds to the financial institution and another for deficit units seeking funds from the financial institution. A viable financial institution must compete success-

18

fully, that is, satisfy some units in both of these markets, in order to earn an adequate return on its shareholders' investment (or for its shareholders' reserve position). In the following paragraphs we discuss some of the difficulties encountered in competing effectively in these two markets.

Most financial institutions obtain the majority of their funds from surplus units. They must, therefore, package their liabilities into forms that appeal to these surplus units. At first pass this might seem easy, since the liabilities of each financial institution possess some distinctive features which cannot be duplicated exactly by any other institution. The location, size, reputation, and policies of the institution often become a part of many of the liabilities that it issues. Such distinctive features, however, often are not sufficient in and of themselves. Surplus units in a dynamic economic environment have changing needs and tastes. Competition among financial institutions has become fierce. In tight financial periods like 1973–1974, financial institutions may be forced to compete with deficit units attempting to attract funds directly from surplus units. In 1973–1974 this competitive pressure was evidenced by a variety of new forms of financing (for example, seven- to ten-year corporate notes or variable rate mortgages) as well as open attempts by deficit units to obtain funds (such as small denomination securities issued by both businesses and the federal government). Clearly, financial management must be innovative. Every financial institution must offer a sufficient return in a form desired by surplus units. In our opinion, the pressure for further changes in the forms of financial institution liabilities will increase in coming years.

The packaging of funds at a sufficiently low cost and in a form acceptable to deficit units is often as difficult as satisfying surplus units. Large, credit-worthy deficit units are generally sought by financial institutions and are directly solicited by some surplus units. For example, a large business seeking short-term funds typically is faced with a choice among several banking groups as well as the commercial paper market. Differentiation of product in this market is more difficult because factors such as location and reputation in the community are less important to deficit units. A financial institution must generally offer the desired amount and type of funds, substantial flexibility in borrowing arrangements, and competitive rates. Even in financially tight periods when financial institutions have access to a large number of potential deficit units, many institutions are forced by competitive pressures to offer the desired quantities in a desirable form at a competitive rate in order to hold existing customers and maintain their industry position. While changes in the desired form of financial institutions' assets (liabilities to deficit units) seem likely to continue, an even greater problem with such assets is to employ them at a rate sufficiently high to recover all costs, including an adequate return to shareholders.

This concern brings us to the heart of the problem facing managers of financial institutions. A financial institution must pay a sufficiently high return in order to attract funds (which must be desirably packaged) from surplus units and charge a sufficiently low rate for these funds (in the desired form) so as to attract deficit units. At the same time, the financial institution must have a wide enough spread between the return paid and the rate charged to cover the costs of transforming its liabilities and assets into desirable form as well as earning at least an adequate return for its shareholders (whether these are owners, depositors, policyholders, etc.). Much of the remainder of this text is concerned with management policies that will enable an individual financial institution to obtain and employ funds at terms (rate and form) which are satisfactory to surplus and deficit units and which allow a sufficient return to compensate shareholders for the risk exposure.

The Primary Objective of Financial Institutions

The first step in the management of a financial institution is to establish a clear-cut set of objectives. Obviously, one major objective is to package assets and liabilities in order to provide desired economic services to surplus and deficit units. The financial institution must somehow balance the conflicting desires of surplus and deficit units; that is, surplus units desire higher returns and deficit units lower costs. How then does the financial institution ascertain when it is operating efficiently?

The answer to this question, as well as other management decisions, should be based on the premise that the primary objective of a financial institution is to maximize the shareholders' wealth. Wealth maximization denotes maximizing the benefits (whether cash payments or increases in the value of holdings) to the residual contributors of funds (generally called shareholders) to the financial institution. Contributors with prior claims are paid contractually promised sums; however, shareholders gain from higher actual or potential residual cash benefits. The maximization of these benefits is consistent with the efficient allocation of scarce financial resources. While we do not wish to de-emphasize the social role, the quantification of social costs and benefits requires one to employ the opinions of individuals rather than to rely on market forces for the efficient allocation of resources. By providing needed financial services in a wealth-maximizing manner, a financial institution will generally perform a needed economic function and will tend to carry out its social and other obligations over a span of time, provided these obligations are brought to bear on management's decisions.

The objective of wealth-maximization needs to be examined further if financial management is to be successful. Wealth-maximization is the maximization of the discounted net cash benefits to shareholders. This condition can be expressed algebraically as:

$$W = \frac{B_1}{(1 + r)^1} + \frac{B_2}{(1 + r)^2} + \frac{B_3}{(1 + r)^3} + \ldots + \frac{B_n}{(1 + r)^n} \quad (1)$$

where W is the wealth position of its shareholders, B denotes the net cash benefits to the shareholders in periods 1, 2, 3, . . . and n, and r is the appropriate rate of discount which reflects both the timing and the risk associated with the net cash receipts.

The key variables comprising B and r are shown in the following equations:

$$B = R - (C + O + T) \qquad (2)$$

$$r = i + p \qquad (3)$$

In equation (2), R denotes the gross receipts from the financial institution's assets (A), C represents the costs of its financial liabilities (L), O is the overhead costs associated with R and C, and T is the taxes the institution must pay. Depreciation and other noncash costs are generally a relatively small percentage of O, so net cash benefits and net income are reasonably similar for most financial institutions. In equation (3), i is an estimated riskless interest rate that reflects the time value of money, and p is the appropriate risk premium associated with the assets (a) and liabilities (L) of the institution. Substituting equations (2) and (3) into equation (1), we obtain:

$$W = \frac{R_1 - (C_1 + O_1 + T_1)}{1 + (i + p)} + \frac{R_2 - (C_2 + O_2 + T_2)}{[1 + (i + p)]^2} + \dots$$
$$+ \frac{R_n - (C_n + O_n + T_n)}{[1 + (i + p)]^n} \qquad (4)$$

The interdependent nature of these variables should be evident. R represents the flow of benefits from the stock of assets A, and C represents the flow of negative benefits (costs) from the stock of liabilities L, which the financial institution has created in order to obtain funds. O, which has both fixed and variable components, will depend at least partially on the nature of the asset and liability positions. For taxable institutions, T can be taken to be a variable cost that is a function of $R - (C + O)$. While the riskless rate (i) is beyond the control of the financial institution, it will tend to be strongly correlated with both R and C. Finally, p is a function of the interaction of the risks associated with the portfolios of assets and liabilities. Conceptually, it is useful to think of the required return $(i + p)$ determined by the markets' perception of the riskiness of the financial institution's asset, liability, and capital composition.

To make prudent financial management decisions, the manager of a financial institution must consider the combined impact of all variables relevant for wealth computation. For example, if management considers purchasing liabilities at 6 percent and investing the proceeds in assets earning 8 percent, they must take account of changes in O, T, and p from the transaction. It may well be that, in spite of the positive spread between R and C, the total effect including increases in overhead, taxes, or risks, may actually reduce the wealth of the financial institution.

The wealth-maximization objective, with only modest adjustments, can be employed for all of the existing organizational forms of financial institutions — the corporate form, the mutual form, and the trusteed organization.[1] *Corporations* are controlled by their common stockholders who elect a board of directors which appoints the management. Common stockholders are entitled to the residual benefits because they supply the risk capital of the corporation. The objective of a corporate-type financial institution should be to maximize the wealth of their common shareholders relative to these shareholders' investment in the institution.

Mutual organizations have no common stock and, therefore, no holders of common stock. For wealth-maximization purposes, one can generally consider the suppliers of funds as shareholders. Legally these shareholders — depositors or policyholders — elect the management which, in practice, tends to be nearly self-perpetuating. Net benefits are usually either returned to depositors and policyholders or accumulated for an indefinite time in the enterprise in a reserve or net worth account. Some mutual institutions, credit unions, in particular, may share their net benefits among borrowers (often with a loan rebate) and depositors. While the objective of wealth-maximization does not indicate how the net benefits should be distributed between these groups, it does seem reasonable that both borrowers and depositors will want the institution to maximize the total wealth available to the two groups.

Trusteed organizations are usually managed by salaried trustees in accordance with the basic documents creating these organizations. The funds accumulated, both prinicpal and net income, accrue to the beneficiary who usually wants the highest possible return for an acceptable risk level; therefore, the wealth-maximization objective also seems appropriate for this form of organization. Differences in the form of contribution and/or benefit may lead to some complexities in this general objective. For example, one may question the coincidence of risk preferences between beneficiaries and contributors if fixed benefits are promised to the beneficiary of a trusteed organization. In such a situation the beneficiary may have a preference for low-risk investments since his return is not affected while the contributor usually prefers higher-risk and higher-return investments since the amount he contributes to the trust is more likely to be lowered. In spite of this risk incompatibility, the wealth-maximization objective seems generally appropriate for trusteed forms of organizations.

The conclusion that wealth-maximization is the appropriate primary objective for nearly all financial institutions leads us to reemphasize two

---

[1]Commercial banks, finance companies, and some types of investment companies must be corporations. Savings and loan associations, casualty insurance companies, and life insurance companies can be corporations or mutual organizations. Mutual savings banks, credit unions, and some forms of investment companies must be mutual organizations. Private and public pension funds generally have trusteed forms of organization.

earlier points. First, we realize (and are in complete support of) the need for financial institutions to fill their socioeconomic roles of serving appropriate surplus and deficit units in the economy. We strongly believe that this need is best served by financial institutions using the wealth- maximization objective rather than seeking to individually help various economic units. In the limited number of situations in which there is conflict between appropriate socioeconomic needs and wealth-maximization by financial institutions, we believe the remedy should be statutory and through administrative regulation rather than by circumventing the appropriate objective of management. Secondly, some may question whether management responsibilities regarding facilities, human resources, and marketing are covered by the wealth-maximization objective. We believe that the wealth-maximization objective is appropriate for these nonfinancial responsibilities. We do, however, emphasize financial management applications in this book.

Application of the Wealth-Maximization Objective

Once wealth-maximization has been accepted as the primary objective of the financial institution, one can turn to the implementation of policy decisions consistent with this objective. Conceptually, every financial management decision should take into account the impact of all variables on the shareholder's wealth position. This can best be demonstrated by the use of a numerical example for a hypothetical financial institution. For simplicity, we assume constant average returns and constant costs over the perpetual life of the institution.[2] Equations (1) and (4) can then be restated as follows:

$$W = \frac{B}{r} \tag{1a}$$

$$W = \frac{R - (C + O + T)}{(i + p)} \tag{4a}$$

We assume our hypothetical institution, ABC Financial Institution, has $10,000 in assets that can be distributed between lower-risk and lower-return asset A_1 and higher-risk, higher-return asset A_2. These assets are financed by $9,000 in liabilities, distributed between lower-cost, higher-risk L_1, and higher cost, lower-risk L_2, and $1,000 in capital or reserves. The returns and costs on these assets and liabilities, the assumed overhead and income tax rate, and the capitalization rates applied to various streams of risky benefits appear in Table 2-1. Given this available menu of alternative assets and liabilities, one may consider the allocation decision facing ABC.

---

[2]With constant returns and costs a series of

$$\frac{B_1}{(1+r)^1} + \frac{B_2}{(1+r)^2} + \frac{B_3}{(1+r)^3} + \frac{B_4}{(1+r)^4} + \cdots + \frac{B_n}{(1+r)^n} = \frac{B}{r}$$

TABLE 2-1   Assumptions About the ABC Financial Institution

Balance sheet totals;			
Assets	$10,000	Liabilities	$9,000
		Capital (or reserves)	$1,000

Available asset returns:

A_1 (a lower-risk asset)	= 8%
A_2 (a higher-risk asset)	= 9%

Costs of acquiring funds, overhead, and taxes:

L_1 (a higher-risk source)	= 6%
L_2 (a lower-risk source)	= 7%
O (overhead per period)	= $100
t (income tax rate)	= 20%
$T = t(R - (C + O))$	

Capitalization rates:

i (riskless rate)	= 8%
P_1 (low-risk premium)	= 2%
P_2 (medium-risk premium)	= 4%
P_3 (high-risk premium)	= 6%

Four possible cases are presented in Table 2-2. In case 1 the entire asset portfolio is invested in A_1 while L_1 is the only liability source. The net income of $128, taking account of overhead and taxes, is capitalized at the 12 percent rate which is assumed to reflect the combined risks of the portfolios of assets and liabilities. This income produces a wealth position for the shareholders of $1,067. In case 2 ABC takes a greater risk, as reflected in the 14 percent capitalization rate, by dividing its assets between the low- and high-risk assets.

TABLE 2-2   Alternative Decisions by ABC Financial Institution

	Case 1	Case 2	Case 3	Case 4
Balance sheet totals:				
A_1	$10,000	$5,000	$10,000	$5,000
A_2		5,000		5,000
L_1	9,000	9,000	6,000	6,000
L_2			3,000	3,000
C	1,000	1,000	1,000	1,000
Returns and costs:				
R	$800	$850	$800	$850
C	540	540	570	570
O	100	100	100	100
T	32	42	26	36˜
B	$128	$168	$104	$144
Capitalization rate and wealth:				
i	8%	8%	8%	8%
p	4%	6%	2%	4%
W	$128	$168	$104	$144
	0.12%	0.14%	0.10%	0.12%
	or $1,067	or $1,200	or $1,040	or $1,200

If the other variables remain unchanged, the higher net income would imply a shareholder's wealth position or $1,200. In other words, the reward is more than sufficient to justify the additional risk exposure.   ABC's shareholders would be better off in case 2 than in case 1. Case 3 illustrates the effects when ABC allocates all of its assets in the lower-risk assets and shifts $3,000 of its liabilities into the higher-cost but lower-risk liabilities. The wealth level resulting from net income of $104 and a capitalization rate of 10 percent is below that in cases 1 and 2 and would be an unfavorable alternative. On the other hand, the wealth in case 4, resulting from shifting to the higher-earning, higher-risk assets *and* the higher-cost, lower-risk liabilities exceeds the wealth obtained in cases 1 and 3 and is equal to the wealth in case 2. Under the wealth-maximization objective, ABC's shareholders should be indifferent to cases 2 and 4.

Many other cases could be presented for even the very simple decisions facing the ABC Financial Institution: other risk–return possibilities and combinations of assets and liabilities could be considered; overhead or taxes could be varied with side effects on asset and liability combinations; different capital or reserve position could affect both net income and risk, and so on. Three basic points seem clear from an analysis of cases 1 through 4: (1) changes in any one variable can affect any or all of the other relevant variables, (2) since risk affects the capitalization rate, one must consider the interactive effect of the portfolio of assets and liabilities, and (3) this example tends to validate our selection of maximizing the net wealth of the shareholders as the primary objective of financial management decisions by a financial institution. We now turn to some of the more detailed aspects of applying the wealth-maximization objective — the subdivisions of our objective for financial management actions, the incremental nature of most of the decision to achieve this objective, and the effects of growth on the wealth-maximization objective.

Subdividing Our Objective for Financial Management Actions

While the criteria for every decision should be its effect on the shareholders' net wealth, practical decision-making will require emphasis on selected variables for day-to-day financial management actions. We believe that most financial institutions can group the key variables affecting their wealth-maximization objective into four interrelated categories: spread management, control of overhead, liquidity management, and capital (or reserve) management.

Spread management emphasizes the difference between the return on assets (R) and the cost of liabilities (C) over time. While a high positive spread is generally desirable, two limiting aspects need to be emphasized by financial managers. First is the fact that it is a high positive spread *over time.* A financial institution using short-term liabilities as a source of funds may not want to buy long-term assets even with a highly favorable spread because of the possible adverse movements in the spread over time. Similarly, a financial institution may use long-term assets rather than face the risk that shorter-term assets, even if they provide a higher spread at this point in time, may yield a low or negative spread later in the life of the liability. Second, the effect on overhead (O) and risk (p) of the manner in which R and C are acquired cannot be ignored. For example, the additional overhead and risk may negate the considerably higher gross spread when financial institutions make consumer loans.

Control of overhead costs is another major area for consideration in proper financial management. Statements on control of overhead costs by some security analysts, such as, "Whenever I see excavation work start on a new building by a financial institution, I sell their stock short," are probably oversimplifications. Nevertheless, two of the major causes of financial stress for any financial institution are being saddled with large fixed overhead costs in periods of stress and ignoring the high overhead costs that might accompany seemingly high-profit opportunities. Our major recommendation for the first problem is that the financial institution examine the impact of any increase in overhead costs on net cash flows at varying levels of activity, not just for the most optimistic projections. For the second problem, we reiterate our earlier statement that rational spread management decisions cannot ignore the effect of overhead costs.

Liquidity management involves the structuring of the interactive portfolios of assets (A) and liabilities (L) so that funds are available to meet the cash flow demands of both existing liability holders and potential deficit customers. Liquidity management should be applied so as to maximize the spread $(R - C)$ at a risk level the financial institution is willing to accept. At an elementary level liquidity management may emphasize matching the maturity structure[3] of an institution's assets and liabilities. Liquidity management is usually more complex. Factors such as expected fund inflows, access to purchased liabilities, credit risks on assets, and purchasing power risks must be considered. For example, a financial institution that expects its annual cash inflows to exceed matured liabilities over the next several years may attain a higher spread without placing excessive pressure on its liquidity position by structuring its portfolio so that the maturities of its assets exceed the maturities of its liabilities. Some financial institutions can legitimately use liability management (the purchase of funds rather than liquidation of assets to meet liquidity needs) if they can purchase the acquired funds at a positive spread in periods of credit ease and tightness. Firms with lower liquidity pressures may take somewhat greater credit risks in their asset portfolios because they will not be under pressure to sell these assets.

The *capital (or reserve) management* position is the final major variable involving financial management decisions. The capital (or reserve) position is based on the residual from assets minus liabilities. If capital is too high, the return per dollar of capital may be low and shareholders may not receive sufficient benefits (dividends, appreciation on common stock, higher interest on savings shares, lower insurance costs, etc.). If capital is

---

[3]The term *matching maturity structure* is used to denote a matching of the time profile of cash flows on assets and liabilities.

too low, higher risk may offset the higher return per dollar of capital. Growth of assets and liabilities may also be constrained by the lack of capital to support that growth. This can be particularly serious for mutual institutions that are unable to raise additional capital from external sources. These four decision-making categories will be discussed in greater detail for each financial institution.

The Incremental Nature of Many Financial Management Decisions

In examples demonstrating our wealth-maximization objective, we ignored the incremental nature of many management decisions in financial institutions. Usually broad choices (such as those portrayed in cases 1, 2, 3, or 4 in Table 2-2) are longer-term decisions and may indicate the direction the institution should move over a period of years. Managers of financial institutions are faced with numerous important but less broad decisions: Should they make auto loans at a given rate? Should they purchase long-term corporate bonds? What should be the maturity of the liabilities they are purchasing? While the wealth-maximization objective is still appropriate, the financial institution should generally base such decisions on changes in revenues, costs, and risks rather than the average levels of these variables.

For example, suppose a financial institution has acquired its funds at an average cost of 7 percent (including overhead, etc.) and is earning an average return of 8 percent of its assets, should it make new loans which will not change its risk level and will return 9 percent? The answer, of course, is that we are not sure, because we do not know the cost of acquiring additional funds. If the additional funds cost 10 percent (the lowest cost of issuing new liabilities or selling currently-held assets), the financial institution would be acting prudently by not making the new loans. For decisions that do not change the risk level of the financial institution, the general rule is that wealth is maximized by undertaking all decisions where marginal revenues exceed marginal costs.

The possible effects of such a decision on the risk level of the financial institution must, of course, be considered. The appropriate evaluative measure is what the change in the total risk level of the financial institution will be due to the decision, not the risk of the individual decision. The portfolio effects of some decisions may even reduce the total risk exposure of the financial institution. The appropriate criterion for decisions affecting both return and risk levels of the institution remains the maximization of the shareholders' wealth.

Size-Maximization or Wealth-Maximization?

One might question the adequacy of the wealth-maximization objective for describing the behavior of some financial institutions. For example, the manager of a mutual financial institution might be expected to equate his personal success with the success of the institution. But the success of the institution from his point of view may be measured by its rate of growth and total size rather than the wealth position of the institution's shareholders. In such a situation, the manager can best achieve the size-maximization goal by reducing the rates charged on loans and increasing the rates paid for funds until average costs equal average revenues. This will usually produce a larger size than is optimal for wealth-maximization since marginal costs are not equal to marginal revenues. However, most of the differences between the two objectives appear to be reconciled since these mutual institutions are depositor-dominated and because managers of such institutions are aware of the added risk that may accompany size-maximization. Charges to borrowers are, therefore, kept at competitive rates and depositors' rebates or higher returns are limited by the desire to have adequate reserves (capital) to serve as a cushion for potential asset losses. In practice, then, even for mutual financial institutions, the wealth-maximization objective appears to be most reasonable.

Linear Programming:
A Management Model for Wealth-Maximization

In recent years, a great deal of effort has been devoted to the construction of mathematical models to facilitate the management of financial institutions. Most have taken the form of mathematical programming models, with management seeking to maximize some measure of performance while satisfying both internal and external constraints on their behavior. Though more elaborate techniques are justified in modeling particular tasks performed by management, the relatively simple linear programming format seems sufficiently powerful for representing the overall management of the institution, and is attractive in its computational ease. A description of the general characteristics of a linear programming model of a financial institution follows. Initially we assume a riskless environment but later relax this assumption as the nature of the model becomes more familiar. Technical notes on linear programming appear in Appendix 1. The adaptations of the general model to fit specific institutions are presented in the chapters in which each institution is discussed.

We begin by formulating the general model in a riskless environment in order to explain its basic features. When there is no uncertainty about the outcome of a particular decision, the objective of management — the maximization of the wealth of the institution — is equivalent to the maximization of the present value of the net aggregate cash flow from its composite portfolio. This goal can be represented in linear form as:

$$\max_i \Sigma \ X_i PV_i \tag{5}$$

where X_i is the amount of dollars invested in the ith asset or provided by the ith liability, and PV_i is the present value of the cash flow received per dollar of the asset held or expended to support each dollar of the liability. Equation (5) says that the wealth of the institution is the residual of the value of its assets less the value of its liabilities. A particular set of X_i's describes the portfolio's composition, the holdings of each portfolio component. The objective of management is to find that set of X_i's which maximizes the expression in equation (5), while satisfying both internally imposed and regulatory constraints on the portfolio's composition. The "optimum" portfolio is that set of X_i's from among the permissable group which maximizes the net value of the portfolio.

Restraints on the portfolio are specified through linear restrictions on the dollars in each component. As an example, if the institution must maintain reserves in cash (c) equal to 7 percent of the amount of the jth liability, we might specify:

$$X_c \geq .07X_j \tag{6a}$$

where X_c and X_j refer to dollars in cash and liability j, respectively. Other restraints on the institution might not be so well defined. For instance, a savings and loan association might feel that it must put at least 90 percent of its loanable funds in mortgages in order not to encounter harsh treatment from its regulatory authority if and when authorization for a branch office is sought. This constraint requires that mortgage holdings be nine times as large as the sum of all other assets and takes the following form in the model:

$$X_m \geq 9 \sum_a X_a \tag{7a}$$

where X_m is dollars invested in mortgages and the X_a's represent amounts in each of the other asset categories. Rewriting equations (6a) and (7a) in standard form, we obtain:

$$.07Xj - Xc \leq 0. \tag{6b}$$

$$9 \sum_a X_a - X_m \leq 0 \tag{7b}$$

$$9X_{a1} + 9X_{a2} + 9X_{a3} + \ldots + 9X_{an} - X_m \leq 0 \tag{7c}$$

where, in equation (7c), we have expanded the summation into its individual components. These two examples are among the more obvious constraints that a financial institution might encounter. The approach, however, is general. One must write each constraint as a linear relationship among the portfolio proportions and same fixed constant (the zero in our examples).

The most direct method of incorporating risk into the model is the use of risk-adjusted discount rates and expected, rather than certain, cash flows in the computation of the present value contributions of the objective function. Since the manner in which these new inputs are obtained is discussed in Chapter 3, we will proceed by assuming they are available. If one recognizes risk in the model, one must usually formulate additional constraints. For example, it might be that the risk-adjusted discount rate used in the objective function for, say, consumer loans assumes that the institution has diversified these loans over individuals with different sources of income. Such diversification minimizes the risk of a large loss from an increase in unemployment in a single industry. To write a restraint assuring that such diversification has been achieved, we could segment the X_{c1} for consumer loans into, say, 10 new $X^i{}_{c1}$ and require that each is at most 20 percent of the total of consumer loans and at least 5 percent:

$$X_i - .20X_{c1} \leq 0 \tag{8a}$$

$$.05X_{c_1} - X_i \leq 0 \qquad \text{for } X_{c1}^1, X_{c1}^2, \ldots, X_{c1}^{10} \tag{8b}$$

We might also be interested in limiting the total risk exposure of the portfolio. If the maximum risk which can be tolerated is 100 units, and asset (liability) i contributes R_i units per dollar, we can insert as a constraint

$$\Sigma_i X_i R_i \leq 100. \tag{9}$$

After the model has been constructed and a solution obtained, several procedures are available for gathering relevant supplemental information. One can investigate the sensitivity of the optimal solution to variations in the form and value of the constraints and the risk-adjusted present value contributions of the portfolio categories. Estimates of the variances and covariances of the cash flow estimates can be used to derive the probability distribution of the expected cash flow.

The single, most-important aspect of the post solution analysis, however, is the consideration of the "reasonableness" of the portfolio composition suggested. Of course, if the model always yielded the a priori expected result, its use would be superfluous. On the other hand, an optimal solution that differs drastically from observed behavior may indicate an error or omission in the construction of the model. As we shall see, several of the appropriate constraints are implicit, not formally stated, and therefore easily overlooked and often difficult to formulate.

Chapter 2

Review Questions

1. State the underlying management principle developed in Chapter 2. Can this principle clash with financial intermediary socioeconomic roles? How can the wealth-maximization principle be justified with socioeconomic roles, if at all?

2. Let us assume that a financial institution can acquire an asset yielding 8 percent. The cost of the required funds is 5 percent. Given only this information, would the institution be making a wise decision to obtain funds at 5 percent and acquire an asset with yield of 8 percent? Why?

3. Three basic types of financial institution organizations have been discussed. Name and describe these organizational types, and briefly indicate how the wealth-maximization principle is applicable to the management of these institutions.

4. The wealth-maximization principle is given in mathematical form in equation (4a). Explain and identify the variables in equation (4a).

5. The discount rate (r) is composed of two factors. Which factor is controllable by the financial institution? What factors affect the magnitude of a financial institution's risk premium?

6. There were four basic categories of financial management decisions. List the four categories and indicate how each is embodied in, or can be related to, the wealth-maximization principle in equation (4a).

7. Besides the four decision areas outlined in question 6 above, there are two other broad problems facing the management of financial institutions. First, there is the incremental nature of decision-making. Second, there is the problem of reconciling size- and wealth-maximization. To effectively make decisions regarding these problems, within the wealth-maximization criterion, what economic principle should be followed?

8. What are the two major components of a linear programming problem? How would risk and uncertainty be incorporated into a linear programming model?

Selected References

Ludtke, James B. *The American Financial System.* Boston: Allyn and Bacon, 1967.

Robichek, Alexander A. and Myers, Stewart C. *Optimal Financing Decisions.* Englewood Cliffs, N. J.: Prentice-Hall, 1965.

Smith, Paul F. *Economics of Financial Institutions and Markets.* Homewood, Ill.: Irwin, 1971

Van Horne, James C. *Functions and Analysis of Capital Market Rates.* Englewood Cliffs, N. J.: Prentice-Hall, 1970.

Weston, J. Fred. *The Scope and Methodology of Finance.* Englewood Cliffs, N. J.: Prentice-Hall, 1968.

Evaluating Returns and Risks
on Assets and Liabilities

HAVING developed the basic objectives of a management model which can be applied by nearly all types of financial institutions, we are now ready to examine how financial institutions evaluate the returns and risks on the available menu of assets and liabilities. We start with a brief description of the most common types of assets and liabilities. The appropriate methods for measuring returns and risks on individual assets and liabilities are also discussed, followed by an explanation of how portfolio theory can be used to analyze the risks and returns from portfolios of assets, liabilities, and the residual capital (reserve) accounts. We conclude this chapter with an example of applying portfolio theory to decisions of savings and loan associations.

Types of Financial Assets and Liabilities

The major purpose in this section is to acquaint the reader with the major types of financial assets and liabilities available to a financial institution.[1] There are many types of financial assets and liabilities and probably as many ways of classifying them. We begin by separating the available financial assets into *debt instruments* and *equity instruments* and then subdivide debt instruments into personalized indebtedness and market in-

---

[1]We limit our discussion here to domestic financial assets and liabilities. Methods for using the foreign exchange market and taking advantage of foreign investment opportunities are briefly discussed in Appendix 2.

debtedness. *Personalized indebtedness* includes direct borrowing by a deficit unit from one or a few lenders. Debt contracts may be short- or long-term and are generally held by the original holder (lender) until maturity. Typically, there is not a secondary market for such debt instruments. Table 3-1 briefly describes the characteristics of some of the principal forms of personalized indebtedness. From this table it is obvious that some personalized forms are direct debts of deficit units, while other forms are indirect obligations of financial intermediaries.

A debt instrument is classified as a *market debt instrument* if it is not associated with a particular lender and is normally traded in a secondary market. The principal forms of short- and long-term market debt instruments are briefly described in the bottom half of Table 3-1.

There are two equity types of financial assets: (1) preferred stock and common stock, and (2) a hybrid, or convertible, form of financial asset which represents a claim on business units. *Preferred stock* is similar to a non maturing debt instrument, except that it has a residual fixed claim on the firm's assets and earnings after payment of all debt claims. *Common stock* has a residual claim against both the assets and income of the firm. The return on common stock varies widely, depending on the firm's performance. *Convertible assets* include debt and preferred securities that are convertible into a stated number of common shares at some specified future period.

The liabilities which financial institutions may employ to attract funds include the previously listed demand deposits, savings and time deposits, negotiable certificates of deposit, commercial paper, and corporate bonds. Additional liability sources for financial institutions include borrowing directly from government agencies; issuing liabilities which feature insurance coverage for specific events; variable payments which are dependent on the institution's ability in managing financial assets; or payments commencing at some stipulated future period, and using the retention of earnings or sale of new external capital. We now consider the way in which a financial institution should measure the risk and return on such financial assets and liabilities.

Measuring Returns (Costs) and Risks on Individual Assets or Liabilities

While the returns (costs) and risks associated with financial assets and liabilities have been widely discussed, the appropriate data is in some cases quite difficult to obtain. We have treated returns and costs (which are negative returns in a measurement sense) as if they were relatively certain when the assets or liabilities were acquired. This assumption may not be appropriate for loans or debt instruments that may have to be sold before maturity or for equity securities. Risk is generally even more complex to measure. Some of the complexities in measuring returns and risks on individual debt and equity securities and the costs and risks of liabilities are considered below.

TABLE 3-1 Brief Descriptions of the Principal Types of Debt Instruments

Category			Type	Issuing Unit	Characteristics
Personalized	Short-term		Demand deposits	Commercial banks	Highly liquid form; used as medium of exchange; explicit interest payments are illegal
			Savings and time deposits	Commercial banks, mutual savings Banks, savings and loan, credit unions	Interest-bearing deposits which can be withdrawn on notice or at specified date
			Commercial loans	Business	Short-term loans to a business; rate usually varies with prime rate
			Consumer loans	Households	Loan to individuals for a specific purpose; generally variable rate
	Long-term		Installment loan	Households	Loan for consumer durables with amortized monthly payments
			Term commercial loans	Business	Loans for permanent working capital or equipment; amortized over 5-10 years
			Mortgages	Consumers	Amortized loans secured by housing; generally fixed rate; limited secondary market
			Privately-placed commercial debt	Business	Business debt placed with one or a few financial institutions
Market	Short-term		Government debt	Federal government	Highly marketable debt with no credit risk; often sold on discount basis
			Agency debt	Government agencies	Obligation of federal agencies; very high quality and nearly as marketable as federal debt
			State and local notes	State and local governments	Short-term tax or bond anticipation obligations of state and local governments; interest is tax exempt
			Commercial paper	Business or finance companies	High quality business promissory notes; sold on discount basis
			Negotiable certificates of deposit	Commercial banks and other financial institutions	Large-size interest-bearing deposits which can be traded before maturity
	Long-term		Government bonds	Federal government	Longer-term interest-bearing notes and bonds which are obligations of the federal government
			Agency bonds	Government agencies	Longer-term interest-bearing bonds of federal agencies
			General obligations	State and local governments	Bonds backed by full faith, credit and taxing power of issuing unit; interest is tax exempt
			Revenue bonds	State and local governments	Bonds backed by revenues from specific project or tax source; interest is tax exempt
			Corporate bonds	Business	Interest-bearing long-term business debt with varying degrees of quality and marketability

Debt securities promise to pay a fixed cash flow for a specified number of periods and a payment of principal at the maturity date. The yield on any maturity debt instrument is the rate of discount (internal rate of return) which equates the discounted value of interest and principal flows to the investor with the current market price of the security. If the interest payments are assumed to occur at the end of the period, then the yield on a debt instrument can be determined by solving the following equation for r,

$$M = \frac{C}{1+r} + \frac{C_2}{(1+r)^2} + \frac{C_3}{(1+r)^3} + \cdots + \frac{C_n + B_n}{(1+r)^n} \qquad (1)$$

where M is the current market price of the instrument, C_i is the amount of annual interest payments to the investor in year i, B_n is the principal payment at maturity, and r is the rate of discount or yield.[2] The rate of discount (r), is readily available in bond yield tables or by using special calculators.

There are several potential weaknesses in this common method for measuring the return on debt securities. First, there may be differences in income tax rates applied to interest (for example, interest payments on state and local debts are exempt from federal income taxes) or differences between purchase price and sale or maturity price. Second, if there is any risk of nonpayment of interest or principal, the rate of discount will be the maximum return and not the expected return. Third, there is an implicit assumption that as cash flows are received they can be reinvested at the rate of discount. Finally, the return calculated from equation (1) is a yield to maturity and may differ from the holding period yield if the debt security is sold prior to maturity.[3]

There are four potential sources of risk for debt securities.

1. There is the risk that the investor will be forced to sell a particular security that does not have broad marketability prior to maturity. Price concessions required in order to sell the security may decrease the security's return appreciably.

2. A second source of risk comes from changes in the general level of interest rates. Changes in the market value of outstanding securities are inversely related to the change in interest rates. For most bonds, the magnitude of such changes will increase with the maturity of the debt instrument. This rate of increase declines as the maturity of the security increases.[4] These changes in security prices are, of course, of greater concern to those institutions whose portfolios are continually revalued and/or of-

---

[2] For more detailed calculations of returns on debt securities — for example, when interest is paid more than once a year — see James C. Van Horne, *Functions and Analysis of Capital Market Rates* Englewood Cliffs, N.J.: Prentice-Hall, 1970).

[3] These potential weaknesses are discussed in greater detail in Sidney Homer and Martin L. Leibowitz, *Inside the Yield Book* (Englewood Cliffs, N.J.: Prentice-Hall, 1972).

[4] See Jess Yawitz, George Hempel, and Bill Marshall, "Average Maturity as a Risk Proxy in Investment Decisions," *The Journal of Finance,* 30:2,(May), 1975, for a discussion of the relationship between maturity and price changes on debt instruments.

fered for sale than for institutions who usually hold debt securities to maturity.

3. A third risk is the possibility of nonpayment of interest and/or principal. The possibility of nonpayment, often labeled the credit risk or default risk, is a relevant consideration for most debt securities except those which are obligations of the federal government.

4. Finally, there is a purchasing power risk associated with all debt instruments. If dollars received as interest or principal payments will purchase less than dollars used to purchase debt instruments, the investor suffers a loss of purchasing power. The investor attempts to overcome this risk by requiring a higher return and/or by having dollar liabilities that are paid in lower purchasing power dollars. To the extent that interest rate and price level changes are positively correlated, it is difficult to separate interest rate and purchasing power risk. That is, nominal (market) interest rates normally adjust to changes in the expected rate of inflation.

The formula for converting nominal rates of return (Rn) to real rates (Rr) is

$$Rr = \frac{1 + Rn}{1 + \dot{q}} - 1 \tag{2}$$

where $\dot{q}$ denotes the actual rate of change in the general price level over the holding period. Equation (2) is commonly expressed as

$$Rr \approx Rn - \dot{q} \tag{2a}$$

which is a simpler approximation of Rr.

The returns on preferred stock are similar to the returns on debt securities except that the preferred stock is generally treated as a claim to a perpetual stream of returns. The appropriate rate of return can be found by solving the following equation for d

$$M = \frac{P_1}{1 + d} + \frac{P_2}{(1 + d)^2} + \frac{P_3}{(1 + d)^3} + \cdots + \frac{P_n}{(1 + d)^n}. \tag{3}$$

Since P is a perpetual stream of equal preferred dividend payments, equation (3) simplifies to

$$M = \frac{P}{d} \tag{3a}$$

where M is the current market price of the preferred stock. The risks associated with preferred stock are similar to those associated with debt securities, with two modifications. The longer maturity (perpetuity) of preferred stock means it will fluctuate more in price for a given interest rate change than nearly all debt securities. Also, credit risk will tend to be higher with preferred stock than debt instruments of the same or similar companies because of the lower claim on assets and earnings of preferred stock compared with the indebtedness of a company.

Because of the greater uncertainty associated with returns on common stock and the greater potential for price change, the methods of measuring the return on a common stock usually differ somewhat from that on fixed income securities. Conceptually, the expected return on a common stock is the rate of discount that equates the present value of the expected future stream of income to the investor with the present market price of the stock,

$$S = \frac{D_1}{1+k} + \frac{D_2}{(1+k)^2} + \frac{D_3}{(1+k)^3} + \ldots + \frac{D_n}{(1+k)^n}. \tag{4}$$

where S is the current market price of the common stock, D_t is the amount of dividend payments to the investor at the end of period (t), and k is the market discount factor which represents the rate of return implied by the market.

The expected return for a given holding period is the rate of discount that equates the present value of dividends expected during the holding period and the present value of the expected market price at the end of the holding period with the current market price of the common stock. If S_h is the market price at which the investor expects to sell the stock at the end of the holding period (h), then

$$S = \sum_{t=0}^{h} \frac{D_t}{(1+k)^t} + \frac{S_h}{(1+k)^h}. \tag{4a}$$

If one assumes that the expected market price at h depends on future dividends beyond h, equation (4a) is the same as equation (4). The appropriate ex post measure of the return on investment in a common stock is the rate of discount (k) in equation (4a) which equates the present value of the sale price and actual dividends paid with the original price paid for the stock.

The risks associated with common stocks are similar to those of fixed income securities, but differ in degree and possible cause. These differences are primarily associated with the uncertain and residual nature of common stock earnings and dividends as opposed to the contractually fixed size and priority in the claim for interest and payments on preferred stock. The cash benefits to owners of common stock tend to vary widely because of risks associated with the stock market and the economy in general. Risks associated with the company are broadly analogous to the credit risk of perpetual bonds or preferred stock. The residual nature of the common shareholder's claim means that variations in return can be quite large. The more general types of risks associated with the economy and the stock market add to the possible variations in returns from common stock.

Because of the large number of variables affecting returns on common stock, the risk on a common stock is often expressed in terms of a statistical measure of past fluctuations in its rate of return.

The costs and risks associated with the fixed cost liabilities of a financial institution are the opposite of the returns and risks to holders of fixed income assets. The rate of discount in equation (1) represents the cost of the liability to the institution throughout the life of the liability. Two primary types of risks are associated with such liabilities. First, there is the possibility of nonpayment at maturity. When a financial institution is unable to meet some of its liabilities at maturity, either from cash inflows or refinancing, it is usually on the verge of failure. The second type of risk is related to the cost of borrowing during the life of the liability and at its maturity. If, for example, the financial institution could borrow funds at a significantly lower cost at some time during the life of the liability, it has foregone an opportunity to refinance at more favorable terms. The reverse is true if rates increase after issuance of the liability. At maturity the institution will be forced to borrow again at the prevailing rate of interest.

Using Portfolio Theory to Analyze Asset, Liability, and Capital (Reserve) Decisions

Portfolio management decisions for financial institutions should not be based on the risk and return of individual assets or liabilities. The main consideration is how such decisions will affect the risk and return of the institution's overall portfolio of assets, liabilities, and capital. With this purpose in mind, one should remember that financial institutions must operate in a world in which asset returns and liability costs are uncertain. This uncertainty or randomness of returns is the *raison d'etre* for portfolio analysis. In a world of certainty, the asset and liability acquisition decisions degenerate into simply obtaining the maximum return on assets and paying the minimum cost for liabilities. Without risk, the quantification of available risk–return combinations and the identification of optimal portfolios becomes a moot question.

The assumption of investor risk aversion serves as the cornerstone for much of portfolio analysis. While any of a number of individual utility functions are consistent with risk aversion, they share the common quality of being concave in wealth. That is, while wealth and utility are positively related, a given increase in wealth has a smaller effect on utility, the greater is the initial level of wealth.

From the assumption that investors are averse to risk, we are able to develop a portfolio model that reflects the "tradeoff" between expected return (cost) and risk. Both the asset and liability acquisition decisions involve a two-step process. On the asset side, one must first ascertain the set of portfolios which offer the highest possible return for each level of risk. Then the manager must choose from among those portfolios the one which is most desirable. Similarly, proper liability management requires one to first generate those combinations which require the least cost commitment for the level of risk, and then choose the wealth-maximizing solution. The complete portfolio decision takes proper account of the tradeoff between net return (return minus cost) and overall risk, where risk encompasses the uncertainty associated with the capital or reserve position as well as the risks associated with assets and liabilities.

Before proceeding with our discussion of the application of portfolio analysis to decisions of financial institutions, we interject a word of caution. While the mathematics of asset selection has been thoroughly developed and is generally straightforward, its application to decisions of financial institutions has been limited. We feel that this lack of application is partially due to the difficulty in obtaining the data required for implementation. A partial remedy to this problem is presented in Appendix 3 where we employ actual return data for the selection of portfolios of fixed income securities.

An Illustrative Two-Asset (or Two-Liability) Portfolio

By investigating the risk–return behavior of a portfolio composed of two assets or two liabilities, we are able to demonstrate the potential benefits from portfolio analysis quite well. The key feature to be noted from this presentation is the relationship between the "risk-pooling" benefits accompanying diversification[5] and the correlation between returns. *Risk-pooling* occurs when the risk of a portfolio is less than the weighted average of the risk from each of the individual assets. If the rates of return on the two assets in question (or the cost of two liabilities) are negatively correlated (inversely related), risk-pooling benefits will be considerable when the assets are combined in a portfolio. As an example, consider a portfolio composed of equity positions in a procyclical steel mill and in a countercyclical residential construction company. In an expanding economy with the accompanying high interest rates, the return from the steel mill will be above average, thereby compensating for the below-average return from the construction firm. The situation would be reversed in a sluggish economy. On the other hand, if the two assets' returns are positively correlated — that is, if variations in return are generally in the same direction — the risk-pooling benefits are restricted.

The mathematics required for computing the risk and return for a two-asset portfolio is quite simple. For assets A and B, let (x_a, x_b), (E_a, E_b), and (σ_a, σ_b) denote the proportions of each asset in the portfolio,[6] the expected rates of return, and the standard deviation in return, respectively. The portfolio's expected return is computed by

$$E_p = X_a E_a + X_b E_b. \tag{5}$$

---

[5]Diversification refers to ownership in more than one asset.
[6]For the two-asset case,

We obtain E_p by weighing each asset's return by its proportion in the port-folio. The standard deviation of the portfolio's return is given by

$$\sigma_p = \sqrt{X_a^2 \ \sigma_a^2 + X_b^2 \ \sigma_b^2 + 2 X_a X_b COVab} \qquad (6)$$

where the covariance between A and B's returns is computed as

$$COVab = \sigma_a \ \sigma_b \ \rho_{ab}, \qquad (7)$$

ρ_{ab} being the simple correlation coefficient.

Earlier, we indicated the importance of the correlation between assets' returns in determining the pooling of risk benefits available from diver-sification. We demonstrate the quantitative significance of this relation-ship with the following numerical example. Let us assume the two assets in question have the following expected returns and risks:

$$
\begin{array}{ll}
E_a = \ 8\% & \sigma_a = 4\% \\
E_b = 12\% & \sigma_b = 6\%
\end{array}
$$

The importance of the correlation coefficient in determining the port-folio's risk is evidenced in Table 3-2. We compute σ_p for values of ρ_{ab} from -1 to $+$ by 0.2 intervals for portfolios composed of proportions of asset A from 0 to 1 by 0.1 intervals. The expected return for every portfolio on a given row in Table 3-2 is identical (column 2). Therefore, the pooling of risk benefits from diversification can be measured by the difference be-tween the standard deviation of the portfolio with $\rho = \ +1$ and that of the portfolio in question.

For an n-asset or n-liability portfolio, the computation of risk and return is slightly more difficult. Return is obtained by

$$E_p = \sum_{i=1}^{n} X_i E_i, \qquad (8)$$

while risk is computed as

$$\sigma_p = \sqrt{\sum X_i^2 \ \sigma_i^2 + \sum_{i=1}^{} \sum X_i X_j COV_{ij}.} \qquad (9)$$

From equation (9), we are aware of the importance of covariability in determining the contribution of a given asset to the risk of the portfolio.

TABLE 3-2 Standard Deviation in Return for a Two-Asset Portfolio for Various Values of ρ ab

% of Portfolio in Asset A	% Return	Correlation Coefficient (ρab)										
		−1	−0.8	−0.6	−0.4	−0.2	0	0.2	0.4	0.6	0.8	1.0
0	12.0	6.0	6.00	6.00	6.00	6.00	6.00	6.00	6.00	6.00	6.00	6.0
10	11.6	5.0	5.09	5.17	5.25	5.33	5.41	5.49	5.57	5.65	5.73	5.8
20	11.2	4.0	4.19	4.37	4.54	4.71	4.87	5.02	5.17	5.32	5.46	5.6
30	10.8	3.0	3.32	3.61	3.88	4.13	4.37	4.59	4.81	5.01	5.21	5.4
40	10.4	2.0	2.51	2.93	3.30	3.64	3.94	4.22	4.49	4.74	4.97	5.2
50	10.0	1.0	1.84	2.41	2.86	3.26	3.61	3.92	4.22	4.49	4.75	5.0
60	9.6	0	1.52	2.15	2.63	3.04	3.39	3.72	4.02	4.29	4.55	4.8
70	9.2	1.0	1.74	2.24	2.65	3.01	3.33	3.62	3.89	4.14	4.38	4.6
80	8.8	2.0	3.35	2.66	2.93	3.18	3.42	3.64	3.84	4.04	4.22	4.4
90	8.4	3.0	3.11	3.28	3.40	3.53	3.65	3.77	3.88	3.99	4.10	4.2
100	8.0	4.0	4.00	4.00	4.00	4.00	4.00	4.00	4.00	4.00	4.00	4.0

The Portfolio Selection Models of Markowitz and Sharpe

Two portfolio models—the Markowitz model and the Sharpe model—have been developed to select "efficient" portfolios of risky assets. A portfolio is deemed efficient if, for a given expected return, it has the lowest possible exposure to risk. While the portfolios selected by the two models are similar, the data and computational requirements vary considerably.

In 1959, Harry Markowitz developed the first model for obtaining efficient portfolios of risky assets. The locus (set) of all such portfolios comprises what is referred to as the *efficient frontier.* The Markowitz procedure utilizes techniques of quadratic programming to determine this efficient frontier. One requires information on E and σ for each asset and the COV between each pair of assets. For a sample of n-assets, the data requirement for the Markowitz model include n-return and n-standard deviation measures and $n^2 - n/2$ covariances.

Before presenting the computational procedures of the Markowitz model, we digress briefly to consider the methods available for obtaining the required data on each asset's risk and return. As indicated earlier in this chapter, data requirements are primarily responsible for the lack of practical applications of portfolio analysis to decisions of financial institutions. The simplest and most commonly used method for obtaining the data required for any portfolio selection model is from historical return observations. While this method generally yields satisfactory results, it has two major shortcomings. First, one may be forced to employ risk–return observations which, for some assets, are contrary with the hypothesis that investors are risk averse. That is, assets having a positive risk sometimes achieve a negative return over a given sample period. Using this return figure as an estimate for the next period's expected return is wholly unsatisfactory since a rational investor would never hold such an asset. The second drawback of employing only historical return data is that one is unable to incorporate specific forecasts of future returns into the asset selection process. In Appendix 3 we indicate how such systematic expectations can be incorporated into model for selecting efficient portfolios.

The objective function of the Markowitz model is the minimization of the portfolio's variance (σ_p^2) for a given expected return. From equation (5) we express σ_p^2 as

$$\sigma_p^2 = \Sigma \chi_i^2 \sigma_i^2 + \underset{i=1}{\Sigma\Sigma} \chi_i \chi_j COV_{ij}. \tag{10}$$

Two constraints are required:

$$C_1: \Sigma \chi_i = 1$$
$$C_2 \quad \chi_i \geq 0 \quad \text{for all } i.$$

The first constraint is simply an adding up condition to assure that the proportions of the portfolio in each asset equal a total of one. The second constraint limits the portfolio to nonnegative holdings of any asset, that is, no short sales.

Observe that while both of the above constraints are linear in the x_i's for this reason conventional techniques of linear programming are incapable of generating the efficient frontier. Rather, one must employ quadratic programming to obtain the minimum value of σ_p^2 for each possible value of E_p.

Figure 3-1 graphs the risk and return of each portfolio contained in the efficient frontier. The Markowitz procedure requires that one first specify a value for the portfolio's return, say E_{p1} as in Figure 3-1, and then the program obtains the leftmost point in the attainable set (shaded area) having a return of E_{p1}. Since the portfolio obtained (M_1) has the smallest possible risk for its rate of return, it satisfies the condition of efficiency. By varying return from E' through E'', the entire frontier can then be traced.

Figure 3-1. Schematic Depiction of the Markowitz Calculation

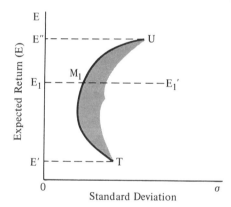

William Sharpe developed a portfolio selection model in 1964 that considerably reduces both the computational and data requirements of the Markowitz model. In spite of this simplification, the Sharpe model has performed well in comparative tests on identical sets of data. The Sharpe model is based on the premise that security price changes can be attributed to two phenomena: (1) factors related to general business conditions in the economy, and (2) factors affecting either one firm or only a small number of firms. Price changes resulting from general economic activity give rise to what is called *systematic risk*. Such price movements are assumed to be perfectly correlated among all assets. On the other hand, price changes that result from factors specific to the firm are uncorrelated (independent) among all assets. Such *nonsystematic risk* commands no premium in the capital markets since it can be eliminated via naive diversification.

In one version of the Sharpe model, an asset's return is related to a single index of economic activity. Candidates for this index include: gross national product, national income, the Dow-Jones Index, and a composite of all stock returns. The following regression equation is employed to obtain estimates of each asset's risk in return.

$$R_{it} = a_i + \beta_i R_{mt} + \epsilon_{it} \qquad (11)$$

In equation (11), R_{it} denotes asset i's return in period t, R_{mt} denotes the index value, ϵ_{it} denotes the random error term, and a_i and β_i are coefficients obtained from the regression. The size of the β coefficient measures the degree of co-movement between the index and the asset's return. Since the index serves as a proxy for economic activity, β can be interpreted as a measure of the procyclical response of the asset's return. While the Sharpe model is general in that it allows for both positive and negative values for β, the evidence suggests that the majority of equity returns move in unison with economic activity $(+\beta$'s).

The data requirements for generating an efficient frontier with the Sharpe single-index model represent a significant simplification over the Markowitz model. The Sharpe model requires estimates for each asset's a and β coefficients and a forecast for the value of the index in the next period (perhaps simply $\bar{X}_m$). The computational time required for the Sharpe calculation has been estimated to be as little as 2 percent of that required for the Markowitz analysis when 2,000 assets are available. From equation (11) we obtain an expression for the expected return on assets i,

$$E(R_i) = a_i + \beta_i \bar{R}_m \qquad (12)$$

where $\bar{R}_m$ is the average value of the index over the period. Note that in this form, $E(R_i)$ is solely a function of historical return behavior.

While the Sharpe-Lintner-Mossin Capital Asset Pricing Model (CAPM) has been shown to provide a reasonable explanation for the structure of historical rates of return in the equity market,[7] its application to practical decisions of financial institutions has been limited. This lack of application can be justified in part by the difficulty in obtaining the required return data for assets and liabilities not traded in efficient capital markets. Furthermore, most financial institutions operate in an environment that places constraints on their activities not found in the assumptions of the CAPM. Such constraints may take the form of limits on asset and liability composition as well as a general cash flow constraint. For these reasons, we

---

[7]As an example, see E. Fama and J. MacBeth, "Risk, Return, and Equilibrium: Empirical Tests," *Journal of Political Economy* 81 (May–June) 1973, pp. 607–636; and M. Miller and M. Scholes, "Rates of Return in Relation to Risk: A Re-Examination of Same Recent Findings," in M. Jensen, ed., *Studies in the Theory of Capital Markets* (New York: Praeger, 1972), pp. 47–78.

hesitate to suggest that optimal management policies for financial institutions simply require that one apply the Sharpe model appropriately in order to maximize valuation.

In the remainder of this chapter we present a general discussion of the financial institution as a portfolio of assets, liabilities, and capital. Particular attention is devoted to the effect of movements in market interest rates on net income. This relationship is explored by first specifying the effect of interest rates on the financial institution's *earnings spread* — the difference between return on assets and cost of liabilities.

The net income (*NI*) before operating costs for a financial institution can be expressed as

$$NI = [\bar{R}_A][A] - [\bar{R}_L][L]$$

where
$$\bar{R}_A = \begin{bmatrix} \bar{R}_{A_1} \\ \bar{R}_{A_2} \\ \vdots \\ \bar{R}_{A_m} \end{bmatrix} \quad \text{and} \quad \bar{R}_L = \begin{bmatrix} \bar{R}_{L_1} \\ \bar{R}_{L_2} \\ \vdots \\ \bar{R}_{L_n} \end{bmatrix} \quad \text{denote}$$

the vector of average returns and average costs on the asset and liability portfolios, respectively,

$$A = \begin{bmatrix} Q_{A_1} \\ \vdots \\ Q_{A_M} \end{bmatrix} \quad \text{and} \quad L = \begin{bmatrix} Q_{L_1} \\ \vdots \\ Q_{L^n} \end{bmatrix}$$

and denote the vector of dollar values in each asset and liability category. Note that average return and cost figures must be employed since most assets and some liabilities have fixed cash flow commitments (i.e., noncallable financial instruments). The difference between the average return on assets ($\bar{R}_A$) and the average cost of liabilities ($\bar{R}_L$) is commonly referred to as the earning spread ($S = \bar{R}_A - \bar{R}_L$). Since the dollar value of assets is approximately equal to the dollar value of liabilities for most financial institutions, the spread should be taken as profit per dollar of assets held.

Any change in money market conditions can be expected to exert an effect on the returns and costs on the financial institution's asset and liability portfolios. The effect on spread, and therefore on profit, from a given change in market interest rates will depend on the specific maturity composition of the assets and liabilities. This point is perhaps best demonstrated with an example.

Savings and Loan Associations in 1966: An Example

The nature of savings and loan associations' (S & L's) asset and liability portfolios causes their spread to be very sensitive to movements in market interest rates. S&L's primary assets are fixed rate home mortgages while they issue demand (callable) liabilities. Thus, the cost of its liabilities is much more responsive to a change in interest rates than is the return on the asset portfolio. At any point in time the average return on the asset portfolio is a function of the historical pattern of mortgage rates. Only a small portion of the mortgages in an S&L's portfolio carry the current rate of interest.[8] On the other hand, the "zero-maturity" nature of the majority of a S&L's liabilities requires that the actual rate paid on deposits (liabilities) be equal to the current rate on new deposits. The differential response of the returns and costs on an S&L's asset and liability portfolio to a change in market interest rates implies that the spread will vary according to the pattern of rates. A prolonged period of rising interest rates has a deleterious effect on the spread since the cost of retaining deposits will rise much more rapidly than will the average return on assets. In such a situation the profitability of the S&L could decrease to the point where its continued viability becomes questionable. The so-called *monetary crunch*[9] of 1966 was just such a period in U.S. monetary history. The rapidly rising interest rates from 1964 to 1966 actually led to the closing of several S&L's with many more having been placed in serious jeopardy.

It should be evident that as the higher level of interest rates continues over time, the S&L's profit spread will be reestablished as it "rolls over" its mortgage portfolio. Since the majority of the mortgages held by S&L's mature in the 20–25-year range, the time required to "roll over" the portfolio is likely to be quite significant.

This example suggests a general rule for assessing the effect of a change in market interest rates on the financial institution's profit spread. If a financial institution holds assets and issues liabilities with approximately equal terms to maturity,[10] its spread will be nearly invariant with respect to a change in rates. On the other hand, if the term of maturity on the asset portfolio exceeds that of the liabilities an increase (decrease) in rates will decrease (increase) the profit spread.

Later in the book, we consider the effect of both legal and institutional constraints on the asset and liability composition and profit spread for specific financial institutions. We will also analyze the effects of specific revisions in these constraints on the risks from interest rate changes.

Chapter 3

Review Questions

1. What are the two broad categories of debt? List some examples of each.
2. Outline the weaknesses in the common (discounting) method for measuring the returns of debt instruments.

---

[8]The suggestion that S&L's make variable rate mortgages is designed to increase the sensitivity of the average return on the asset portfolio to a change in interest rates.

[9]See H. P. Minsky, "The Crunch and its Aftermath," *Banker's Magazine,* February, 1968.

[10]While maturity is sometimes taken as a proxy for risk exposure, it has several undesirable qualities. See Yawitz, Hempel, and Marshall, "Average Maturity as a Risk Proxy in Investment Decisions," for a discussion of the shortcomings of maturity as a risk proxy.

3. List and explain the four sources of risk for debt securities. What is probably the biggest risk of all, given our present economic conditions?
4. Briefly, why is common stock more risky than debt instruments?
5. Why would a management objective directed toward minimizing the risk of particular assets lead to disaster in a financial environment? What is a more appropriate approach?
6. Within the context of portfolio analysis, how should management select an efficient asset–liability mix?
7. What does diversification mean? How does one effectively diversify?
8. What are the two major shortcomings in using historical observations in a portfolio selection model?
9. Briefly describe the difference betweeen the Markowitz and Sharpe models for portfolio selection.

Selected References

Francis, Jack Clark and Archer, Stephen H. *Portfolio Analysis.* Englewood Cliffs, N.J.: Prentice-Hall, 1971.

Homer, Sidney. *A History of Interest Rates.* New Brunswick, N.J.: Rutgers University Press, 1963.

Homer, Sidney and Leibowitz, Martin L. *Inside the Yield Book.* Englewood Cliffs, N.J.: Prentice-Hall, 1972.

Kessel, R. A. *The Cyclical Behavior of the Term Structure of Interest Rates.* New York: National Bureau of Economic Research, 1965.

Malkiel, B.G. *The Term Structure of Interest Rates.* Princeton, N.J.: Princeton University Press, 1966.

Michaelson, J. B. *The Term Structure of Interest Rates: Financial Intermediaries and Debt Management.* New York: Intext Educational Publishers, 1973.

Money Market Instruments. 2d ed. Cleveland: Federal Reserve Bank of Cleveland, 1965.

Norgaard, R. L. "An Examination of the Yields of Corporate Bonds and Stocks." *Journal of Finance,* September 1974, pp. 1275–86.

Sharpe, W. F. *Portfolio and Capital Markets.* New York: McGraw-Hill, 1970.

Van Horne, James C. *Functions and Analysis of Capital Market Rates.* Englewood Cliffs, N.J.: Prentice-Hall, 1970.

Yawitz, Jess; Hempel, George; and Marshall, William. "Average Maturity as a Risk Proxy in Investment Decisions." *Journal of Finance,* 30:2, May 1975.

```
44444444444444444444444444444444444444444444444444444444444444444444444444444444
44444444444444444444444444444444444444444444444444444444444444444444444444444444
444444444444444444444444444444   444   444444444444   44444444444444444444444444444
444444444444444444444444444444   4444   44444444444   44444444444444444444444444444
444444444444444444444444444444   44444   444444444   444444444444444444444444444444
444444444444444444444444444444   444444   4444444   4444444444444444444444444444444
444444444444444444444444444444   4444444   44444   44444444444444444444444444444444
444444444444444444444444444444   44444444   444   444444444444444444444444444444444
444444444444444444444444444444   444444444   4   4444444444444444444444444444444444
444444444444444444444444444444   4444444444     44444444444444444444444444444444444
444444444444444444444444444444   4444444444   444444444444444444444444444444444444444
44444444444444444444444444444444444444444444444444444444444444444444444444444444
44444444444444444444444444444444444444444444444444444444444444444444444444444444
```

The Environment
of Financial Institutions

Up to this point we have implied that nearly all financial institutions should follow the conceptual models developed in Chapters 2 and 3. If this implication was valid, we would probably find that different types of financial institutions would be very similar. Furthermore, we probably would not find some of the seemingly contradictory asset and liability structures found in financial institutions. As an example, the practice of savings and loan associations of financing long-term assets with short-term liabilities. A quick look at the real world indicates that neither condition exists—there are significant differences among financial institutions and some asset and liability structures are inconsistent with the wealth-maximization objective. This disparity cannot be attributed to weakness in our conceptual models, but rather to the environment in which financial institutions are forced to operate. Two elements stand out: the historical development of the institutions and their regulatory environment.

If the historical development of financial institutions in the United States may be said to have followed a pattern, it has been like the pattern of a crazy quilt. The opposing strands of warp and woof have been both functional and structural. The basic functional opposition has been the struggle between the provision of ample credit and safety in financial institutions. The structural opposition has been twofold. There has been the continuing conflict between state-chartered institutions and those established under the aegis of the federal government; and there has been the opposition between the advocates of home-town unit institutions and the more extensive branch and holding company systems. The result of this interweaving has been a design which contains a little of everything, including continued controversy. The pattern was developed in four historical periods: the formative years, 1781-1860; the rapid but irregular growth from 1861-1900; the movement toward more competition and more regulation, 1901-1945; and the postwar period, 1946-1976.

The Formative Years: 1781–1860

Few of our current financial institutions existed prior to American independence. There were government-owned land banks—institutions that issued paper money against mortgages on land—and some branches of foreign financial institutions, such as banks and insurance companies. Merchants who needed credit or who had obtained credit to offer to their customers often carried on a bankinglike business as a sideline to merchandising. Finally, in late 1781, the first incorporated bank, The Bank of North America, was established by Robert A. Morris in an effort to support the credit of the newly formed United States. The Bank of New York and the Massachussetts Bank were established in 1784. These three banks served as a good example for successful banking, and they were joined by the federally chartered Bank of the United States in 1791. Other state banks were chartered in the following years, and the American pattern for a number of privately owned independent banks was established. This pattern was in keeping with the frontier spirit of competition and the need for credit to finance the expanding nation.

Commercial banks were the first and the dominant financial institutions in this period. Both the banking system and the country grew. In 1820 there were approximately 300 individual banks; by 1845 there were 506; the number passed 1,000 in the early 1840s, and reached 1,601 by the end of 1860, at which time a bank credit of $800 million was in effect.[1] Bank credit flowed into agriculture, merchant inventories, transport facilities, key industrial enterprises, and government. Banks served as the primary means of funneling savings and foreign capital into domestic investment.

The creation of purchasing power by banks aided the growth of the American economy. Before the Revolution, the American economy consisted mostly of self-sufficient farms. By the end of 1860 the growth of commercial enterprise necessitated the development of a financial structure that would enable business to take full advantage of a national market giving full scope to specialization and exchange. From 1790 to 1861 the economy's production expanded eighteenfold. During this period the quantity of money increased fortyfold to $600 million with no adverse inflationary effects.[2]

The extension of bank loans to finance the expanding economy fluc-

---

[1]Controller of the Currency, *Annual Report for 1876* (Washington, D.C.; GPO, December 2, 187), p. 159, and Paul B. Trescott, *Financing American Enterprise* (New York: Harper & Row, 1963), pp. 16–23. About a thousand additional banks were started but also closed, nearly all within ten years of opening, through 1860.

[2]Trescott, Ibid., p. 18.

tuated greatly at this time. During periods of boom, bank credit was vigorously expanded; in downturns, bank credit fell precipitously. For example, bank notes expanded 56 percent from 1834 to 1837, fell by 60 percent from 1837 to 1843, then expanded by 119 percent from 1843 to 1848.[3] These savings in the extension of bank credit helped to accentuate variations in economic activity over this period. The economic decline tested the strength of banking institutions. Many banks had inadequate capital and held loans that were highly speculative and backed by insufficient security. When economic activity declined, there were numerous bank failures which created large losses for depositors.

Efforts to promote "safe" banking during this period stressed the ability of banks to exchange bank notes for specie (currency). This emphasis on safety resulted in the restriction of bank credit and caused a steady increase in unsatisfied credit demands and eventual relaxation of credit controls at the expense of monetary responsibility. These gyrations tended to underscore the importance of both monetary responsibility and the credit function of banks, neither of which could be subordinated to the other.

The various attempts made by states to control banking excesses met varying success. The most concerted efforts were undertaken by the First and Second Banks of the United States which were chartered by Congress. The First Bank of the United States was chartered in 1791, and established branches in major port cities. It served as a clearinghouse for notes and checks of other banks when they were presented as payment to the government. State-chartered banks were forced to keep a sufficient amount of specie on hand to meet the demands of the First Bank when their notes and checks were presented for payment. This requirement served to limit the amount of notes issued by state-chartered banks.

The First Bank's charter was not renewed in 1811 because state's rights sentiment ran high and because the growing country needed additional sources of credit. During the next several years state-chartered banks extended vast amounts of credit (partially to aid in financing the War of 1812) and greatly expanded their notes and deposit liabilities. There was a rapid inflationary spiral and in 1814 and 1815 many banks were forced to suspend specie payments.

Cries for reform were strong and a Second Bank of the United States was chartered in 1816. It was similar to the First Bank of the United States, but much larger. The Second Bank started poorly by continuing to expand loans during the period primarily because some of its branches were directed by corrupt speculators. America experienced its first monetary panic in 1819 when upheavals in the international financial situation caused a drain of gold and silver from the country. Later, the Second Bank followed a policy of spirited credit reduction and gained the amity of a large sector of the American populace.

The Second Bank gradually developed into a more efficient instrument

[3]Lester V. Chandler, *The Economics of Money and Banking*, 4th ed. (New York: Harper & Row, 1964).

of banking control under Nicholas Biddle. The Bank's lending policy was controlled so as to offset fluctuations in economic activity and, through its vigilance, state-chartered banks were forced to maintain reasonable credit positions. The result was moderate growth in credit and a relatively safe banking system.

This period of safe banking with moderate credit growth ended when Andrew Jackson became president. Jackson strongly favored a rapid expansion of credit to finance the growing country. In 1836 he refused to renew the charter of the Second Bank. Jackson's emphasis on credit rather than safety encouraged a rapid expansion of economic activity, financed to a large extent by a massive increase in state bank notes. This rapid expansion culminated with a serious depression in the late 1830s and early 1840s. Bank failures, lack of confidence in bank notes, and the precipitous decline in bank credit contributed heavily to the depression. While the problems encountered during this period would seem to vindicate the central bank concept, there was not sufficient support for the establishment of a third bank of the United States. The job of bank regulation was left to the states who exercised the function with varying degrees of success.

Commercial banks, nevertheless, remained the dominant financial intermediary — accounting for about seven-eighths of the assets of all financial intermediaries in 1860. The banks of that period differed greatly from present-day commerical banks. Common equity, consisting of common shareholders' original contributions and retained earnings, furnished about half of the total sources of funds. The remaining half was divided about evenly between bank notes and deposits. Most of the funds were used for fairly short-term loans to businesses. Most commercial banks were not interested in financing governments or consumers.

Even though commercial banks were by far the dominant financial institution, many other of today's financial institutions can trace their development in the United States to the early 1800s. Most commercial banks emphasized self-liquidating commercial loans financed by larger demand-type accounts. To fill the need for lending on real property and to supply a competitive outlet for small savings, mutual savings banks appeared in the boom years after the War of 1812. The Massachusetts Hospital Life Insurance Company, the first trust company, was created in 1818 to provide an investment outlet for colonists as well as income for Massachusetts General Hospital. The forerunner of our modern savings and loan associations, Oxford Provident Building Association, was founded in Philadelphia in 1831 as a cooperative engaged in financing the building and purchasing of homes. The first investment banking concerns began operations in the 1830s. While private insurance companies are as old as the country itself, the first mutual life insurance companies did not begin operation until the 1840s. Figure 4-1 shows that no major financial institution appeared from the mid-1840s through 1900. Most of the institutions not appearing by the 1840s were formed in the period from the early 1900s through the 1929-1933 depression.

In summary, throughout the nation's formative years, financial institu-

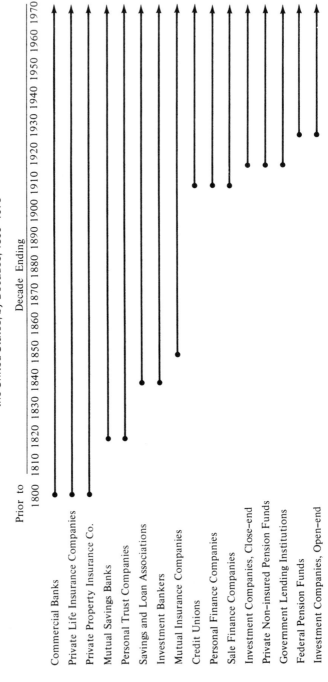

Figure 4-1. Appearance of Different Types of Financial Institutions in the United States, by Decades, 1800–1975

52

tions played a vital role in increasing the circulation of money and in the establishment of an efficient market economy. Banks were by far the dominant financial institution during this period. Most nonbank financial institutions were established to fill an economic void not covered by banking. The creation of money in the form of bank notes and bank deposits furnished a large proportion of the money needed to fuel the country's growth as the economy became increasingly specialized and dependent on exchange. Unstable, and at times unsound, bank lending policies contributed heavily to the recurrent problem of instability in the economy. Nevertheless, economic development proceeded more rapidly, although unevenly, because of the creation of purchasing power by banks in excess of the amounts generated out of current savings.

Rapid but Irregular Growth: 1861 to the Early 1900s

The period from the beginning of the Civil War through the early 1900s was a time when financial intermediaries experienced rapid financial growth. During this period of wildcat financing, financial institutions were not heavily regulated and it was reasonably easy to start (or terminate) a financial institution. The U.S. economy and the total assets of financial institutions grew irregularly but at a much more rapid average rate than in the first six decades of the nineteenth century. Most of the increased savings which fed the financial institutions flowed through commercial banks, savings banks, life insurance companies, and trust companies. Commercial banks remained by far the dominant financial institution. As shown in Table 4-1, financial institutions in 1900 controlled more than 11 times as many assets as they did in 1850.

The demand for funds to finance the Civil War led to the National Banking Act of 1863, which legalized the creation of a national bank note currency backed by United States securities. Existing state-chartered banks were strongly encouraged to obtain national charters because these notes could be issued only by banks with national charters. So many amendments were submitted for the improvement of the 1863 act that it was replaced by the completely revised National Banking Act of June 3, 1864. This legislation did not establish a system of central banks but only made possible the chartering of banks by the federal government. The 1864 act provides the basis for our present national banking laws.

The combined effects of these acts were limited but led to essential reforms of the monetary system. These acts tended to stress the monetary function of banks over the credit function. Banks were effectively restrained from extending private credit through note issues. In order to encourage liquidity and safety, another provision of the acts prohibited national banks from making mortgage loans. In addition, national banks were prohibited from making loans on their own stock. They were forbidden to make an individual loan in excess of 10 percent of their capital accounts. The banking acts opened the way for easy entry into banking

TABLE 4-1   Growth of Major Types of Financial Institutions

A. Growth in Number of Units and Offices (in thousands)

	Number of Units					Number of Offices*				
	1850	1900	1929	1949	1974	1850	1900	1929	1949	1974
Commercial banks	0.7	12.9	24.3	14.2	14.5	0.9	13.0	27.8	18.7	42.9
Life insurance companies	0.0	0.7	0.8	0.6	1.8	—	—	—	—	—
Property insurance companies	0.2	0.7	1.4	1.0	3.0	—	—	—	—	—
Mutual savings banks	0.1	0.6	0.6	0.5	0.5	0.1	0.6	0.7	0.7	2.1
Savings and loan associations	0.0	5.4	12.3	6.0	5.0	0.0	5.4	12.4	6.2	13.9
Credit unions	—	—	1.0	10.1	23.0	—	—	1.0	10.1	23.0
Trust companies and departments	0.0	0.1	3.5	3.0	2.6	—	—	—	—	—
Investment companies	—	—	0.5	0.2	0.7	—	—	0.5	0.2	0.7
Finance companies	—	—	1.3	5.4	3.5	—	—	—	—	—
Investment bankers	0.1	1.0	3.0	2.9	0.8	0.1	1.1	5.0	4.2	3.9

B. Growth in Total Dollar Assets (billions of dollars)

	1850	1900	1929	1949	1974
Commercial banks	$0.5	$10.0	$ 66.0	$157.7	$916.3
Life insurance companies	0.0	1.7	18.3	61.6	263.3
Property insurance companies	0.0	0.5	4.7	11.0	81.3
Mutual savings banks	0.0	2.4	9.9	21.5	109.6
Savings and loan associations	—	0.5	7.4	14.5	295.6
Credit unions	—	—	0.0	0.8	32.0
Trust companies and departments	0.0	3.0	30.0	50.0	377.8
Investment companies	—	—	3.0	3.3	62.7
Finance companies	—	—	2.6	6.4	93.4
Investment bankers	—	0.6	10.0	2.7	16.8
Government lending institutions	—	—	0.4	23.7	87.0
Private noninsured pension funds	—	—	0.5	6.0	133.7
State and local pension funds	—	—	0.5	4.9	93.9
Federal pension funds	—	—	0.0	34.3	84.6
Total covered institutions	$0.6	$18.7	$154.7	$398.4	$2,648.0

Sources: 1850-1949 data from Raymond W. Goldsmith, *Financial Intermediaries in the American Economy Since 1900* (Princeton, N.J.: Princeton University Press, 1958). 1974 data from Table 1-1, Chapter 1.

*Shown only when the concept of ''office'' is clear and information is available.

throughout the country. Since states no longer monopolized the chartering of banks, many states were forced to ease the requirements for bank chartering.

While the acts succeeded in shoring up the underpinnings of the banking structure, their very restrictive posture led to the development of a dual banking system. The capital requirements for national banks were onerous to the western and southern portions of the nation. In the West, much capital was needed to develop land and resources. The South needed capital to rebuild a war-ravaged economy. Substantial sources of capital were not available in either area and export of capital from the eastern portion of the nation was erratic and often not sufficient to satisfy expansionary needs. These shortages can be attributed, in part, to the prohibition of nationwide branch banking. Large eastern banks were prohibited from establishing branches in order to funnel savings into other areas of the country. Even if eastern banks could have established branches in these areas, they would have been prevented by law from supplying the strong demand for mortgage credit.

Another major factor in the revival of state-chartered banks after the Civil War was the gradual acceptance of bank deposits as money. The state banks that retained their state charters after Congress imposed the 10 percent tax on state bank notes adopted the practice of making loans in the form of deposits against which the borrower could write checks. This lending process was a great stimulus for checking accounts, which were already being adopted across the nation because of their increased spread of communication and transportation.

After the Civil War the nation embarked upon an era of rapid economic growth. Real output of goods and services is estimated to have increased at roughly a 6 percent compound annual rate from the late 1860s to the early 1900s. An increase in population, a large increase in the amount of land under cultivation, the creation of a national transportation system, and America's industrial revolution were all important contributing factors to this growth. Banks remained by far the most important financial institution in the United States — rarely holding less than three-fifths of the assets of all financial institutions. Banks continued to supply the essential credit to finance farming, railroads, and industry; however, the character of their operations and the structure of their sources and uses of funds underwent great changes during this period. The ease in obtaining state charters and the ease in regulations and supervision by state banking authorities permitted state-chartered banks to grow roughly 70 percent of the total number of banks holding nearly 50 percent of the total assets of commercial banks by the early 1900s. Bank notes had fallen below 5 percent of total sources of bank funds compared to about 25 percent half a century earlier, while their share of net worth fell to less than 20 percent compared with a share of about 50 percent in 1860. By the early 1900s deposits were the dominant source of bank funds and demand deposits accounted for more than three-fourths of this total. Short-term loans to businesses remained the dominant bank asset throughout this period; however, banks also made some longer-term loans to businesses in order to finance capital expenditures.

The economic growth from the end of the Civil War through the early 1900s was not continuous, and the contributions of banking to this growth were not completely salutary. At times the extension of credit was overoptimistic; furthermore, banking declines and failures contributed to the depressions in the mid-1870s and the mid-1890s. The role of banks in precipitating the Panic of 1907 led to demands for a safer banking system.

While deposits in mutual savings banks climbed fiftyfold in the last half of the nineteenth century, most of this growth occurred in the first twenty-five years of this period. The rate of growth of savings banks slowed as population expanded west of the Mississippi River. Westerners who wished to deposit their savings in a bank were able to open time deposit accounts in most banks west of the Mississippi. Life insurance assets grew 100-fold in the last half of the century, allowing life insurance companies to increase their share in the total assets of all intermediaries from 2 to 13 percent. The reasons for this rapid growth included aggressive marketing, the rise in national income, and the increase in the number of people dependent upon someone else for their jobs. Trust companies also grew rapidly during the latter half of the nineteeth century — growing from a few in 1850, to 35 by 1875, approximately 200 by 1890 and slightly over 500 by 1900.[4]

More Competition and Regulation: The Early 1900s to 1945

Both the environment and structure of financial institutions changed markedly from the early 1900s through World War II. At the start of this period competition among different types of financial institutions was limited. Later, new types of financial institutions were formed to fill some of the existing gaps in financial services and the situation grew more competitive. The creation of the Federal Reserve System changed the regulatory environment for banks. The 1929–1933 Depression weakened confidence in all financial institutions, and was particularly damaging to commercial banks and savings and loan associations. Many new regulations and regulatory bodies appeared as a result of these financial problems. Finally, repercussions from World War II severely limited the actions of most financial institutions.

As late as the early 1900s each type of financial institution was highly specialized, performing distinctive functions that rarely overlapped. For example, most larger commercial banks were not interested in time deposits, consumer loans, or long-term loans. Mutual savings banks and savings and loan associations used time deposits as their major sources of funds and were not interested in short-term loans.

Three new consumer-oriented financial institutions — credit unions, personal finance companies, and sales finance companies — were started in the early 1900s. The fact that most existing financial institutions were unable or unwilling to make short- and intermediate-term loans to individuals was probably the primary reason for the formation of these institutions. Their growth was aided by the rapid growth in the demand for consumer durables during this period. Credit unions were mutual organizations obtaining their funds from and making loans to individuals who qualified as members. The finance companies, on the other hand, usually raised over half of their funds by borrowing from commercial banks. The proceeds from these loans and other funds raised (primarily from issuing corporate bonds or stock) were then lent to customers.

The other financial institutions started in this period emphasized income

---

[4]Murry E. Polakoff, et al., *Financial Institutions and Markets* (Boston: Houghton Mifflin, 1970).

assurance systems for retired persons or investment management for moderate savers. Private pension funds — both corporate, and state and local — were started in the 1910s. Their growth was slow; the assets of state and locally administered funds reached the $1 billion mark in 1936, while assets of corporate funds reached this plateau in 1938. Federal government pension funds began appearing in the 1920s, but the majority of such funds, which exist at the present time, were started in the 1930s. Finally, both closed-end and open-end investment companies were started during the 1910s and 1920s as vehicles to allow smaller investors to enjoy the investment expertise and diversification previously available only to large investors.

Competition among financial institutions increased as businesses expanded into larger-scale enterprises and professional management brought a greater degree of sophistication into financial activity. Businessmen and the public began to take advantage of improving transportation and communication. The public also became much more familiar with the securities market when the federal government financed World War I by borrowing over $25 billion. Public familiarity with insurance increased through the federal government's program for insuring members of the armed forces.

Faced with a loss of customers to other financial institutions, commercial banks became more aggressive. They entered the retail business by welcoming time deposits and they moved away from the real bills doctrine with its emphasis on short-term, self-liquidating commercial loans. Banks also moved into new areas — laws were passed allowing national banks to purchase investment securities and enlarging their power to make real estate loans. In spite of this aggressiveness on the part of banks, their dominance over other financial institutions began to slip nationally in the 1920s (Table 4-2). Other financial institutions, particularly savings and loan associations and life insurance companies, grew more rapidly than banks.

Then came the Depression from 1929 to 1933. Both the volume and the rate of savings fell sharply with demands for funds from credit-worthy businesses and individuals declining rapidly. With the shift toward greater risk aversion, investment bankers and investment companies were the major casualties, not fully recovering for the next two decades. Commercial banking was also badly hurt by the Depression, partly because the public feared for the safety of its deposits. When the "banking holiday" was declared in 1933, commercial bank assets were below what they had been in 1922. Between 1930 and 1933, 9,096 commercial banks, with deposits of $6.8 billion (approximately 13 percent of total deposits in 1930), were suspended. Final losses to depositors were estimated to be nearly $1.3 billion. During the same four-year period 526 savings and loan associations, with assets of $0.4 billion (roughly 5 percent of deposits in 1930) failed. On the other hand, mutual savings banks (only 10 banks whose assets totaled less than $30 million failed), life insurance companies, and

TABLE 4-2 Percent of Financial Assets of Selected Financial Institutions in Selected Years, 1900–1974

	1900	1912	1922	1929	1933	1939	1949	1959	1965	1974
Commercial banks	66.2%	67.3%	69.1%	58.1%	49.7%	52.6%	55.0%	41.5%	37.5%	44.7%
Life insurance companies	11.3	13.6	12.7	16.1	22.5	23.2	21.5	20.5	17.0	12.8
Property insurance companies	3.3	3.7	4.1	4.8	4.9	4.8	3.8	4.9	4.3	4.0
Mutual savings banks	15.9	12.3	9.6	8.7	11.7	9.4	7.5	7.4	6.5	5.3
Savings and loan associations	3.3	3.1	4.1	6.5	6.7	4.3	5.1	10.8	14.4	14.4
Private noninsured pension funds	—	—	.1	.4	.8	.8	2.1	5.6	7.8	6.5
State and local pension funds	—	—	.1	.4	.9	1.3	1.7	3.9	5.0	4.6
Investment companies	—	—	.2	2.6	1.4	1.3	1.2	2.6	3.9	3.1
Finance companies	—	*	*	2.3	1.5	2.4	2.2	2.9	3.5	4.6
Total selected financial institutions . . .	100.0%	100.0%	100.0%	100.0%	100.0%	100.0%	100.0%	100.0%	100.0%	100.0%
Amount of assets (in $ billions)	$15.1	$32.4	$68.7	$113.9	$92.7	$126.1	$286.9	$509.8	$898.6	$2,049.8

Sources: Raymond W. Goldsmith, *Financial Intermediaries in the American Economy Since 1900* (Princeton, N.J.: Princeton University Press, 1958), and Table 1-1, Chapter 1.

*Assets were less than 0.1 percent of total financial assets.

public and private pension funds escaped the Depression with little or no decline in total assets.[5]

During the 1900-1945 period two new major bank regulatory bodies were formed. Both are still in existence today. The first of these bodies, the Federal Reserve System, was created as a result of the inherent weakness in the United States banking system as it existed in the early 1900s and because of the new demands on banking which developed as the economy expanded during the late 1800s and early 1900s.

Decentralization resulted in banks that were local in character and owned by residents of the communities in which they were located. In the absence of a central bank, there was a wide variety of legal reserves. Reserve balances of country banks at city banks and reserve city banks were, in many cases, used to purchase securities and make call loans by the bank to which they were entrusted. These investments supposedly could be liquidated at once with minimum capital loss; however, in times of financial distress they could only be liquidated at a great loss. Therefore, while on paper reserves might have appeared to be sufficient to meet a liquidity crisis, the scattering of reserves left the banking system constantly exposed to swings in demand for currency which might trigger a financial collapse.

Another major problem was the inflexibility of national bank notes. When the national banking system was established, it was envisioned that national bank notes would expand during periods of heavy credit demands and contract during periods of inactive business. The volume of national bank notes, however, was realistically governed not by the need for credit but rather by the availability and price of government bonds. The increases and decreases in note circulation often ended up having the effect of increasing cyclical pressure on the economy.[6]

There were several other noticeable weaknesses and new problems. First, the volume of bank loans was only marginally more responsive to credit needs of the economy than were bank notes. Rigid legal minima for bank reserves in many cases stifled the ability to extend credit. Bankers Acceptances had been ruled illegal by the courts and the rediscount business among commercial banks was almost nonexistent. Second, banks were facing an increasing operational problem trying to handle the expanding volume of checks. With no centralized location to effect the efficiencies of size and organization, the collection of checks drawn on banks scattered throughout the country was a complicated and expensive task. Third, the banking system was subject to the unsettling influence of government receipts and expenditures. The amount of Treasury funds deposited in banks varied greatly during the year because of the uneven pattern of federal government revenue collection and expenditures.

The cries for banking reform intensified when banks were blamed for the short but severe Panic of 1907. A National Monetary Commission was

---

[5]Polakoff et al., *Financial Institutions and Markets.*
[6]J. Martin Peterson and D. R. Cawthorne, *Money and Banking* (New York: Macmillan, 1949), p. 117.

formed in 1908 to survey the activities of U.S. banks here and abroad and to offer suggestions as to how to strengthen our banking system. Their efforts were culminated with the passage of the Federal Reserve Act in December of 1913.

The Federal Reserve System, which became effective in 1914, was a compromise between the system of independently owned banks in existence in this country and the central banking systems of such countries as Canada, Great Britain, Spain, and Germany. Many of the proponents of central banking stressed the need for an efficient central bank; however, the opening of the vast western frontiers in addition to the local autonomy of the southern areas created an atmosphere of distrust for centralized financial control. The resulting compromise took the form of a series of 12 central banks, each representing a specific region of the United States, and hence being more responsive to the particular financial problems of that region.

The Federal Reserve System did not supplant the system that existed under the National Banking Act but rather was superimposed upon it. All national banks were required to become members of the Federal Reserve System. State-chartered banks were permitted to join the system upon the presentation of evidence of a satisfactory financial condition. All member banks were required to purchase capital stock in the individual Federal Reserve bank in their district up to a maximum of 6 percent of their paid-in capital and surplus. The Federal Reserve banks were, therefore, private institutions owned by the many member banks of the Federal Reserve System. Member banks could receive dividends of up to 6 percent on the stock of their Federal Reserve bank.

A Board of Governors in Washington, D.C., was responsible for coordinating the activities of the 12 district Federal Reserve banks. The Board's powers were severely limited prior to the mid-1930s. The primary tool used to influence the cost and availability of credit was the rate charged to member banks when additional funds were borrowed from the Federal Reserve System. Each of the 12 district Federal Reserve banks had the power to independently set this "discount" rate. Member banks were required to hold reserves against demand and savings deposits in the form of deposits at their Federal Reserve bank; however, such reserve ratios could not be employed to control credit availability since the percentage of reserves to be held against deposits was fixed, by an act of Congress, until the mid-1930s. While the Board of Governors and some Federal Reserve banks experimented with the purchase and sale of government securities in the mid-1920s, it was the mid-1930s before the Federal Open Market Committee was formally established with the power to control these purchases and sales.

Even in the early years of its existence, the Federal Reserve System was successful in overcoming some of the previous banking weaknesses. Federal Reserve banks became the main source of currency in the United States. These banks bore the cost of minting, shipping, and issuing their currency, which served to replace the previously inflexible monetary system. As the public's demand for currency changed, the Federal Reserve bank automatically adjusted the flow of such currency from the reservoirs of funds. The Federal Reserve System also facilitated the clearance and collection of checks for the banks of the nation. Each Federal Reserve bank served as a clearinghouse for all the banks in its district, and checks were cleared between districts through the Inter- district Settlement Fund. The Federal Reserve System also provided other needed services such as acting as the government fiscal agent and providing supervision and regulation of member banks.

The early years of the Federal Reserve System were generally favorable. The country experienced a brief, but severe, economic decline a year or so after the end of World War I. From 1922 to 1929, however, the country experienced prosperity and stable economic growth marked by only very mild recessions. There was a close correlation in time between movements in economic activity and the explicit policy measures taken by the Federal Reserve System. This close synchronism produced confidence that the monetary mechanisms of the Federal Reserve System offered a workable approach to smoothing and sustaining economic growth. This presumption was rudely shattered by the 1929 Depression.

The Depression years of 1929 to 1933 led to significant changes in the Federal Reserve System and to the creation of a new regulatory body. There was a period of uncertainty in banking circles following the stock market crash in 1929; however, most banks managed to survive the initial shock. The number of bank failures started to accelerate in late 1931, and by March of 1933 over 9,000 banks (roughly one-third of the total number of banks) were forced to close their doors. The causes of these failures included: the inadequate capital of many banks; the illiquid nature of many secured bank loans; monetary tightness in late 1931 (when the Federal Reserve, fearing inflation and gold outflows, allowed bank credit to decline for several months at a rate of approximately 25 percent per annum); and the lack of public faith exemplified by conversions of deposits into currency.[7]

In 1933 the Federal government took decisive action to restore confidence in the banking system. First, there was a temporary "banking holiday." Second, a federal system of deposit insurance became operational. Finally, several changes were enacted to centralize and strengthen the power of the Federal Reserve System. The latter two events are discussed in the following paragraphs because they are the basis for much of our current regulatory environment.

As the number of bank failures grew in the early 1930s, there was an insistent demand for an effective form of deposit insurance. This demand was not new. States such as New York (initiated in 1829), Vermont, In-

[7]Rudolph L. Weissman, *The New Federal Reserve System* (New York: Harper & Row, 1936), p. 34.

diana, Michigan, Ohio, and Iowa developed plans to afford protection to both the notes issued by banks in those particular states and the deposits of bank customers. Meager resources and the lack of economic diversification severely limited the effectiveness of most state plans. In addition to the state plans, approximately 150 bills for federal guarantee or insurance were introduced in Congress from 1886 to 1933. Finally, the 1934 Steagall Amendment to the Glass Bill of 1933 established a temporary form of deposit insurance. In 1935 Congress agreed on a permanent insurance plan that provided for the establishment of a corporation to be known as the Federal Deposit Insurance Corporation (FDIC).[8]

The FDIC initially afforded a single depositor maximum deposit insurance of up to $5,000. Membership was required for all members of the Federal Reserve System. In addition, any state bank that was not a member of the Federal Reserve was free to join the FDIC if it desired to do so. Mutual savings banks were also permitted to join the FDIC and most did. Ironically, however, federal deposit insurance practically eliminated an important competitive advantage of mutual savings banks, their excellent performance under adverse economic conditions. The FDIC has changed slightly over the years. Its current status is reviewed later in this chapter.

The Federal Reserve System changed appreciably during the decade of the 1930s. Hindsight indicates the sharp contraction of credit in late 1931 was an error. The existence of commercial bank deposits at Federal Reserve banks was not effective as a method of preventing numerous bank failures. The lack of real coordination or flexibility was evident. For example, one of the reasons bank excess reserves rose rapidly in the mid-1930s was the fixed nature of reserve requirements.

There were three notable changes in the Federal Reserve System during the mid-1930s. First, the Federal Open Market Committee was formalized and given full control over all purchases and sales of government securities by the Federal Reserve banks. Second, the Board of Governors was given broader powers to alter the legal reserve requirements within a broad range set by Congress and to require approval of changes in the discount rate charged in the various Federal Reserve district banks. Third, the Board of Governors was given special powers to regulate the credit terms on which transactions in certain segments of the economy, such as stock market securities, were financed.

Commercial banks began to change in the 1930s. By the mid-1930s banks were faced with low demand for short-term loans to businesses and farmers, and very low interest rates on high-quality bonds. While banks wanted to avoid illiquid loans and loans for speculative purposes, they desperately needed new outlets for income funds. Three outlets, in addition to the traditional self-liquidating, short-term business and farm loans, were explored. Many banks expanded their amortized mortgage lending to

---

[8]Carl A. Dauten and Merle T. Welshans, *Principles of Finance* (Cincinnati: South Western, 1975), pp. 57³60.

consumers. A few banks began making loans to consumers to finance automobile purchases and other personal needs. Other banks soon followed because of the high profits on these loans. Finally, some banks began to make loans to businesses with scheduled maturities of several years. Even with these new forms, loan demand was low and the extension of business and consumer credit was severely limited during World War II.

The Postwar Years: 1946-1976

Economic decisions during World War II strongly influenced the immediate postwar period. About 60 percent, or $228 billion, of total government expenditures during World War II were financed by borrowing. Most of this indebtedness was held by financial institutions. From 1940 to 1948 the money supply had more than tripled, money incomes had multiplied more than two and one-half times, and wholesale prices had more than doubled.[9] The liquid asset holdings of the general public and of the financial system were greatly expanded. For example, slightly over 56 percent of all bank assets on December 31, 1945 were U.S. government bonds.[10]

During the immediate postwar period the Federal Reserve could not use its major stabilizing weapon — open market operations — to control the continuing inflationary pressures. This limitation was the result of Federal Reserve policies regarding the purchase and sale of government securities initiated during the war to aid Treasury financing. When the United States entered World War II it was understood that in time of national emergency the primary responsibility of a central bank was to facilitate the financing of necessary government expenditures. It was the duty of the Federal Reserve to insure that funds to finance the war would be forthcoming. In order to facilitate the acceptance of debt issues of the Treasury, the Federal Reserve System adopted a policy of establishing and maintaining rates on government securities. The Federal Reserve would buy or sell government securities to maintain these predetermined rates. This "pegged" rate structure would assure the Treasury of a market for its bonds and remove the incentive for investors who believed that higher rates might be offered on later issues to defer purchases of bonds.

These pegged rates severely handicapped the Federal Reserve in dealing with the recession of 1948. When business activity declines the Federal Reserve should normally follow a policy of easy money, creating bank reserves to encourage credit expansion and bolster total demand. But with demand for credit weak, banks tended to purchase government securities. This demand forced the price of government securities up, forcing the Federal Reserve to sell securities to check the declining rates. The sale of

---

[9]Milton Friedman and Anna Jacobson Schwartz, *A Monetary History of the United States* (Princeton, N.J.: Princeton University Press for NBER, 1963), pp. 493 and 546.

[10]Based on figures from *Federal Reserve Bulletins* (Washington, D.C.: Board of Governors, 1975).

securities by the Federal Reserve absorbed bank reserves, making credit more difficult to obtain. The Federal Reserve felt it could not properly affect the supply and availability of credit if forced to maintain the pegged rates.

With the outbreak of hostilities in Korea in mid-1950, the dispute between the Federal Reserve and the Treasury intensified. Defense expenditures soared with concommitant inflationary pressures. A large government deficit and strong private demand fueled credit expansion. The Federal Reserve became increasingly anxious about their responsibility to prevent inflation. Treasury officials, on the other hand, were concerned with any disturbance in the government security market which might complicate the financing of the burgeoning government deficit.

The result was an agreement in March of 1951 popularly referred to as the Accord. The Accord, while reiterating the duty of the Federal Reserve to maintain an orderly market in government securities, freed the Federal Reserve from a commitment to support government bond prices. The Accord was a milestone in Federal Reserve history. Not since the early 1930s had the Federal Reserve been in a position to regulate the money supply and reserves. Excess reserves were large for several years prior to World War II; therefore, open market operations were ineffectual as a means of fundamentally altering reserve positions or influencing interest rates. With the advent of World War II, open market operations were conducted to maintain a prescribed rate on government securities to facilitate Treasury financing. The post-accord period was, in many respects, the first real test of monetary policy since the 1930s.

The decade of the 1950s saw irregular growth in the American economy. A strong underlying demand for capital assets was a prime factor in moving the economy forward. Recessions in 1953 and 1957 and the pressure of the Korean War (1950-1952) interrupted the overall growth of the decade. The Accord enabled the Federal Reserve to end the rise in prices engendered by the Korean involvement. Economic activity continued at a high level for some two years after prices peaked in eary 1951. By 1953 the Federal Reserve was again concerned with inflationary pressures and initiated a series of restrictive actions which produced a rapid tightening of money markets. The Federal Reserve changed its policy to one of monetary ease and the downturn reversed itself in mid-1954. The economy continued upward until mid-1957 when another downturn began. At this time the Federal Reserve found itself battling both inflation and a recession. The Federal Reserve adopted an easy monetary policy and aided the recovery from the economic downswing. The economy slowed down again in 1960 after the Federal Reserve again tightened monetary policy to fight inflation.

The period from the end of World War II through 1960 was the start of a new era for commercial banks. Commercial banks were the major and most diversified source of loan funds to finance the substantial but erratic growth of the 1950s. Banks provided a substantial portion of the credit to finance the purchase of capital assets by business and agriculture, public improvements by governments, and durable goods by consumers. While continuing to supply short-term credit to business and agriculture, banks also supplied substantial amounts in consumer loans and for the financing of fixed-capital outlays by business through term loans.[11]

Several other bank-related developments in this period seem worthy of mention. First, bank loan-to-deposit ratios had a sharp upward trend and bank liquidity declined throughout this period. Such trends could not continue indefinitely. Second, the trend of interest rates was upward following the Accord. While this trend increased the return on bank assets, it created potential liabitity problems. With considerably higher returns available, the holding of large demand deposit balances was less attractive. Also, competing financial intermediaries, such as savings and loan associations, mutual savings banks, and credit unions, tended to pay a significantly higher return on their savings deposits. Such financial intermediaries grew considerably faster, albeit from a lower base, than commercial banks. Annual average interest rates on the savings deposits of commercial banks, savings and loans, and mutual savings banks and rates on Treasury bills appear in Figure 4-2.

During the 1950s savings and loan associations experienced an incredible rate of growth. In addition to their interest rate advantage cited above, savings and loans prospered because they were located in the capital-scarce far West, and because they were often managed by aggressive entrepreneurs. Credit unions grew at an equally rapid rate from a much smaller base because of their favorable return differential during the 1950s. Mutual savings banks, on the other hand, grew at a much slower rate. The advantages of the higher interest rates they paid on savings deposits compared with rates available from commercial banks were partially mitigated by their reputation of being overly conservative.

Other financial institutions fared unevenly from the affluence and prosperity of the 1950s. Life insurance company growth slowed, while pension funds and investment companies grew faster than average (see Table 4-2 for the proportionate holdings of financial assets of most financial institutions).

An economic downturn that began in 1960 continued into early 1961.

[11]According to Trescott, *Financing American Enterprise*, pp. 219-230, business firms obtained about $44 billion in bank credit directly from commercial banks and an additional $32 billion through securities purchased by bank-administered trusts and pension funds from 1945 through 1960. To finance much-needed capital expenditures, state and local governments obtained $14 billion directly from commercial banks through bond issues and an additional $4 billion through trust fund investments. The banks also played a major role in marketing these bonds to other buyers. Commercial bank credit also provided a major part of the financing for consumers. By 1960 more than one-fifth of all bank credit was going to individual households. Commercial banks furnished about one-sixth of home mortgage funds in the postwar period. Commercial banks were also major suppliers of consumer credit for automobile purchases. Directly and indirectly, banks extended nearly one-half of the consumer credit by 1960. Finally, one-third of all farm borrowing was done at commercial banks.

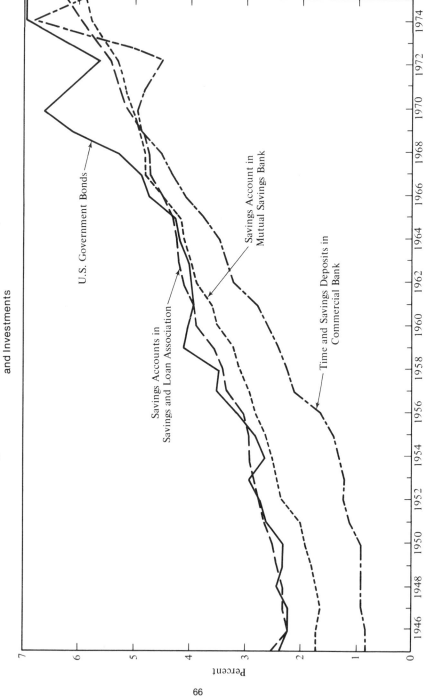

Figure 4-2. Annual Average Yield on Selected Deposits and Investments

U.S. Government Bonds

Savings Accounts in Savings and Loan Association

Savings Account in Mutual Savings Bank

Time and Savings Deposits in Commercial Bank

Percent

1946 1948 1950 1952 1954 1956 1958 1960 1962 1964 1966 1968 1970 1972 1974

Source: *Savings and Loan Fact Book, 1975* (Chicago: U.S. Savings and Loan League, 1976). p. 17.

66

After a promising recovery, activity eased again during the latter part of 1962, and there was widespread feeling that another recession was imminent. The recession did not occur. Neither the slowing of activity in 1962 nor a more substantial dip in late 1966 and early 1967 was of sufficient intensity to be classified as a recession. Thus, the economy grew impressively without decline through most of the 1960s. Until 1966 this growth was accompanied by only modest price increases and was aided by moderately expansive monetary and fiscal policies and excess labor and productive capacity.

In the early 1960s commercial banks, concerned with their slower than average growth in the 1950s, began to compete more effectively for savings deposits in two ways. First, they progressively raised their rates on passbook accounts and savings certificates to compete with other financial intermediaries. Second, starting in 1961 with the large New York banks, commercial banks began to offer negotiable certificates of deposit (CD's) and other liability forms in order to attract savings. These CD's often allowed banks to retain the deposits of large corporate customers who were making serious efforts to economize on demand balances and to attract funds that might have otherwise gone into short-term marketable securities. As the interest paid on bank deposits rose Regulation Q, the regulation which limits both the rate and the other terms banks can use to attract savings, became increasingly significant.[12] Most bank rates were at or close to the maximum rates under Q when these rates were increased in the early 1960s. The rates that banks were paying soon climbed to the new maximum rates and remained at or close to these rates throughout the 1960s and early 1970s.

The relatively noninflationary and rapid growth of the first half of the 1960s changed by late 1965. Inflationary pressures increased drastically because (1) the excess labor and physical capacity of the early 1960s disappeared, (2) the nation had substantial increases in defense expenditures associated with the Vietnam War, and (3) consumer and business spending grew rapidly. The demands for credit by all sectors of the economy increased to a level of more than twice the average in the late 1950s and early 1960s.

Three attempts were made to slow the inflationary trend. Most of the burden was placed on the monetary authorities in 1966. The Federal Reserve used its policies, including Regulation Q, to slow the growth of money and credit in 1966. Their policies led to an alleged near-liquidity crisis in the bond markets and outflows rather than inflows in many nonbank financial intermediaries. The effects of this "credit crunch" proved temporary. Inflationary pressures moderated for a few months, but the pressures, spurred by expansionary monetary and fiscal policy, became even more intense in 1967 and 1968.

---

[12]Regulation Q was part of the Banking Act of 1933. Regulation Q permits the Federal Reserve Board to regulate the rate of interest which banks pay on savings and time deposits having different maturities, different conditions of withdrawal or repayment, or different locations.

In 1969 both monetary and fiscal policies were aimed at curbing excessive spending and price inflation. This time Regulation Q was used as the cutting edge of monetary policy. When the maximum return on deposit forms was below existing market rates, both commercial bank and nonbank financial intermediaries had deposit outflows. Despite attempts by banks to attract funds from unregulated sources, the growth of money and credit was slowed appreciably. There was a great deal of turbulence in the money and capital market and a second and more severe credit crunch resulted, causing a mild but prolonged recession throughout 1970. By mid-1970 monetary policy had eased substantially and banks and other financial institutions began attracting substantial net savings inflows. In 1971 and 1972 most financial institutions found themselves with more savings inflows than demand for credit, and both savings and lending rates fell.

The credit ease in 1972 and most of 1973, as well as the relaxation of the wage and price controls, led to rapid inflation in the latter part of 1973 and most of 1974. Monetary policy was used as the primary tool to ease these inflationary pressures. Regulation Q was not used as extensively and interest rates were allowed to rise even more during this period than in the earlier period of tight money. *Disintermediation* (loss of funds by financial institutions because more funds flow directly between savers and investors) was more pronounced in financial institutions where the return paid was limited by high proportions of fixed return assets. The housing industry seemed to suffer even more than in earlier slowdowns. The economy experienced a sharp downturn starting in the fall of 1974. Both monetary and fiscal policy turned expansive by early 1975 to combat this decline.

Commercial banks were in a substantially different position in 1975 than they were at the start of the 1960s. By growing rapidly through most of the 1960s, banks returned to a position of great relative importance as a source of credit. Banks paid for this growth with a greater reliance on purchased money and by continuing decreases in their liquidity positions. By 1975 time and savings deposits had risen to roughly 60 percent of all bank deposits (excluding interbank deposits). A significant proportion of these time and savings deposits were acquired by banks paying rates that compared favorably with rates paid by other financial institutions and in the open market. Throughout the 1960s and early 1970s, banks' cash and short-term securities declined and banks' loans increased relative to total bank assets.[13]

These trends obviously affected individual banks in different ways. Some aggressive banks had acquired three-fourths of their deposits through rate-competitive funds and had loan-to-deposit ratios of over 100 percent in 1974, while some smaller conservative banks had little, if any, rate-competitive money and had loan-to-deposit ratios under 50 percent.

Other financial institutions also changed in this decade of inflationary pressures and credit crunches. The position of life insurance companies

---

[13]Based on figures from *Federal Reserve Bulletins.*

relative to other financial institutions continued to decline. They had held over 20 percent of the financial assets of the selected financial institutions in Table 4-2 in the 1930s, 1940s, and 1950s; but their share of these assets had fallen to 13.5 percent at the end of 1973. In the late 1960s some life insurance companies made an attempt to combat the negative impact of inflation on their traditionally fixed return policies by offering variable return annuities and variable amount policies. These innovations failed to encourage significant amounts of new insurance business. In addition, the composition of the long-term financial assets held by life insurance companies changed over the last decade or so — for example, they held relatively more lower-rated corporate debts and fewer home mortgages. The reasons for these types of changes are discussed in Chapter 7.

The performance of thrift institutions — mutual savings banks, savings and loan associations, and credit unions — also varied widely over the 1960s and 1970s. The average mutual savings bank grew at a slower rate than the average of all financial institutions, while S&L's and credit unions grew faster than average. In order to combat this trend, many mutual savings banks became much more aggressive in obtaining funds and in managing their asset portfolios. Both mutual savings banks and savings and loan associations grew irregularly because of the long-term nature of their assets and the short-term nature of most of their liabilities. Credit stringency in 1966, 1969, and 1974 brought the growth of these institutions to a standstill because they were unable to compete ratewise with commercial banks and/or direct market instruments. The two major shifts which these two institutions have attempted to employ in order to improve this situation — variable rate mortgages and intermediate-term liabilities — are discussed in Chapter 6. The possible impact of structural changes recommended by the Hunt Commission and other parties, such as liberalizing asset regulation, allowing demand deposits, and reducing tax advantages, are discussed in Chapter 10.

Financial institutions with large amounts of common stock (private pension funds and investment companies) tended to find their growth slowed as inflation seemed to hurt stock prices more than it helped them in the late 1960s and 1970s. The growth of open-end investment companies was dampened the most because of the noncontractual nature of most of their liabilities. These so-called mutual funds suffered two periods during which people withdrew more funds than they invested in these institutions. Current financial management practices in the investment-type financial institutions are discussed in Chapter 9.

The Regulatory Framework for Banks

Regulation of banking is currently divided among three federal agencies and fifty state agencies. Areas of responsibility overlap yet the duties of the diverse regulatory agencies are generally carried out smoothly and efficiently. Indeed, the pluralism of bank regulatory authority in the United

States may have led to a regulatory environment superior to an environment charted by a single authority.

Bank regulation encompasses a wide variety of technical functions relating to the operation of banks. These concern (1) the issuance and enforcement of regulations; (2) the chartering of banks; (3) the periodic examination of banks and the requirement that bank management take steps to correct unsatisfactory or unsound conditions found through such examinations; (4) the review and analysis of periodic reports of conditions, earnings, and expenses; (5) the rendering of counsel and advice, when requested, on bank operating problems, particularly in the case of smaller banks; (6) the approval of proposed changes in the scope of corporate functions exercised by individual banks and of proposed changes in their capital structures; (7) authorization for the establishment of branches and for the exercise of trust powers; (8) the approval of bank mergers and consolidations; (9) the organization and regulation of bank holding companies; (10) the regulation of bank service corporations; and (11) the liquidation of banks. The four types of supervisory agencies do not each perform all of these functions, but all are the responsibility of one or the other. The purpose of this section is to summarize the broad aspect of the regulatory environment in which commercial banks must operate.[14]

The diffusion of bank regulatory authority does not mean that banks are not closely regulated. Banking in the United States is more closely regulated than in any other developed country in the world. At the same time, no other country has as many banks in relation to its population. These facts are not unrelated. On the contrary, the degree and character of bank regulation in the United States springs directly from the nature of our banking structure.

As noted in the preceding section, our diverse banking structure developed in response to the often conflicting desires of different segments of the public. Despite recent trends toward consolidation, we still have thousands of banks, chartered by both state and federal governments and, for the most part, locally owned and operated. Left to their own and often inadequate devices in the past, hundreds of banks failed. Americans appeared to want to preserve this diverse structure without sacrificing banking safety. The American system of bank regulation, therefore, has developed over the years in response to the desires for a sound banking system that is, at the same time, responsive to the credit needs of a dynamic economy. To assure the continuance of such a system should be one of the basic responsibilities of bank regulatory authorities.

The limitation of banking activities through detailed provisions of regulation and law is a distinctive feature of banking in the United States. All banks derive their powers from the banking laws which are, in this

---

[14]More complete descriptions of the Regulatory Framework for Banks are contained in part 10 of *The Bankers' Handbook* William H. Baughn and Charles E. Walker, eds. (Homewood, Ill.: Dow-Jones-Irwin, 1966), and *Bank Supervision* by the Federal Reserve Bank of St. Louis.

sense, permissive. On the other hand, the banking laws specifically limit the powers granted and are thus essentially restrictive. The restrictions are designed to prevent, if possible, our banks from making the mistakes which led to widespread bank failures in the past.

The regulatory authorities, both state and federal, are concerned with regulation and supervision. They administer the banking laws, promulgate and interpret regulations issued thereunder, and exercise impersonal and objective judgments with respect to bank policies in order to further the public interest. They use the examination process to keep themselves informed of both the legality and the soundness of an individual bank's operations.

As noted earlier, the historical development of the American banking structure has given rise to a multiplicity of regulatory agencies at both the state and federal levels. Under our concept of dual banking, national banks are chartered and supervised by the Office of the Comptroller of the Currency, while state banks are chartered and supervised (in the first instance) by the banking authorities of the respective states. Most state-chartered banks, however, have come under federal supervision and regulaton of one kind or another. With the establishment of the Federal Reserve System, those state-chartered banks that became members submitted themselves voluntarily to many of the restrictions imposed by law on national banks and to examination and supervision by the Board of Governors of the Federal Reserve System. Most of the larger state banks have chosen to become members.

With the advent of federal deposit insurance, nearly all of the remaining state banks accepted supervision by the Federal Deposit Insurance Corporation as a condition of insurance. There remain fewer than 200 nonmember, noninsured commerical banks subject to no direct federal supervision.

The three federal regulatory agencies, moreover, have overlapping jurisdictions, and individual banks are subject to the rules of more than one agency. The extent of this overlapping is shown in Figure 4-3. National banks, for example, while chartered and supervised solely by the Comptroller of the Currency, are required to be members of the Federal Reserve System, and their deposits are insured by the Federal Deposit Insurance Corporation. Both of these latter agencies have the power to examine national banks—a power seldom exercised—but both review reports of examinations made by national bank examiners. National banks are also subject to some state laws such as those governing branching authority, "legal" holidays, and so on.

The crisscrossing of regulatory responsibility is further illustrated by the rules regarding changes in banking structure. All holding company transactions, including those involving nonmember banks, are subject to the jurisdiction of the Board of Governors of the Federal Reserve System. The establishment of *de novo* branches requires the approval of the chartering authority, state or national, and for state banks, the additional approval of either the Board of Governors or the FDIC, depending on member or

Figure 4-3. Supervision of the Commercial Banking System
Principal Relationships

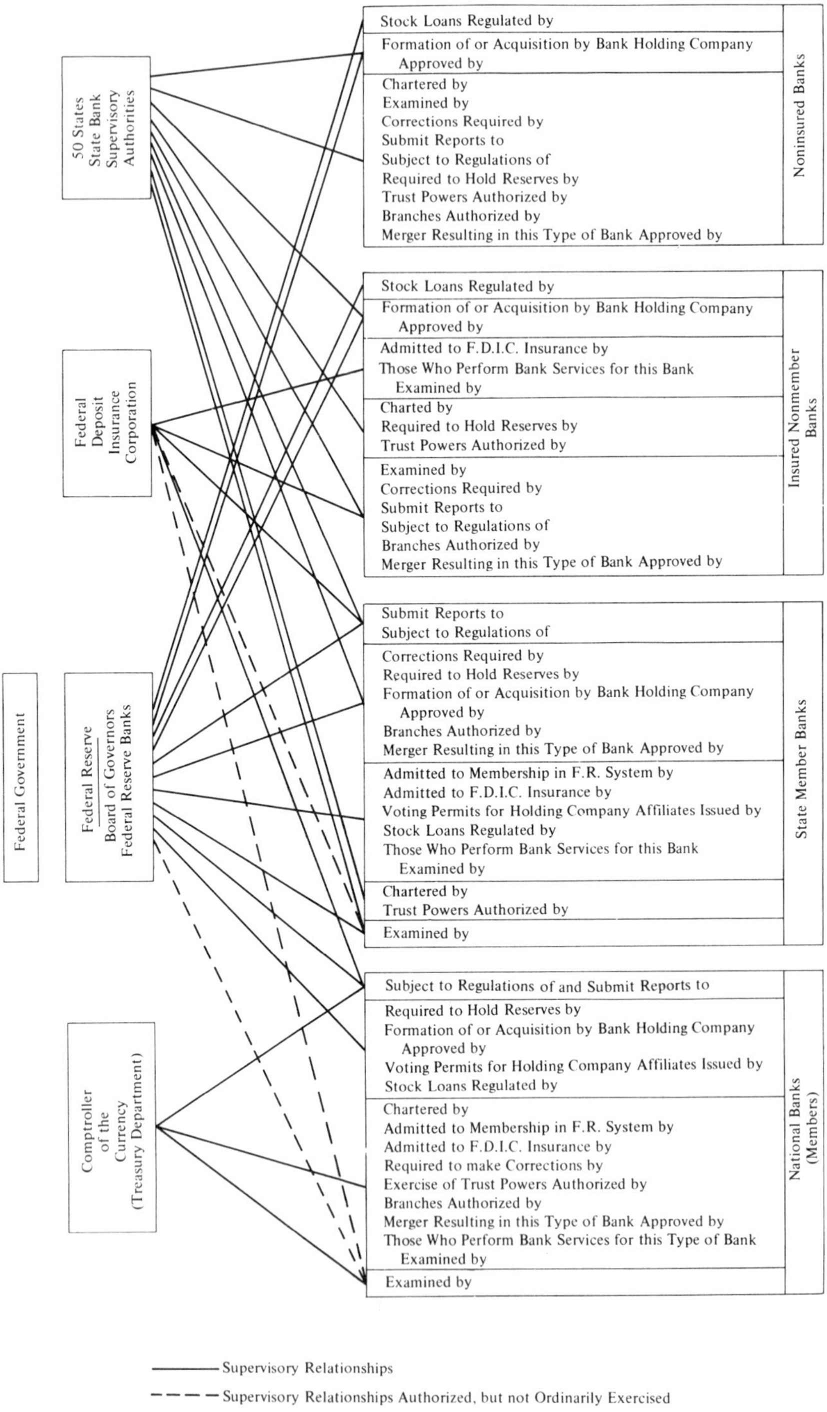

Federal Government

50 States State Bank Supervisory Authorities

Federal Deposit Insurance Corporation

Federal Reserve Board of Governors Federal Reserve Banks

Comptroller of the Currency (Treasury Department)

Noninsured Banks

Stock Loans Regulated by
Formation of or Acquisition by Bank Holding Company Approved by
Chartered by
Examined by
Corrections Required by
Submit Reports to
Subject to Regulations of
Required to Hold Reserves by
Trust Powers Authorized by
Branches Authorized by
Merger Resulting in this Type of Bank Approved by

Insured Nonmember Banks

Stock Loans Regulated by
Formation of or Acquisition by Bank Holding Company Approved by
Admitted to F.D.I.C. Insurance by
Those Who Perform Bank Services for this Bank
Examined by
Charted by
Required to Hold Reserves by
Trust Powers Authorized by
Examined by
Corrections Required by
Submit Reports to
Subject to Regulations of
Branches Authorized by
Merger Resulting in this Type of Bank Approved by

State Member Banks

Submit Reports to
Subject to Regulations of
Corrections Required by
Required to Hold Reserves by
Formation of or Acquisition by Bank Holding Company Approved by
Branches Authorized by
Merger Resulting in this Type of Bank Approved by
Admitted to Membership in F.R. System by
Admitted to F.D.I.C. Insurance by
Voting Permits for Holding Company Affiliates Issued by
Stock Loans Regulated by
Those Who Perform Bank Services for this Bank
Examined by
Chartered by
Trust Powers Authorized by
Examined by

National Banks (Members)

Subject to Regulations of and Submit Reports to
Required to Hold Reserves by
Formation of or Acquisition by Bank Holding Company Approved by
Voting Permits for Holding Company Affiliates Issued by
Stock Loans Regulated by
Chartered by
Admitted to Membership in F.R. System by
Admitted to F.D.I.C. Insurance by
Required to make Corrections by
Exercise of Trust Powers Authorized by
Branches Authorized by
Merger Resulting in this Type of Bank Approved by
Those Who Perform Bank Services for this Type of Bank
Examined by
Examined by

——————— Supervisory Relationships

— — — — Supervisory Relationships Authorized, but not Ordinarily Exercised nonmember insured status. Merger applications follow the same course except that each of the three federal agencies must seek the advice of the other two and the Department of Justice with respect to the competitive factors involved.

The three federal regulatory agencies and the state agencies are responsible for bank examination, the foundation of bank regulation. American banking is highly competitive because of the large number of banks in the country. In most communities there are two or more sources of banking services. Bank examinations in the United States are primarily designed to protect depositors from unsound banking practices rather than provide a substitute for competition. Bank examinations, by any of the four major types of regulatory agencies, emphasize review and appraisal of asset quality, capital adequacy, and the ability of management.

Inherent in banking are two factors which give rise to the need for examination. The first involves the bank's loans and investments which lead to the creation of demand deposits. Since these demand deposits make up the major portion of the nation's money supply, the quality of bank credit underlies the value of our money. The second factor is the nature of the financial intermediary role that banks fulfill in the economy. Banks receive savings and demand deposits that are highly liquid. These deposits are invested by banks in other less-liquid assets. To prevent a liquidity crisis banks must hold some liquid assets, have adequate capital, and maintain professional management. The three federal regulatory agencies and an example of a state agency are briefly described in the following paragraphs.

The Federal Reserve System

The Federal Reserve System is concerned with national credit and monetary policies as well as its bank regulatory responsibilities. Indeed, the primary function of the Federal Reserve System is to foster a flow of money and credit that will facilitate orderly economic growth, a high level of employment, a stable dollar, and a long-run balance in our international payments. The commercial banks are the main institution used by the Federal Reserve to perform this function because almost all of the money in the economy comes either directly or indirectly from commercial banks. The Federal Reserve influences the availability of bank reserves which, in turn, influences the amount of bank credit that will be extended and the cost borrowers must pay for these funds.

In the past the Federal Reserve System has relied primarily on three complementary instruments to control banks' reserve positions: (1) open market operations, (2) discount operations, and (3) the level of reserve requirements. Open market operations and discount operations influence the level of bank reserves directly. The reserve requirements affect the money supply by changing the monetary multiplier. The availability of bank credit and money is a major influence on the levels of interest rates and the availability of credit.

The major portion of Federal Reserve operations affecting the reserve position of banks are accommodating in that they are undertaken in response to short-term variations in the economy's needs for bank credit and are affected through open market operations. *Open market operations* consist of purchases and sales of government securities in the open market. Open market operations are undertaken at the initiative of the Federal Open Market Committee. The Federal Open Market Committee is composed of the seven appointed members of the Board of Governors and five of the twelve presidents of the district Federal Reserve banks.

In *discounting operations,* member banks borrow from their district's Federal Reserve bank to obtain additional reserves. When a member bank borrows at a Reserve bank, the amount of the loan is added to its Reserve balance at the Federal Reserve bank. There is a charge against the borrowing bank's reserves when it repays the loan. These loans are usually of short maturity, rarely exceeding 15 days.

Regulation A states the conditions under which a member bank may borrow from its Federal Reserve bank. This function is administered in light of the credit policy which the Federal Reserve System wishes to follow. Regulation A is supplemented by "Operating Letter No. 7." This operating letter outlines many of the procedural steps in borrowing, such as the forms that must be submitted. The rates at which Federal Reserve member banks can borrow are set by each district's Federal Reserve bank, subject to approval by the Board of Governors.

The Federal Reserve can also affect bank reserves by changing the *reserve requirements.* When the reserve requirements are changed, there is no change in the amount of reserve balances at the Federal Reserve. Instead, the amount of demand deposits, time deposits, or savings deposits that a bank can support with a given amount of reserves is changed. Changes in required reserves are less flexible and continuously adaptable than open market operations and discounting. In the post-World War II period, reserve requirements were altered when it was felt that nontemporary adjustment of bank reserves and credit were necessary.

Regulation D covers the reserve requirements of member banks. It defines demand deposits, time deposits, savings deposits, and similar bank liabilities. Another part of the regulation contains instructions for the computation of reserves. It also states the ranges within which reserve requirements may vary.

Another instrument of Federal Reserve policy, Regulation Q, has assumed an increasingly important role in monetary policy in recent years. Regulation Q prohibits the payment of interest on demand deposits and allows the Federal Reserve to establish the maximum rates of interest that may be paid on various classes of time and savings deposits. In the last half of the 1960s, banks attracted substantial amounts of funds from corporations through the use of certificates of deposit. The rates established under Regulation Q determine the competitive ability of banks in attracting these funds. For example, in late 1969, banks had net outflows of certificates of deposits and were less able to make new loans and increase demand deposits because the maximum rates set under Regulation Q were below existing market rates.

The Federal Reserve is also responsible for: (1) approving the establishment of branches or the absorption of other banks by state member banks; (2) allowing holding companies to acquire the stock of banks; (3) chartering foreign banks and financing corporations; (4) allowing member banks to engage in banking in foreign countries; (5) administering the disclosure requirements of the Securities Act of 1934, as amended, concerning securities of banks within the System's jurisdiction and registered under the provision of the 1934 act; (6) regulating credit extended by banks, brokers, and dealers in securities for the purpose of purchasing or carrying stock or securities convertible into stock; and (7) establishing the banking-related field in which bank holding companies may operate. The Federal Reserve also has the power, although it has not used it in recent years, to regulate consumer credit and real estate credit.

In addition to these more general powers, the Federal Reserve System also has a varied list of supervisory functions. It is particularly concerned with admission of state-chartered banks to membership in the System; the field review of state member banks and the analysis of operations of each member bank; the correction of unsatisfactory conditions in state member banks or violations of the banking law; and the issuance and enforcement of regulations pertaining to banking of member banks. In all phases of supervision, there is full recognition of the distinction between the Federal Reserve System's responsibilities relating to bank supervision and those pertaining to monetary policy. Examinations are not made with a view of implementing the monetary policy in effect at the time, but with the purpose of determining whether the bank is in sound condition.

Every state member bank is subject to examination (made under the direction of the vice-president in charge of examination of the Federal Reserve bank in the district in which it is located) by examiners approved by the Board of Governors. In these examinations, the examiner appraises the quality of bank assets, the nature and amount of liabilities, and the adequacy of capital. He also attempts to uncover any unsound or unsafe banking practices, review compliance with applicable laws and regulations, and make an evaluation of bank management.

It is the operating policy of the Federal Reserve System to conduct at least one regular examination of each state member bank during each calendar year. Additional examinations are made if deemed necessary. In most states concurrent examinations are made with state banking authorities, while in others the Reserve bank makes an independent examination.

National banks, as members of the Federal Reserve System, are also subject to examination by direction of the Board of Governors or the Federal Reserve banks. In practice, however, they are now examined by either since the Comptroller of the Currency is charged directly with this task. The Comptroller provides reports on the examination of national banks to the Board upon request, and each Federal Reserve bank purchases copies of the bank examination reports in its district.

In addition to the above-mentioned duties, the Federal Reserve, in pursuing its policy of maintaining proper levels of credit throughout the nation, conducts certain operations and imposes certain requirements on member banks. The power and authority of the Federal Reserve System arises from the Federal Reserve Act, first adopted in 1913 and amended many times since. Every member bank is supplied by the Board of Governors with a copy of this act because it is the basis of most of bank regulation. Each Federal Reserve bank also prepares printed instructions outlining various procedures. These instructions describe the specific procedures to be followed by member banks in dealing with the Federal Reserve bank.

Table 4-3 shows that at the end of 1974 member banks constituted 43 percent of the number of all commercial banks in the United States and held approximately 81 percent of the total deposits in such banks. Table 4-3 also shows that state member banks accounted for 13 percent of the number of all state-chartered commercial banks and held 54 percent of the total deposits in state-chartered commercial banks.

The Comptroller of the Currency

The Office of Comptroller of the Currency was created by the Currency Act of 1863. It was the intention of Congress that the establishment of banks chartered by the federal government would aid the Civil War financing effort by strengthening the market for U.S. Treasury bills. The Comptroller of the Currency was to be the administrator of the act; so in the period before the establishment of the Federal Reserve, the Comptroller of the Currency was the only regulatory body for national banks.

The Comptroller of the Currency has continued to oversee examination of national banks, sharing its findings with the Federal Reserve, which is also concerned with the condition of national banks. Table 4-3 shows that at the start of 1975 the Comptroller of the Currency was responsible for examining 4708 national banks. The Comptroller appoints 14 regional national bank examination staffs who examine national banks at least once during the calendar year.

The Comptroller must determine the adequacy of applicants for all national bank charters. In considering applications, the Comptroller takes into consideration the adequacy of a prospective bank's capital structure, its future earnings prospects, the character of its management, and the convenience and needs of the community it would serve. The Comptroller must also certify the establishment of branches by national banks and acquiesce in mergers involving national banks.

The Comptroller of the Currency, while maintaining a large staff for administrative and research purposes, makes the final decision on all questions of national bank regulation. Because the Comptroller is not required to compromise with other members of a board or committee, the per-

TABLE 4-3 Number and Deposits of All Commercial Banks, December 31, 1974
(Banks grouped by class and deposit size)

| Deposit Size (in dollars) | Insured Commercial Banks | | | | Noninsured Banks and Trust Companies[a] |
| | total | Members Federal Reserve System | | Nonmembers FR System | |
		National	State		
	(number of banks)				
Less than 1 million	85	20	9	56	134
1 to 2 million	356	54	15	287	23
2 to 5 million	2,252	360	108	1,784	33
5 to 10 million	3,201	743	200	2,258	16
10 to 25 million	4,638	1,666	349	2,623	16
25 to 50 million	1,951	888	162	901	6
50 to 100 million	933	490	107	336	10
100 to 500 million	635	369	85	181	21
500 million to 1 billion	93	61	15	17	0
1 billion or more	84	57	24	3	1
Total	14,228	4,708	1,074	8,446	260
	(in thousands of dollars)				
Less than 1 million	$ 60,423	$ 15,127	$ 6,294	$ 39,002	$ 29,868
1 to 2 million	564,358	88,489	22,739	453,130	37,987
2 to 5 million	8,100,779	1,361,549	390,333	6,348,897	114,485
5 to 10 million	23,635,770	5,663,694	1,476,739	16,495,337	113,643
10 to 25 million	74,667,687	27,644,777	5,709,299	41,313,611	281,316
25 to 50 million	68,090,248	31,450,645	5,666,883	30,972,720	284,335
50 to 100 million	64,524,317	33,975,967	7,404,585	23,143,765	702,773
100 to 500 million	120,276,022	77,417,153	19,500,005	33,358,864	4,497,069
500 million to 1 billion	68,184,384	44,274,555	10,751,636	13,158,193	0
1 billion or more	308,308,934	211,269,632	93,870,300	3,169,002	1,155,743
Total	$746,412,922	$433,161,588	$144,798,813	$168,452,521	$ 7,217,219

Source: *Annual Report of the Federal Deposit Insurance Corporation, 1974* (Washington, D.C.: Federal Deposit Insurance Corporation, 1975).
[a]Includes 72 state-chartered, nondeposit trust companies.

sonality and abilities of the person in the office give the Office of the Comptroller its force and account in large part, for the creativity of a particular administration. The Office of the Comptroller has shown wide swings in its exercise of influence because of the varying personalities of the Comptrollers since the inception of the office.

The Federal Deposit Insurance Corporation

The Federal Deposit Insurance Corporation was created to restore confidence in the banking system after the banking problems in the 1929 Depression period. While some banks had failed in the 1920s due to poor management practices, the large number of failures in the early thirties threatened to topple the entire banking system. By the end of 1935, a few months after the permanent plan of federal deposit insurance was introduced pursuant to the Banking Act of 1935, more than 90 percent of the United States commercial banks came under the insurance protection of the Federal Deposit Insurance Corporation. Establishment of the FDIC brought back some measure of federal control of bank formation under State charter. Considerable power is exercised over state chartering by the FDIC because federal authorities could now withhold deposit insurance.

Table 4-3 shows that at the start of 1975 less than 2 percent of the commercial banks were nonmembers of the FDIC. Note that most of the noninsured banks were small. A depositor in an insured commercial bank is currently protected up to $40,000 of the aggregate of all deposits maintained in the same right and capacity. This maximum amount fully protects roughly 99 percent of all depositors; however, the depositors that exceed the insurance maximum usually do so by a substantial amount. It is estimated that the insurance coverage within the $40,000 maximum covers approximately 62 percent of total deposits in all insured commercial banks.[15]

The authority and responsibility of the FDIC related to deposit insurance extends to all insured banks. To avoid duplication of effort among the federal supervisory agencies, the FDIC confines its examinaiton activities to insured banks that are not members of the Federal Reserve System. For national and state member banks a review of the examination reports of the other federal agencies has been satisfactory for the FDIC's needs.

It is the FDIC's policy to examine insured nonmember banks at least annually, and more often if necessary. In over half of the states, the FDIC's examinations are usually conducted jointly or concurrently with the state authorities. All banks under the insurance protection of the FDIC are required to submit various reports and comply with rules and regulations of the FDIC. Certain activities of banks, such as the establishment of branches, changes in location, or acquiring other banks through merger, require the FDIC's approval.

The FDIC is managed by a three-member Board of Directors. The chairman and the directors are appointed for a six-year term by the president with the advice and consent of the Senate. The Comptroller of the Currency, also a presidential appointee, serves ex officio as the third member of the Board. The regional directors of the fourteen regions are appointed by the Board of Directors.

It is the ability of the FDIC to withhold insurance that gives federal authorities considerable influence over the state-chartering of banks. Regarding applications of commercial banks for coverage by federal deposit insurance, the FDIC is required by statute to consider several fac-

---

[15]*Annual Report of the Federal Deposit Insurance Corporation, 1974* (Washington, D.C.: Federal Deposit Insurance Corporation, 1975).

tors, such as (1) the financial history and condition of the bank, (2) the adequacy of its capital structure, (3) its future earnings prospects, (4) the general character of its management, (5) the convenience and needs of the community to be served by the bank, and (6) the consistency of its corporate powers with the purposes of the Banking Act of 1935. Banks chartered by the states and not members of the Federal Reserve System must apply to and be approved by the FDIC to obtain deposit insurance. Banks beginning operations either as national banks or members of the Federal Reserve System become insured upon certification by the appropriate agency that the above six factors have been given consideration.

State-chartered banks comprise approximately two-thirds of all commercial banks and are supervised by a banking commission or department in each of the states (Table 4-3). The states were supervising banks before the introduction of federal regulation of banks, but the record of states in this field was uneven. It was the spotty record of state banking regulation that produced the Federal Reserve Act of 1913, in part, "to establish a more effective supervision of banking in the United States." The trials of the banking system during the 1930s led to the expansion of supervision of state banks through the establishment of the Federal Deposit Insurance Corporation in 1935.

State statutes and regulatory agencies are still particularly important in these areas. First, the form of banking allowed in each state — type of branching or bank holding companies, if any — is determined by the state. Second, all state banks, whether they are members of the Federal Reserve and/or FDIC or not, are chartered by the state's regulatory agency. Third, all state banks that are not members of the Federal Reserve are typically examined by state examiners. This examination is often concurrent with the examination by the FDIC.

The present Missouri "examination" statute is typical of state legislation.[16] Omitting unnecessary material it reads as follows:

361.160. Examination of Banks and Trust Companies
1. The commissioner, at least once each year, either personally or by deputy or examiner appointed by him, shall visit and examine every bank . . . doing business under the laws of this state. . . .
2. The commissioner, or the deputy or examiners designated . . . shall have power to examine any such corporation, whenever, in his judgment, it may be deemed necessary or expedient. . . .
3. He and his deputy and examiners shall have power to administer oaths to any person whose testimony may be required in such examination . . . and to compel . . . attendance of any person for the purpose of any such examination. . . .
4. On every such examination inquiry shall be made as to the condition and resources of such corporation, the mode of conducting and managing its

[16]Most Missouri banking statutes date from 1907; however, a legislative tradition of bank regulation, including examination, has been in effect in Missouri since 1837. The statute presented was revised slightly in 1949.

affairs, the actions of its directors or trustees, the investment of its funds, the safety and prudence of its management, the security afforded to its creditors, and whether the requirements of its charter and of law have been complied with in the administration of its affairs, and as to such other matters as the commissioner may prescribe.

In summary, the regulatory framework for commercial banks is divided among three federal agencies and fifty state agencies. It is the product of the historical development of banking and of bank traditions. Bank regulation seeks to foster an effectively functioning and sound banking system in which the public interest is properly safeguarded. Bank management should operate within this framework, but should not look to it as a crutch or a substitute for good bank management.

Because the regulatory frameworks among other financial institutions vary widely, we have chosen to place the framework for each institution in the chapter dealing with the financial management of that institution. For example, the regulatory framework for insurance companies is discussed in Chapter 7.

We realize that the environment in which financial institutions are managed is dynamic rather than static. Furthermore, we believe the management decisions of well-run financial institutions must adjust to change in the economic or regulatory environment. In Chapter 9 we discuss what the future environment for financial institutions may look like and how these institutions' management decisions should adjust to such changes.

Chapter 4

Review Questions

1. Why was the Bank of the United States formed? Why was it opposed?
2. What banking reforms arose from the Banking Acts of 1863 and 1864?
3. What were the major problems that caused the formation of the Federal Reserve? Why did we develop a Federal Reserve System rather than a central banks system as in Great Britain or France?
4. What changes in the federal banking system stemmed from the Depression of 1929?
5. What limitations did the Federal Reserve face in its attempt at controlling inflation immediately after World War II? What was the significance of the Accord of 1951?
6. Compare the asset and equity positions of a bank in 1890 to one in 1970. What factors led to the significant changes in these positions?
7. What two inherent factors of banking give rise to the need for periodic examination? Explain why this is so.
8. What are the Federal Reserve's three basic tools for affecting monetary policy? State how each affects the money supply and interest rates.
9. There were three important regulations placed on banks. List and describe them.

10. The American economy is based on capitalism and free enterprise, yet the banking industry in this country is heavily regulated. Reconcile this heavy regulation of the industry with the free enterprise basis by briefly describing the evolutionary process of our banking system.

Selected References

The Banker's Handbook. Baughn, William H. and Walker, Charles E., eds. Homewood, Ill.: Dow-Jones-Irwin, 1966.

Chandler, Lester V. *The Economics of Money and Banking.* 4th ed. New York: Harper & Row, 1964.

Dewey, D. R. *Financial History of the United States.* 12th ed. New York: Longmans, Green, 1934.

Friedman, Milton and Schwartz, Anna Jacobson. *A Monetary History of the United States.* Princeton, N.J.: Princeton University Press, 1955-1956.

Goldsmith, R. W. *Financial Intermediaries in the American Economy Since 1900.* Princeton, N.J.: Princeton University Press, 1958.

Hammond, Bray. *Banks and Politics in America from the Revolution to the Civil War.* Princeton, N.J.: Princeton University Press, 1957.

Jacobs, D. P. et al. *Financial Institutions.* 5th ed. Homewood, Ill.: Irwin, 1971.

Kroos, H. E. and Blyn, M. R. *A History of Financial Institutions.* New York: Random House, 1971.

Kuznets, Simon. *Capital in the American Economy: Its Formation and Financing.* Princeton, N.J.: Princeton University Press, 1961.

Trescott, Paul B. *Financing American Enterprise.* New York: Harper & Row, 1963.

U.S. Congress, House Banking and Currency Committee, Subcommittee on Domestic Finance. *Comparative Regulations of Financial Institutions,* Washington, D.C.: U.S. Government Printing Office, 1963.

Weisman, Rudolph L. *The New Federal Reserve System.* New York: Harper & Row, 1936.

Financial Management
of Commercial Banks

COMMERCIAL banks are America's oldest and dominant financial institution. Throughout our history we have had a unique system in which all commercial banks are privately owned institutions seeking to maximize the return on their owners' investments. The banking sector's share of total financial assets has declined from roughly 80 percent throughout the nineteenth century to between 35 and 40 percent in recent years. In this chapter we will (1) discuss the unique characteristics of commercial banks as a financial institution; (2) apply our wealth-maximization model to a typical commercial bank; (3) examine actual banking performance against the criteria developed from our model; and, (4) evaluate the major financial decisions facing managers of commercial banks.

Regulatory Characteristics Affecting Bank Financial Decisions

One of the most important characteristics of commercial banks is their ability to influence the growth of the major component of our money supply—demand deposits. This ability to create money was fundamental to the historical conflict between safety and credit discussed in Chapter 4 and is a basic determinant of the regulatory environment in which bank management must operate. Currently, commercial banks are allowed to choose among a wide range of primary and secondary financial assets. A notable exception is the prohibition on holding corporate stock. In contrast to this relatively liberal choice among types of financial assets, banks are probably the most regulated financial institutions in the United States. Nearly every banking decision is subject to the scrutiny of one or more of the major bank regulatory bodies—the Federal Reserve System, the Federal Deposit Insurance Corporation, the Comptroller of the Currency, and the regulatory body in the bank's state. Many banking decisions are also regulated by agencies such as the Securities and Exchange Commission, the Fair Trade Commission, and the Consumer Protection Agency.

Four forms of controls have tended to exert the strongest impact on bank management in recent years.

1. Certain proportions of demand, savings, and time deposits and selected other liabilities cannot be invested in earning assets but must be held in the form of reserves. The Federal Reserve determines the reserve ratio percentage required for the various deposit forms for its member banks and permits member banks to hold these reserves in vault cash or on deposit in their region's Federal Reserve bank. Nonmember bank reserve requirements are determined by the state regulatory body and can usually be held as vault cash or deposits with a correspondent bank. The original purpose of these required reserves was to insure a minimum level of bank liquidity. Now, the reserve ratio requirement allows the Federal Reserve to control the money supply. Later, we will discuss how this requirement acts as a constraint on many banking decisions.

2. The capital position of a bank is closely checked by bank regulatory authorities. Future expansion of banking assets and deposits can be severely constrained by demands from regulators to raise more capital following a period in which asset and deposit growth exceeded the growth in capital from retained earnings. Many economists believe that this capital constraint may severely limit banking growth in the coming decade.[1]

3. Both regulatory authorities and bank management carefully monitor a bank's liquidity position, that is, its ability to satisfy the needs for funds to meet loan demands or deposit withdrawals. Such liquidity needs have traditionally been met by unpledged short-term securities and cash. In recent years, regulatory authorities have recognized that the purchase of liabilities is another liquidity source for many larger banks. Nevertheless, the asset allocation decisions of most banks are affected by management and regulatory desires to maintain adequate liquidity.

4. The Federal Reserve has in the past employed Regulation Q to restrict the interest rates banks are able to pay for some categories of deposits. In periods of generally high interest rates, this constraint has restricted banks' ability to compete with other financial institutions and with some primary security instruments. As long as Regulation Q remains in effect, banks must take into account its impact before reaching financial management decisions.

---

[1]As an example, see George H. Hempel, "Bank Capital: Issues and Answers," *The Magazine of Bank Administration*, 51:3, March 1975, for a discussion of the bank capital issue.

Applying the Wealth-Maximization Model to Banking Decisions

Recognizing the constraints facing bank management, we examine the risk–return tradeoffs by applying the general wealth-maximization model to a hypothetical commercial bank. To keep the example simple, we employ equation (4a) (Chapter 2)

$$W = \frac{R - (C + O + T)}{(i + p)} \tag{4a}$$

which assumes constant average returns and costs for the perpetual life of the bank.

It is assumed that our hypothetical bank, Third National Bank, has $100 million in assets which can be allocated among (1) required reserves (A_0), which are determined by the Federal Reserve and earn a zero return; (2) short-term securities (A_1), which offer a relatively low risk and a low return; (3) longer-term securities (A_2), which have higher returns and risks than A_1; and (4) loans (A_3), which offer the highest return and highest risk of all the bank's assets. These assets are financed by $92 million in deposit and other liabilities (composed of lower-cost, high-risk D_1, and higher-cost, lower-risk D_2) and $8 million in capital. The returns and costs on these assets and liabilities, the assumed overhead and income tax rate, and the capitalization rates applied to various risky income streams appear in Table 5-1. Given the available alternatives one may inquire as to the optimal asset and liability allocation decisions of Third National Bank.

TABLE 5-1   Assumptions About Third National Bank

Balance Sheet Totals

Assets	$100,000,000	Deposits and other liabilities	$92,000,000
		Capital	$ 8,000,000

Available Asset Returns

A_1 (short-term securities) =   6%
A_2 (long-term securities) =   8%
A_3 (loans) = 10%

Costs of Acquiring Funds, Overhead, and Taxes

D_1 (low-cost deposits) =   5%
D_2 (higher-cost deposits) =   7%
O (overhead per period) = $1,000,000
t (income tax rate) = 40%
$T = t(R - (C + O))$

Reserve Requirements (A_0 earns 0%)

A_0 for D_1 = 15%
A_0 for D_2 =   5%

Capitalization Rates

i (riskless rate) = 8%
P_1 (low-risk premium) = 2%
P_2 (medium-risk premium) = 4%
P_3 (high-risk premium) = 6%

Six possible situations are presented in Table 5-2. In the first case, it is assumed that Third National Bank obtained \$52 million of D_1 and \$40 million of D_2 and had \$8 million of capital. Approximately \$9.8 million were required as reserves in A_0, Third National Bank lent \$60.2 million (A_3) and chose to invest \$20 million in short-term securities (A_1) and \$10 million in longer-term securities (A_2). These asset, liability, and capital decisions produced net benefits, after overhead and taxes, of \$972,000. When benefits are capitalized at a 12 percent rate, the wealth of the bank owners is \$8 million. The capitalization rate reflects the combined risk of the bank's portfolios or assets and liabilities.

In cases 2 and 3, it is assumed that Third National Bank's fund sources (deposits, other liabilities, and other capital) were as in case 1, while the bank has chosen to emphasize higher earnings and lower risk, respectively, in its asset allocation decisions. In case 2, Third National Bank had a higher proportion of its assets in loans and a lower proportion in short-term securities. The results, as expected, were a higher net after-tax benefit of \$1,212,000 and a higher capitalization rate, assumed to be 14 percent. The total effect was a slight improvement in the owners' wealth position to \$8,657,000. In case 3, it was assumed that Third National's desire for lower risk resulted in an increase in its holdings of short-term securities (A_1) and a decrease in loans (A_3). The lower level of net benefits,

TABLE 5-2 Alternative Decisions by Third National Bank

	Case 1	Case 2	Case 3	Case 4	Case 5	Case 6
Balance Sheet						
A_0	\$ 9,800,000	\$ 9,800,000	\$ 9,800,000	\$ 7,800,000	\$ 9,800,000	\$ 9,800,000
A_1	20,000,000	10,000,000	25,000,000	12,000,000	10,000,000	24,000,000
A_2	10,000,000	15,000,000	10,000,000	10,000,000	10,000,000	15,000,000
A_3	60,200,000	70,200,000	50,200,000	70,200,000	71,200,000	50,200,000
D_1	\$52,000,000	\$52,000,000	\$52,000,000	\$32,000,000	\$52,000,000	\$52,000,000
D_2	40,000,000	40,000,000	40,000,000	60,000,000	40,000,000	40,000,000
E	8,000,000	8,000,000	8,000,000	8,000,000	9,000,000	7,000,000
Returns and Costs						
R	\$ 8,020,000	\$ 8,420,000	\$ 7,720,000	\$ 8,540,000	\$ 8,520,000	\$ 7,660,000
C	5,400,000	5,400,000	5,400,000	5,800,000	5,400,000	5,400,000
O	1,000,000	1,000,000	1,000,000	1,000,000	1,000,000	1,000,000
T	648,000	808,000	528,000	696,000	848,000	504,000
B	972,000	1,212,000	792,000	1,044,000	1,272,000	756,000
Capitalization Rate and Wealth						
i	8%	8%	8%	8%	8%	8%
p	4%	6%	2%	4%	6%	2%
	\$ 972,000	\$ 1,212,000	\$ 792,000	\$ 1,044,000	\$ 1,272,000	\$ 756,000
W	12%	14%	10%	12%	14%	10%
	or \$8,100,000	or \$8,657,000	or \$7,920,000	or \$8,700,000	or \$9,086,000	or \$7,560,000
$W - E$	\$100,000	\$657,000	\$80,000	\$700,000	\$86,000	\$560,000

$792,000, capitalized at the appropriately lower risk rate of 10 percent, implies an owners' wealth position of $7,920,000.

The mixture of deposits, other liabilities, and capital are allowed to vary in cases 4, 5, and 6. In case 4, it is assumed that Third National Bank obtains $32 million in D_1 and $60 million in D_2 and that their capital remains at $8 million. Under the assumptions presented in Table 5-1, these sources constitute a higher cost but lower risk liability structure than the sources for cases 1, 2, and 3. After meeting its required reserves of $7.8 million, our bank chooses a fairly aggressive asset structure of $70.2 million in loans, $12 million in short-term securities, and $10 million in long-term securities. The bank's owners have a wealth position of $8.7 million if one assumes that the net benefits of $1,044,000 is capitalized at a 12 percent (medium-risk) rate.

Cases 5 and 6 indicate an additional dimension of Third National Bank's management tradeoffs. In case 5, it is assumed that Third National chose to aggressively seek high returns on assets (as in case 2) but that its regulatory authorities forced the bank to raise $1 million of additional capital. If $1 million was lent out and the bank's other assets and liabilities were as in case 2, the bank's net benefits would be $1,272,000 and its capitalized value would be $9,086,000. In case 6, it is assumed that Third National chose the low risk, lower return approach and because of this lower risk, its regulatory authorities had required the bank to have $7 million rather than $8 million of capital. If that bank had $1 million less in short-term securities and the bank's other assets and liabilities were as in case 2, the bank's net benefits would be $756,000 and its capitalized value would be $7,560,000.

While many other situations could be presented for even the relatively simple asset and liability decisions facing the Third National Bank (other risk–return possibilities and combinations of assets and liabilities could be considered; overhead or taxes could be varied with side effects on asset and liability combinations; a different capital position could affect both net benefits and risks; etc.). Three basic points seem evident. First, changes in any one variable will normally affect nearly all other variables. Second, since risk affects the capitalization rate, one must consider the interactive effect on risk from decisions regarding the portfolio of assets, liabilities, and capital. Finally, while the effect on the net wealth of the common shareholders is the primary consideration in bank management decisions, further elaboration on the specific decision-making criteria is needed for bank management to decide on its objectives.

The overall decision-making criterion should be to maximize the *net* wealth of the owners, which is the wealth (W) of the owners less their investment in the bank (E). Thus, among the cases considered in Table 5-2, case 4 would be the optimal choice. Case 6 is preferable to case 5 if the regulatory authorities have varying capital requirements. A possible exception to this criterion would be the situation in which the owners' investments were markedly different. For example, would W of $7.5 million and E of $7 million be preferable to W of $10.6 million and E of $10 million? In unusual situations where this disparity exists, the ratio of W to C is the appropriate decision criterion. (In the example, 1.07 of the first case would be preferable to 1.06 for the second case.) When the assumption of similar size is relaxed, nearly all decisions relating to management policies causing changes in asset, liability, and capital should employ maximization of net wealth of the owners (W—E) as the objective.

Subdividing Bank Objectives for Management Actions

As we indicated in Chapter 2, most financial institutions can divide the key variables affecting their wealth-maximization objective into four categories: spread management, control of overhead, liquidity management, and capital management. Commercial banks are certainly no exception. Rather than repeat the relevant material from Chapter 2, we present a brief summary of the overall guidelines.

Throughout this book we have emphasized the goal of management to be the maximization of shareholder wealth. Since any present value calculation requires estimates of future profits and the required capitalization rate, one must take account of the total effect of any bank management decision. That is, not only should one consider the effect of a given decision on current profits, but also the long-run effects on profit and risk. The wealth-maximization objective requires that bank managers take a "longer view" to their decision-making. At any point in time a manager could quite easily structure the composition of the bank's asset and liability portfolios so as to maximize the current spread between the return on assets and the cost of liabilities. By simply looking at the current spread one might infer that management is acting in the best interest of the stockholders. Most likely, this would not be the proper conclusion. In order to demonstrate the possible problems incurred when management seeks to maximize the current spread, we assume an initial environment in which the term structure of interest rates is sharply sloping upward. Normally, such a "shape" to the yield curve reflects the expectation that rates will rise in the future. Table 5-3 contains data on the rates for each of two types of assets and liabilities available to the bank.

If the bank pursues a policy of maximizing current spread, the asset and liability choices are obvious—obtain funds from time deposits at 5 percent and allocate these funds to five-year installment loans. The gross operating spread from the bank's portfolio would be a "healthy" 3 percent. Un-

TABLE 5-3   Rate and Cost Data for Third National Bank

Available Asset Returns

   $A_1 = 6\%$; a callable business loan at prime plus $\frac{1}{2}\%$
   $A_2 = 8\%$; a five-year installment credit loan

Costs of Acquiring Funds

   $D_1 = 5\%$; a time deposit account at approximately $\frac{1}{2}\%$ under prime.
   $D_2 = 7\%$; a five-year maturity certificate of deposit.

fortunately, such a policy of borrowing short to lend long, in an environ-ment with an upward sloping yield curve, almost insures that the spread will deteriorate in the future. In order to demonstrate this point, we assume that after two years the anticipation of higher rates is evidenced in the money market. Specifically, the rates on the financial instruments listed in Table 5-3 have increased by a full 3 percent. Since the bank originally elected to borrow at the short-term rate, it must now pay a full 8 percent on time deposits in order to remain competitive with alternative financial instruments (Treasury bills, savings accounts, etc.) and thereby avoid a runoff in its deposit base. The return on the asset portfolio which seemed to be quite profitable two years earlier is now equal to the cost of obtaining funds, that is, the gross spread is now zero. The lesson to be learned from this example is obvious. By "locking-in" the 8 percent rate on assets two years earlier the bank created a situation in which its spread is highly sensitive to interest rate movements. The strategy of maximizing the current spread had serious implications for the future profitability of the bank.

As an alternative, suppose the bank had elected to finance the 8 percent installment loans by emitting 6 percent CD's having the same maturity. Regardless of the movements in rates over the five-year period, the bank has guaranteed itself a stable 2 percent spread since it will not be forced to pay a higher rate on its liabilities.

The bank could have also pursued a policy of financing short-term assets with short-term liabilities and been fairly certain of the stability of its spread over time. Such a policy would have generated a 2 percent spread with the original array of rates — 7 percent, 5 percent. After two years, the 3 percent increase in all rates would have again resulted in a 2 percent spread.

The Incremental Nature of Bank Management Decisions

In these examples which demonstrate the wealth-maximization objec-tive, we have ignored the incremental nature of many management deci-sions by commercial banks. Usually broad choices, such as those in cases 1–6 in Table 5-2, are longer-term decisions and may indicate the direction the bank is moving over a period of years. Managers of banks are faced with numerous important but less broad decisions: should they make auto loans at a given rate? Should they purchase long-term municipal bonds? What should be the maturity of the liabilities they are purchasing? While the wealth-maximization objective is conceptually appropriate, bank management should generally base such decisions on changes in revenues, costs, and risks rather than on the average levels of these variables.

For example, if a bank has acquired its deposits and other funds at an average cost of 7 percent (including overhead, etc.) and is making an average return of 8 percent on its assets, should it make new loans that will not change its risk level and will return 9 percent? The answer, of course, is that we are not sure because we do not know the cost of acquiring additional funds. If the additional funds cost 10 percent (the lowest cost of issuing new liabilities or selling currently held assets), the bank would maximize its wealth by not making the new loans. For decisions that do not change the risk level of the bank, the general rule is that wealth is maximized by undertaking all decisions where marginal revenues exceed marginal costs.

Any effects that such a decision might have on the risk level of the bank must, of course, be considered. The appropriate evaluative measure is the change in the total risk level of the bank due to the decision and not the risk of the individual decision. The portfolio effects of some decisions may even reduce the total risk exposure of a bank. The appropriate criterion for decisions affecting both the return and risk levels of a bank remains the maximization of common stockholder wealth.

Bank Decisions in Differing Environments

The normative model for commercial bank decisions described in the preceding paragraphs should be useful to most managers of commercial banks. If this model is appropriate, however, one might wonder why the assets and liabilities of most banks have changed so drastically in the last two or three decades. Table 5-4 indicates that loans which constituted 30.9 percent of bank assets in 1950 rose to 47.2 percent of assets in 1962 and 59.7 percent in 1974. U.S. government securities which composed 36.7 percent of bank assets in 1950 fell to 5.9 percent by 1974. The changes in commercial banks' sources of funds are equally startling. While commercial banks obtained 70.3 percent of their resources from demand deposits in 1950, this proportion fell to 55.2 percent and then to 34.6 percent. Time and savings deposits rose from 21.6 percent of total resources in 1950 to 33.1 percent in 1962, then to 46.9 percent in 1974. Observe that from 1962 through 1974 most of the increases in bank loans of $406.6 billion and other securities of $109.5 billion were financed by increases of $33.3 billion in time and savings deposits and of $95.5 billion in borrowings and other liabilities.

Furthermore, even at a given point in time, commercial banks differ markedly. Table 5-5 demonstrates that in 1974 the average small bank obtained roughly 85 percent of its resources from deposits — 37 percent from demand deposits and 47.9 percent from time and savings deposits — while the average larger bank obtained 77 percent of its resources from deposits and 15.6 percent from federal funds and other borrowings. In terms of employment of these resources, the average smaller bank favored U.S. Treasury and agency obligations and the selling of federal funds, while the average larger bank held a much larger proportion of its assets in the form of loans.

Such differences are primarily attributed to differences in the environment in which banks must operate rather than from substantial management objective differences. A brief summary of the changes in the overall banking environment in recent decades and differences in the en-

TABLE 5-4   Principal Assets and Liabilities of All Commercial Banks
(at end of year)

	1950	1962	1974
Assets (in $ billions)			
Cash and due from banks	$ 40.3	$ 54.0	$126.1
U.S. government securities	62.0	66.4	54.4
Other securities	12.4	29.3	138.8
Loans	52.2	140.1	546.7
Other assets.	2.0	7.3	50.3
Total assets	$168.9	$297.1	$916.3
Liabilities and Capital			
Demand deposits	$118.7	$163.9	$317.3
Time and savings deposits	36.5	98.2	429.5
Borrowings	.1	3.6	55.9
Other liabilities	2.0	7.3	50.5
Capital accounts.	11.6	24.1	63.1
Total liabilities and capital	$168.9	$297.1	$916.3
Assets (% of total)			
Cash and due from banks	23.9%	18.2%	13.7%
U.S. government securities	36.7	22.3	5.9
Other securities	7.3	9.9	15.1
Loans	30.9	47.2	59.7
Other assets.	1.2	2.5	5.5
Total assets	100.0%	100.0%	100.0%
Liabilities and Capital			
Demand deposits	70.3%	55.2%	34.6%
Time and savings deposits	21.6	33.1	46.1
Borrowings	.0	1.2	6.1
Other liabilities	1.2	2.5	5.5
Capital accounts.	6.9	8.1	6.9
Total liabilities and capital	100.0%	100.0%	100.0%

Source: Federal Reserve Bulletins (Washington, D.C.: Board of Governors of the Federal Reserve System, 1951-1975).

vironments banks may face in the mid- and late 1970s should prove interesting. The presentation demonstrates how bank management employing similar objectives could and often should formulate substantially different policies in order to satisfy its goals.

The overall banking environment has changed markedly in the last few decades. From 1930 through the mid-1940s private loan demand was limited by the Depression and World War II. Interest rates remained low throughout this period. The banking industry itself suffered from a tarnished image and restrictive legislation as a result of the bank failures during the Depression. During this period, most banks attempted to reduce the risk in their asset portfolios. Loans declined and U.S. government securities were often acquired as the replacement. Banking resources

TABLE 5-5　Percentages of Assets and Liabilities of Different-sized Commercial Banks at the End of 1974

	Banks with Deposits of:	
	$2–5 million	*$1 billion or more*
Assets		
Cash and due from banks	11.3%	16.1%
U.S. Treasury and agency obligations	22.4	5.7
State and municipal obligations	6.8	7.2
Other securities	1.0	.5
Federal funds sold (loaned)	9.0	3.3
Loans	46.5	58.2
Other assets.	3.0	9.0
Total assets	100.0%	100.0%
Liabilities and Capital		
Demand deposits	37.0%	34.2%
Time and savings deposits	47.9	42.8
Federal funds purchased (borrowed)	.3	8.7
Borrowings and other liabilities	3.5	6.9
Reserves on loans and securities	.5	1.1
Long-term debt	.1	.6
Other capital accounts.	10.7	5.7
Total liabilities and capital	100.0%	100.0%

Source: Annual Report of the Federal Deposit Insurance Corporation, 1974 (Washington, D.C., FDIC, 1975).

declined in the early 1930s, then grew slowly from the mid-1930s through the end of World War II.

Private credit demands grew rapidly from the end of World War II through the early 1960s. Banks responded to the growth by participating in new forms of loans to consumers and businesses and by increasing loans as a percent of their total assets. Most banks appeared to emphasize the maintenance of a wide spread in order to maximize value to their owners. Banks remained relatively passive in competing for funds from surplus units and, as a result, grew considerably slower than most other types of financial intermediaries.

In the late 1950s and early 1960s this general strategy came under criticism as spreads began to narrow in spite of the lower returns banks were paying to savers relative to many other financial intermediaries. Banks began to change their strategy in the early and mid-1960s from high spreads and slow growth to lower spreads with more rapid growth. Regulators appeared to encourage this trend by relaxing Regulation Q, which set the maximum rate banks could pay on time and savings deposits, and by allowing banks to use certificates of deposits and other liability forms to compete more effectively for funds. The strong demand for credit from the mid-1960s through the mid-1970s allowed banks to employ the substantially larger amounts of funds that they were able to attract. The structure of banking also began to change rapidly in the mid-1960s. Bank holding companies were able to buy into (hopefully) more profitable lines of nonbank financial business and were also encouraged by congressional and regulatory actions. The ability to increase profits with greater volume as margins fell proved to be difficult. When the economy slowed in late 1974, many banks found themselves with high loan-to-deposit ratios, a capital shortage, and some unprofitable lines of business. The industry was further shaken by the failure of three large banks, U.S. National Bank, Franklin National Bank, and Security National Bank.

Figures 5-1 to 5-4 provide graphical support for four of the major trends discussed in the preceding paragraphs. Figure 5-1 indicates that costs have

Figure 5-1. Revenues, Expenses and Earnings as Percentages of Assets
for All Insured Commercial Banks, 1959–1975

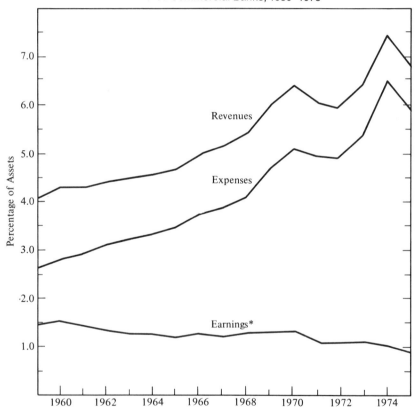

*Before taxes.

Source: Annual Reports of the Federal Deposit Insurance Corporation, Washington, D.C., 1960–1976.

Figure 5-2. After-Tax Earnings on Capital for All Insured Commercial
Banks, 1959–1975

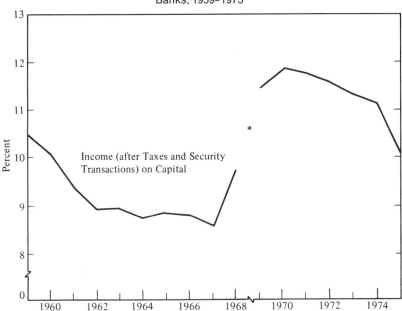

*Because of changes in the form of reporting by banks, FDIC figures since 1969 are not fully comparable with those for 1968 or earlier.

Source: Annual Reports of the Federal Deposit Insurance Corporation, Washington, D.C., 1960–1976.

risen even more rapidly than revenues, causing before-tax earnings to decline from 1.5 percent of assets to 0.9 percent of assets in the last fifteen years. From Figure 5-2 it is apparent that the after-tax return on capital also fell steadily over this period in spite of the rapid growth in banking assets, greater reliance on tax-exempt income sources, and lower amount of capital. Figure 5-3 illustrates one aspect of the greater risk in bank asset structures as banks have attempted to maintain their earning margin — the deterioration of bank liquidity over the last three decades. Finally, Figure 5-4 illustrates the capital position for all insured commercial banks during the past several decades. It is interesting to note that while bank capital has remained a relatively stable proportion of total assets and deposits over this period, capital steadily declined in relation to risk asset measures over the last two or three decades. This has occurred in spite of the marked increase in long-term debt as a source of external bank capital.[2]

The banking environment in the mid-1970s and in future years remains uncertain. It appears that most banks will become less interested in growth

---

[2]From 1966 to 1974 banks sold approximately $7.5 billion of long-term debt and $0.8 million of common stock. *Cf.* Hempel, "Bank Capital."

Figure 5-3. Cash Assets and U.S. Government Securities to Total Deposits

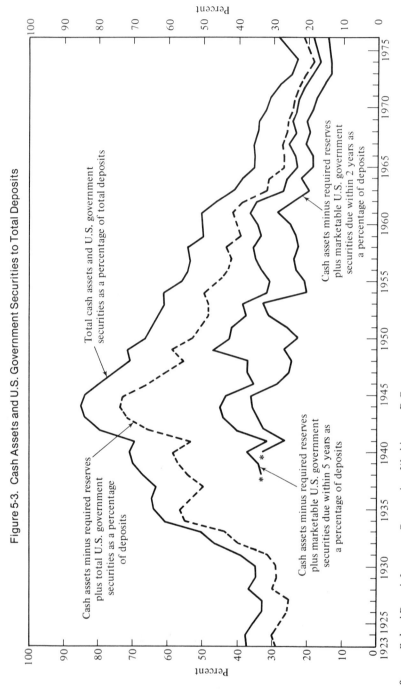

Total cash assets and U.S. government securities as a percentage of total deposits

Cash assets minus required reserves plus total U.S. government securities as a percentage of deposits

Cash assets minus required reserves plus marketable U.S. government securities due within 5 years as a percentage of deposits

Cash assets minus required reserves plus marketable U.S. government securities due within 2 years as a percentage of deposits

Source: Federal Deposit Insurance Corporation, Washington, D.C.

*First year of series.

94

Figure 5-4. Conventional Capital Ratios for Insured Commercial Banks

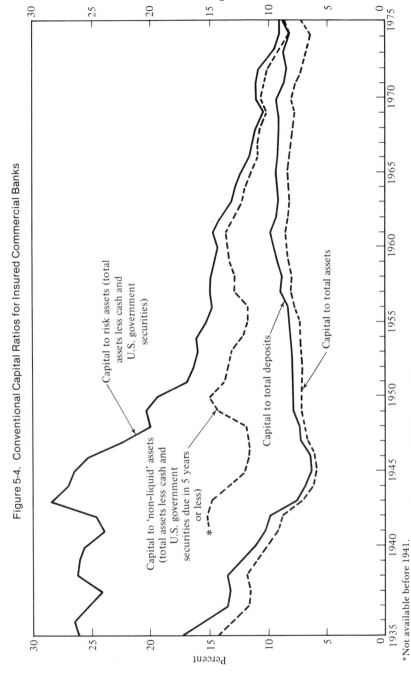

Capital to risk assets (total assets less cash and U.S. government securities)

Capital to 'non-liquid' assets (total assets less cash and U.S. government securities due in 5 years or less)
*

Capital to total deposits

Capital to total assets

*Not available before 1941.
Source: Federal Deposit Insurance Corporation, Washington, D.C.

95

and more interested in widening spreads. A trend toward accepting better-quality loans has already been evidenced by many banks. Regulators appear likely to be more strict in their capital adequacy requirements while at the same time limiting bank growth to new nonbanking activities. Competition with other banks, other financial institutions, and even some nonfinancial corporations will become more intense. Banks will have to react to these and other changes as they occur.

Even ignoring the degree to which the environment and regulation have changed commercial banking over the last few decades, one is often amazed to find the great differences among bank balance sheets at any point in time. Such differences arise primarily from the large disparity among bank market areas. A bank in a rural area must, of necessity, emphasize loans to its customers that are quite different from the loans made by a bank located in an industrial center. A bank in a suburban area is more likely to have a lower loan-to-deposit ratio and a higher proportion of mortgages and savings deposits than a similar bank in a commercial area. The size of the bank itself significantly affects its ability to assess certain forms of financing. The liberalizing of branching laws in some areas and the permission to use electronic banking units seems likely to reduce the effects of some environmental factors in the near future. We will probably, however, continue to see varying strategies and performance among banks employing the same basic objective and fundamentals of bank management.

Policies Consistent with Wealth-Maximization

We now turn to specific areas where bank management must make policy decisions. These areas include decisions for attracting funds, liquidity, lending, investments, and capital. After discussing each area separately, we discuss how policies can be coordinated among the areas. We emphasize those management policies and actions that we believe will be useful in the environment of the mid- and late 1970s and that are consistent with our wealth-maximization objective.

Attracting Funds

Attracting funds has become one of the key ingredients of most banks management policies and actions. More and more bankers are acting as if they believe that attracting funds deserves equal status with the managing of funds. Our brief discussion emphasizes the attraction of deposits (some of which may be purchased money) and outlines some of the other available principal forms of funds.

While bank managers do not have complete control over the level of deposits, they do have the ability to considerably influence their amount. Because deposits are so important to the profitable operation of a bank, most banks tend to compete aggressively for deposits. Many of the factors which determine the level of deposits in a bank are beyond the control of an individual bank. For example, monetary and fiscal policy, Regulation Q, and the general level of economic activity are exogenous factors which an individual bank must recognize but cannot control. The individual bank can exert a varying degree of control over an intermediate group of factors—for example, the size and physical location of the bank. Finally, the individual bank determines directly such factors as its physical features and personnel, its marketing effort, the interest rates (within Regulation Q) it pays on time and savings accounts, the type of loans it is willing to make, and the level of services it offers its depositors.

At the present time, a bank cannot pay interest on demand deposits. For this reason, banking services are typically offered in order to attract such deposits. Ideally banks should carefully calculate the costs of such services and assure themselves that the value of the related deposits compensates them for that cost and provides a reasonable profit margin. This is usually done by calculating a service charge representing the actual cost plus profit margin and offsetting this charge, in whole or in part, by an earnings credit. This credit is usually related to some money market rate representing the value of the funds to the bank.

Of almost equal importance in attracting demand deposits, particularly business accounts, is the willingness to lend. The availability of credit is essential to most businesses. When funds are in short supply (as they are predicted to be in the foreseeable future), banks will give preference to those customers who maintain demand deposit accounts. *Credit accommodation* is a primary factor in deposit solicitation, and banks frequently offer "solicitation" lines of credit to businesses that have no present need to borrow, and by the same token, businesses maintain deposit balances in anticipation of their possible need to borrow in the future. One outstanding example of this relationship is the so-called backup line of credit supporting a corporation's sale of commercial paper. A company actively using commercial paper to finance its current needs will obtain and advertise the availability of its unused bank lines of credit. These unused lines are typically supported by demand deposit balances of at least 10 percent of the credit available.

Passbook savings are a second form of bank deposits. The passbook savings market is primarily a market of convenience. Since competing mutual thrift institutions are permitted to pay higher interest rates than commercial banks (theoretically in the interest of channeling savings funds into the residential mortgage market), commercial banks must emphasize greater convenience. The main thrust of commercial bank advertising in this field has concentrated on "one-stop, full-service" banking. The fact that commercial banks, even when they are in close competition with strong mutual institutions, still have large amounts of passbook savings is evidence of the effectiveness of this marketing technique.

Small-denomination certificates of deposit are a third deposit category. Banking regulations permit the payment of slightly higher rates of interest on savings instruments with fixed maturities of at least 30 days. For savers who are interest responsive, the savings certificate may serve as an attractive alternative to passbook savings. Certificates are issued in a variety of forms to suit the needs and tastes of various classes of savers. They are usually sold in minimum denominations of $1,000. Interest may be paid by check on a monthly or quarterly basis or, in some cases, accumulated to maturity. For savers who prefer the passbook concept, such certificates may be issued in the form of a special passbook.

The most recent interest regulations permitting mutual thrift institutions to pay slightly higher rates of interest on similar certificates as well as on passbook savings has given them a competitive edge in the market for savings certificates. Certificate buyers are prima facie interest rate conscious and the mutuals advertise their higher rates aggressively. Nevertheless, there are enough potential customers who will sacrifice a modicum of interest for the convenience of dealing with only one bank to make the promotion, or at least the availability, of the full spectrum of savings certificates worthwhile for a commercial bank that is actively seeking deposits.

Large certificates of deposit are a fourth deposit category. Under present regulations, certificates of deposit in minimum amounts of $100,000 are not subject to interest rate regulation. Such certificates represent the most fruitful source of funds to larger banks.

For the small and moderate-sized bank, the market for large denomination certificates will be confined to those few corporate customers who from time to time may have excess cash. To be effective in this market a bank must be sufficiently large and well-known so that its certificates will trade in a reasonably broad secondary market.

While most corporate treasurers will buy the certificates of any recognized bank, when rates are comparable they are more likely to acquire certificates issued by one of the banks with which they have an account. In times of tight money, banks may put considerable pressure on their customers to purchase the CD's. In normal time periods, the major banks post their issuing rates and, if they are seeking money, telephone the corporate treasurers with whom they have established contacts. By the same token, the treasurer with funds to invest will call a number of banks and "shop the market." Actual rates are often negotiated slightly off the posted rates for large blocks of funds of especially desirable maturities.

From the standpoint of attracting deposits, it is important for the bankers to be acquainted with many treasurers and other potential buyers of CD's. Although rate is always the primary factor, personal acquaintance is a definite factor when rates are nearly equal. The solicitation of large state and local deposits is carried out in a similar fashion. In this market, however, willingness to hold pledgeable securities is an additional consideration.

The attracting of nondeposit sources of funds has become important for some larger banks in recent years. These sources include borrowing from a Federal Reserve bank, purchasing federal funds, repurchase agreements (the agreement by a bank to purchase, at a specific price and time in the future, a security it is currently selling), Eurodollars, capital notes, and the issuance of commercial paper through a holding company. Most of these sources are highly interest-sensitive and banks should realize that their cost can vary considerably over a short period of time. Furthermore, most bankers typically assume that they could always purchase funds through these sources by paying a sufficiently high rate. This assumption proved to be a myth in mid-1974 when a few financially weak banks found these sources of funds not always available and many other banks found they were forced to pay up to 1 percent above the going market rate to obtain such funds.

Nevertheless, these nondeposit sources will remain an important means of attracting funds in the coming years.

A final major source of funds, *bank capital,* has other characteristics in addition to providing funds and is discussed later in this chapter.

Liquidity

Liquidity management encompasses the measurement of the liquidity needs of a bank as well as decisions as to how these needs should be met. Over time, the liquidity needs that individual banks experience will be equal to the difference between loan increases and deposit growth. The simplest method for making such an estimate is to assume that history will repeat itself, that seasonal patterns will not vary significantly from year to year, and that secular trends will continue.[3] Adjustments are then made for any cyclical forecast. Loan demands tend to rise above the normal trend in times of high business activity and to fall below expectations when the economy as a whole experiences a recession. Demand deposits, on the other hand, tend to rise (for all banks) in times of slack business activity because the Federal Reserve System makes reserves more easily available in order to encourage credit use and to stimulate an increase in the money supply. In periods of high levels of business activity, demand deposits tend to increase more slowly because the Federal Reserve System pursues more restrictive policies. The application of this method of estimating liquidity requirements to several hundred banks over a three-year period has indicated that it is a reasonable approach. It is an assumption, however, that needs at all times to be modified by managerial judgment and foresight.[4]

Providing for a bank's liquidity needs is often more complex than

---

[3]For detailed techniques for measuring a bank's liquidity, see Howard D. Crosse and George H. Hempel, *Management Policies for Commercial Banks,* 2d ed. (Englewood Cliffs, N.J.: Prentice-Hall, 1973), pp. 143-151.

[4]The Bank Examinations Department of the Federal Reserve Bank of New York has used a simplified version of this approach in connection with examinations of state member banks. The majority of banks examined could meet the requirements thus calculated; many of those that did not had to resort to borrowing in larger amounts and for longer periods than the examiners considered appropriate.

estimating such requirements. In many banks, directors and senior managers have available some estimates of their bank's liquidity needs but do not have adequate policies and procedures for securing these needs. One approach to providing for needed liquidity is through liability *management* — the purchase of liabilities at market rates to meet loan demands or other deposit withdrawals. This became a fairly common practice for many larger banks in the late 1960s and early 1970s. Proponents of such a policy hold that it is no longer necessary to depend entirely on liquid reserve assets to meet probable liquidity needs; instead, as such needs arise, they can be met by the management of liabilities. Banks can acquire needed liquidity by paying a high enough rate to sell large certificates of deposit, purchase federal funds (borrowing other banks' excess reserve), or borrow in the Eurodollar market.

Proper management of liabilities can significantly improve the performance of banks that have good access to the money markets. On the other hand, the contribution of liability management in providing liquidity needs during cyclical boom may be limited and is likely to be very costly. Loan demands tend to run high in such periods, and liability sources (1) tend to become expensive, (2) may be limited by the ceiling on interest rates that banks can pay on deposits, and (3) may be restricted to only better-quality banks. For instance, in the summer of 1974 many businesses were only willing to purchase the CD's of large, money-market banks (regional banks could acquire funds only by offering a 1 percent premium above the going rate) and most banks refused to sell their federal funds to the troubled Franklin National Bank.

Although liability management may be useful to large, money-market banks, in our opinion regional banks should only use liability management to reduce their seasonal liquidity needs and medium- and small-sized banks should rely primarily on assets to meet most liquidity needs. By holding an adequate amount of liquid assets — an approach that may involve some loss of current income during the early stage of a cyclical expansion — most banks will avoid higher costs and possibly far greater capital losses (from the sale of depreciated bonds) during the later stages of expansion. Put in more precise terms, the essence of liquidity management is to equate the probable earlier loss of income with the subsequent higher cost and possible capital losses.[5]

For most banks, sound liquidity management requires that the liquidity position consist primarily of assets that are of highest quality and short maturity and that can be readily sold without adverse effects on any of the bank's customers. Assuming that this position is accepted, we now describe briefly the primary means of attaining the highest return while insuring an adequate liquidity position.

The basic procedure to follow in managing the liquidity position is that of matching, over time, the cash flows from the assets with the liquidity re-

---

[5]Walter Woodworth, "Bank Liquidity Management: Theories and Techniques," *The Bankers' Magazine*, Autumn 1967, p. 78.

quirements. Assets used to meet volatile demand deposit fluctuations and seasonal loan demands will obviously differ from assets used to meet possible residual outflows of savings deposits and secular increases in loans.

Seasonal loan demands should basically be covered by assets that either mature very close to the time the demands materialize or can be readily sold with a high probability of no loss of principal. The bank can choose from a broad menu of liquid assets (as described in Chapter 4) and should make its acquisition decision on the basis of the highest available after-tax yield. Since the other category of liquid assets must be highly marketable, they should be limited to Treasury bills and possibly some agency obligations that mature within a year. The basic concept is that if the yield curve for Treasury bills has a positive slope (which is the normal situation), the yield of a longer-term bill for the period held (remember that one year is the maximum maturity) will usually be higher than the yield to maturity for a bill with a maturity that matches the holding period.

An example should help clarify this concept. Suppose a bank feels that it will need $100,000 to meet seasonal loan demands in approximately three months. Should the bank purchase 91-day bills yielding 4.5 percent or 182-day bills yielding 5.0 percent? Using the yield formula for the estimated holding period,[6] the bank would find that the yield over 91 days for the 182-day bill will be 5.5 percent if interest rates remain constant. Further, the bank should find that unless the rate on 91-day bills rises above 5.5 percent,[7] the bank will be better off buying the 182-day bills. Thus, unless the bank believes that the rates on 91-day bills will increase from 4.5 to above 5.5 percent in the next three months, the 182-day bills would be the preferable financial instrument.

Possible liquidity needs arising from cyclical or secular increases in loan demands might be satisfied by holding longer-term liquidity instruments. The major forms of assets acceptable for this purpose are U.S. government securities, federal agency securities, and higher-quality, marketable state and local securities.[8] Under most circumstances these securities will have maturities of one to three years at the time they are bought. Short-term

---

[6]The formula for determining the yield for the holding period (Yh) is

$$Yh = Yo + \frac{Tr(Yo - Ym)}{Th}$$

where Yo is the original yield, Ym is the market yield when sold, Tr is the remaining time to maturity, and Th is the time held (in units consistent with Tr).

[7]The break-even market yield (Yb) is determined by

$$Yb = Yo + \frac{Th(Yo - Yc)}{Tr}$$

where Yc is the market yield for a security maturing at the end of the holding period and the other symbols are the same as those in footnote 6 above.

[8]The marketability of state and local bonds varies widely. For example, see George H. Hempel, *Measures of Municipal Bond Quality* (Ann Arbor: University of Michigan Press, 1967), pp. 15–44; and "Liquidity and Muni Bonds," *Monthly Review*, Federal Reserve Bank of San Francisco, January 1968, pp. 10–12,

securities are appropriate if the bank feels there is a high probability that rates will rise over the next year or so. The potential price fluctuations for securities maturing much over three years disqualifies such securities for even longer-term liquidity needs.[9] Acceptable securities with maturities exceeding three years should be considered part of the investment portfolio.

Lending

Lending is the primary function of commercial banking; consequently, the formulation and implementation of sound lending policies are among the most important responsibilities of bank managers. Well-conceived lending policies are essential if a bank is to perform its credit-creating function effectively, earn a high return, and minimize the risk inherent in any extension of credit.

A bank's loan portfolio differs from its investment portfolio in three basic ways: (1) most bank loans are on a personal basis, therefore, the bank usually does not desire to sell its loans and often is unable to sell them because of their lack of marketability; (2) many bank loans are essential in attracting depositors and customers for other banking services; and, (3) the interest rate charged on an increasing proportion of loans varies with general interest rate movements. We believe a bank's loans should earn a high enough return to compensate the bank for the risk associated with the loan. The risk associated with a loan must not only include the credit risk from a potential nonpayment, but also some additional risk due to the lack of marketability and an interest rate risk for those loans with fixed rates. The return must include not only the borrower's interest payments, but also some imputed return on the funds attracted and net income from additional services provided to the borrowing customer.

We now summarize the three broad areas of bank lending policy. The first addresses the question of the appropriate size of the loan portfolio. Basic to decisions about the size of the loan portfolio is an assessment of the legitimate credit needs of the community or credit markets that the bank serves and an appraisal of the bank's ability to meet such demand. In some communities the demand for credit is virtually insatiable. In more fully developed and stable communities management may have to search out opportunities in order to make sound loans. In any event, the bank should formulate lending policies based on the community's needs and the bank's lending ability rather than on an arbitrary set of ratios representing preconceived ideas of appropriate or average statistical relationships.[10]

The second broad area of lending policy is the composition of the loans

---

[9]For example, the price of five-year Treasury notes declined over 7 percent in the five-month period from March 1974 to August 1974.

[10]At the end of 1974, loans were less than 40 percent of all assets for nearly 9 percent of all commercial banks, and loans exceeded 60 percent of all assets for roughly 12 percent of all banks. This disparity tends to support the considerable differences in credit needs and in the ability to meet these needs. *Source: Annual Report of the Federal Deposit Insurance Corporation, 1974,* Washington, D.C., 1975, p. 225.

in the bank's loan portfolio. A bank's lending policies serve as a screening device by which bank managers seek to limit the bank's loans to the type and character that they think appropriate, particularly when loan demand is pressing hard against a bank's available funds. From a policy viewpoint, the character of a loan should take precedence over its form. In other words, it is more important that loans be sound than that they be mortgage loans, business loans, consumer credit, and so on. The form of lending should reflect the demands of the community.

Here again, simple statistical relationships, although widely used as rough guidelines, should not be determinative. A bank in a rapidly growing residential community should normally have a higher proportion of mortgage loans than a bank in a stable industrial area. The latter, by the same token, normally should have a higher proportion of commercial loans and perhaps of consumer credit.[11] While it is desirable for the directors and top management to establish ceilings on the various forms of lending, they should do so primarily to distribute available bank credit in proportion to the community's needs so that one form of demand will not be slighted because another is too liberally supplied.

There are several special considerations that may play a part in determining the types of loans that some banks are willing to make. Whether a bank, particularly a medium- or small-sized bank, should accept business loans (or leases) with maturities in excess of three to five years is a problem that vexes many bank managers. If the bank has an adequate staff to evaluate the payment, purpose, and protection for such loans, and if the bank is willing to allow the interest rate on such loans to vary with general interest rates,[12] it should usually fill its community's credit needs for this form of borrowing. The regular cash flows from such loans or leases normally compensate the bank for the longer time to final maturity.

Business loans made to two types of firms may present some special problems. Lines of credit to finance companies typically represent long-term loan commitments by the bank. A bank cannot turn these loans on and off in response to credit ease or tightness. Also, many loans to finance companies are rather impersonal. Although compensating balances tend to be high, they are seen as a part of the interest charge and will be withdrawn immediately if the bank cancels the line of credit. Unless the bank's management feels that lines of credit to a finance company are clearly part of the credit needs of the community that the bank must serve, they should compare lines of credit to finance companies with alternative long-term investments.

Lending to small concerns on any but a short-term seasonal basis also often presents special problems. Many of these companies are closely held

---

[11]It is important that the bank be flexible about such relationships. The authors know of suburban banks in unit-banking states that have a high proportion of commercial loans to smaller businesses. (For a written example, see "Aggressive Commercial Lending Policy Helps Double Bank's Size," *Banking*, June 1971, pp. 22–24.) Furthermore, widespread branching systems and bank holding companies are often heavily involved in all types of loans.

[12]A bank is taking significant additional risk if the interest rates on such loans are fixed.

corporations that, as a matter of tax policy, show minimum profits and operate with a nominal net worth. Salaries paid to the principal stockholders are often larger than net profits, and the real net worth is reflected either in loans made to the company by its principals or in the net worth of the principals themselves. Banks should try to serve the legitimate credit needs of such small concerns (this is an essential banking function and generally leads to profitable customer loyalty if the firm grows); however, sound policy requires that debt to stockholders be subordinated formally to bank debt, and that the endorsement or guarantee of the principals be obtained by the bank as additional protection. If quality of management is a vital consideration in the extension of credit, banks may also require the assignment of life insurance on the principals.

Whether to confine a bank's consumer lending to direct loans or to purchase loans from automobile and appliance dealers is another matter that perplexes bank managers. The major virtue of indirect lending is its volume. Because of the keen competition for dealer business, a bank usually has to accept average credit risks on dealer loans, even though it formally reserves the right to be selective. Financing the dealer's inventory, another necessary step, entails its own risks and expensive procedures. As a result of all these factors, the rate of return from indirect financing is generally lower than that from direct lending. However, it is possible for a large volume to be generated and the business to be profitable if carefully handled; witness the success of some major finance companies specializing in this field.

Lending directly to the bank's own customers is, by contrast, a safer and less expensive means of extending consumer credit. Mistakes involve no more than a single borrower here and there, and most of the applicants for loans will be already known to the bank. Direct lending promotes good customer relations and generates future business. Many banks that can obtain a satisfactory volume of direct consumer loans have learned that for these reasons they can offer lower rates to selected borrowers and still enjoy a higher rate of return. [13]

Mortgage loans outside a bank's primary market area should be evaluated as an investment. Policies regarding mortgage loans within a bank's primary market are more difficult to formulate. Nearly all banks will make mortgage loans to valued customers. However, the long term and fixed return on most mortgage loans, as well as the lack of compensatory balances or service requirements from most mortgage borrowers, serve to discourage a sizable number of banks from seeking other mortgages. One of the suggested remedies for this reluctance is the variable rate mortgage discussed in Chapter 6.

Construction lending presents a different sort of problem. While such loans are short-term, there are several types of risks that must be

---

[13]Figures furnished to us by a large suburban bank clearly justify its policy decision to withdraw from dealer financing and concentrate heavily on advertising for direct loans which, it had concluded, were considerably more profitable.

understood and assessed. Banks that do not have the expertise to evaluate construction loans carefully should probably avoid them. On the other hand, if appropriate managerial expertise is available and credit needs for such financing exist in the bank's community, this type of lending provides a useful service and is often very profitable.[14]

The third broad lending policy area encompasses the terms a bank charges for lending its funds to deficit units. A bank's terms of lending are determined by policies establishing the desirable levels of interest rates, compensating balances, repayments, and collateral.

The range of rates that a bank may charge on various types of loans will be largely determined by forces beyond its control, that is, the level of rates in the market and the forces of competition. Within these limits, the individual bank retains some degree of flexibility for establishing interest rate policies that will help to determine the volume and character of the bank's loan portfolio and to bring about changes therein over time.

The marginal cost of lending should be the floor for a bank's lending rates. The rates that banks charge must be sufficiently high to cover (1) the marginal cost of the funds loaned; (2) the cost of making and servicing different kinds of loans (including a proportionate share of the overhead expenses of the bank); (3) a cost factor representing the probable losses that may be incurred over time; and, (4) a reasonable margin of profit. It is important that a bank's management be aware of these costs. Differences in the second and third categories of these costs, in particular, are important in explaining why (at any given time) rates on different kinds of loans may vary widely. Banks quite naturally tend to set lower rates on loans that cost less to process and that entail less risk—larger, short-term, or secured loans, for example. Processing costs per dollar of loan decrease both with the size of the loan and as less collateral is required. Collection cost and potential losses diminish as the term of the loan decreases and the responsibility of the borrower increases. It is the most credit-worthy borrower who is most likely to be granted a large or an unsecured loan.

Above this theoretical floor, bank lending rates are established in a highly complex and competitive market that includes a variety of other lenders, many of whom are specialists in particular types of credit instruments. For example, when large corporations need capital financing they may arrange term loans with their banks or private placements with insurance companies, or they may go to the public capital markets. Their choice will be influenced partly by rate and partly by the various terms imposed by different lenders. For short-term financing the same corporations (if their credit standing is high) may choose between banks and the commercial paper market. The purchaser of a home who seeks mortgage

---

[14]The high rates on construction loans appear to result more from the belief of many lenders that construction loans are very risky, rather than from actual losses. For an analysis of the risk factors involved and the yields and losses on construction loans, see Peter A. Schulkin, "Construction Lending at Large Commercial Banks," *New England Economic Review*, July/August 1970, pp. 2–11,

financing may choose among a commercial bank, a savings bank, a savings and loan association, a life insurance company, and a private lender. Finance companies and credit unions compete with commercial banks for consumer loans, as do various government agencies for farm loans. There is, in short, no lack of competition in most of the broad segments of bank lending activities.

Despite the pervasive competition, however, direct rate competition among banks serving the same market is rare. In fact, the more competitive a bank's situation, the greater the likelihood that its lending rates will conform closely with those of its close competitors. Such a bank cannot long charge higher rates for the same kinds of loans without losing many of its best customers. If it offers lower rates, it is likely to receive more applications than it can reasonably accommodate.

Traditionally, most commercial banks have varied the rates on outstanding seasonal commercial loans and lines of credit in accordance with changes in the prime interest rate or some other index of the general level of interest rates. On the other hand, the rates on consumer installment loans, mortgage loans, and many commercial term loans have typically been fixed for the life of the loan at the rate agreed on when the loan was made. The limited maturity of most consumer installment loans may explain the prevalence of fixed rates on these loans. However, many banks have begun to question fixed rates on longer-maturity loans, such as mortgage loans and commercial term loans. Some banks have already shifted to variable rates on one or both types of loans.[15] This questioning and changing of policy has been encouraged by periods of rapid increases in interest rates during the 1960s and 1970s.

The basic argument in favor of fixed rates is that planning for the bank and the borrower will be simplified because both know the size of the required interest payments. Furthermore, proponents argue that over long periods of time the interest return with fixed rates would be similar to the overall return if the banks were to use variable rates. The basic argument for variable rates is that the cost of a sizable proportion of a bank's funds is affected by the general level of interest rates. Thus, the bank's profits and cash inflows may be severely eroded in periods of rising interest rates. On the other hand, profits and cash inflows may increase drastically when interest rates fall. It is generally felt that profits and fund inflows will be more stable (possibly at a somewhat higher level) with variable interest rates since the bank will have greater flexibility to match maturities on assets and liabilities.

We tend to favor the charging of variable interest rates, where appropriate, for both commercial term loans and consumer mortgage loans. Two means of adjusting a variable rate contract are available—changing the rate or changing the term to maturity. Generally, rate changes have been the preferable means for most variable rate contracts. In addition to

---

[15]For a discussion of the impact and use of variable rates on mortgages by commercial banks, see "Variable Rates on Mortgages: Their Impact and Use," *New England Economic Review*, Federal Reserve Bank of Boston, March/April 1970, pp. 3-20.

the logical arguments favoring variable rates, both simulated and real-life experiences provide favorable support for the use of variable rates.[16] Such problems as misinterpretation, apprehension, and downright anger on the part of bank customers when rates increase can hopefully be overcome if the banking community is willing to put forth the effort.

The terms on a given loan encompass not only the rate charged but also the size of the balance that the commercial bank requires the borrower to maintain. In essence, the matter of compensating balances arises out of a quite natural relationship between banks and their customers. Individuals and companies find it necessary to maintain deposit accounts for operating purposes at levels presumably related to the scale of their operations. Once this relationship is established, normal practice would be to channel loan requests to the bank where deposits are maintained. Under ordinary circumstances, the size of an appropriate loan would seem to be related to the amount of the bank deposits normally maintained.

Under many conditions, this natural relationship appears to be valid. Banks typically required the demand deposits of a business to average 10 to 15 percent of the business' unused line of credit and 15 to 25 percent of its actual loan outstanding. Although these proportions might cause the borrower to maintain slightly higher than normal demand deposit balances, there is usually a good deal of flexibility in the arrangement and the cost of the money required in order to maintain the required balance probably would not be very substantial. While in the case of consumer installment loans or mortgage loans many banks give preferential treatment to their depositors, few banks explicitly require deposit balances.

Other major lending terms include repayment plans and collateral. It is prudent for all loan requests to include realistic, stated repayment plans. The cleanup period for lines of credit should also be explicitly stated. The maturity and form of repayment that are acceptable will vary from bank to bank depending on the credit needs of the bank's community and the ability of the bank to meet these needs. Collateral requirements should remain relatively constant. A realistic collateral policy should serve to improve credit-worthiness enough to enable bank management to make economically desirable loans and should not be used to restrict credit.

Investments

Investment analysis seems to be short-changed in many banks. The investment portfolio is usually secondary in importance to meeting the credit

---

[16]Simulations under several types of economic conditions have come out favorable for variable rates on commercial term loans (for example, in "A Profitability Model Comparing Variable and Fixed Rate Loan Policies," an unpublished study by Robert Hayes, over longer periods of time the variable rate policy resulted in a 10 percent higher profit to the bank). In three of four simulated economic situations—in sharply rising, widely fluctuating, and mildly fluctuating rate markets, but not in sharply falling rate markets—and in several real-life experiences, variable rates on mortgages seemed preferable to fixed rates (see "In Simulation and Real Life Variable Rates Really Work," *Savings and Loan News*, January 1971, pp. 21–26).

function of the bank and to providing sufficient liquidity for foreseeable demands; however, the investment portfolio is important for three reasons: (1) it is a primary source of liquidity, (2) it is a relatively important source of income, and (3) unplanned investment decisions tend to lead to results that may not be consistent with the bank's desired objective.

The first reason for the investment portfolio is easy to understand. Most banks do not have adequate liability sources for liquidity. In a period of heavy loan demand, for example, most banks either obtain funds by liquidating investments or are unable to make desired loans. The option to purchase liquidity by issuing CD's or other loanable funds is appropriate for some larger banks but is simply not available on a reasonable basis to most banks.

The second reason is supported by FDIC data. For example, interest on investments provided 21 percent of aggregate revenues for all insured banks in 1974. Investments provide an even larger proportion of these banks' net incomes because of the significantly lower costs associated with revenues from investments. If the typical bank could improve its average yield on investments by just 20 basis points (0.2 percent), it would increase its return on capital by roughly one-half of 1 percent.[17]

The perverse nature of many unplanned investment decisions is more complex but equally important. Short-term investments appear desirable in boom periods when loan demand is strong and interest rates are high. Yields on short-term investments may exceed those on long-term investments, and many banks are particularly aware of liquidity in their portfolios. The facts that reinvestment yields may be much lower in a few months and that the bank did not tie down some very attractive yields for longer periods of time never seem to become apparent until the opportunity has disappeared. Opposite pressures appear to exert themselves in recessionary periods when loan demand and interest rates tend to be low. Faced with declining returns on its loan portfolio, a bank finds itself under pressure to purchase longer-term securities that have relatively higher yields than shorter-term securities. The problem, of course, is that when loan demand accelerates and interest rates rise, the bank may be forced to take large losses or be "locked in" with an unfavorable investment position.

These three reasons indicate the importance of managing the bank's investment portfolio. We now examine rational investment policies pertaining to investment media, quality levels, maturities, and switching strategies.[18]

The essence of establishing flexible portfolio policies pertaining to investment media and quality levels is the matching of the type and quality of investment instruments with the investment needs of the bank. Both the needs and the related policies should be reviewed periodically.

---

[17]Figures are based on data in tables 111 and 116 in the *Annual Report of the Federal Deposit Insurance Corporation, 1974,* Washington, D.C., 1975.

[18]The interested reader can obtain a more technical knowledge of bond portfolio management by consulting Appendix 3.

The first need affecting a bank's investment media and quality levels is the bank's need for liquidity. Usually the estimated liquidity needs plus some margin of safety are met primarily by highly marketable, good quality securities. Even with reasonable maturity policies, most banks should use federal funds, U.S. government securities, or federal agency securities to cover their major liquidity needs. If a bank chooses to employ a more aggressive maturity strategy, such as trading on the yield curve (discussed later), to meet some of its liquidity needs, highly marketable, good quality securities become even more essential.

Another investment need affecting investment media is the level of the bank's pledging requirements. The bank must have acceptable quantities of U.S. government securities, federal agency securities, or state and local securities to meet these requirements. In cases where more than one type of security can be used to satisfy the pledging requirements, the choice will depend on the bank's risk and tax positions. In practically all banks, policymakers should insist that the bank pledge those eligible securities that they are least likely to want to sell in the future. Substitution of pledged securities, while possible, can be a time-consuming process.

The bank's risk position will also have a strong impact on the policies affecting the media and quality levels of a bank's portfolio. Banks taking considerable lending risks (in relation to their capital position) and banks lacking managerial expertise or time should limit their purchases to U.S. government securities, agency obligations, state and local securities, corporate bonds rated Aaa or Aa, and federally insured or guaranteed mortgages. Such a policy (in conjunction with reasonable maturity policies) should effectively place a limit on the risks in the investment portfolio and should require limited managerial expertise and effort for its implementation. Banks with limited senior managerial resources, in particular, should adopt this type of policy.

On the other hand, banks which have the necessary managerial capacity and are in the position to take additional risks in their investment portfolio should usually be less restrictive in their quality requirements. Such banks should be able to purchase state and local securities or corporate bonds rated below Aa that have higher yields than higher-quality bonds.

The tax position of the bank is essential in determining whether bank policy should encourage concentration in state and local securities with tax-exempt interest payments or in other investment instruments paying taxable interest. If the gross yields on state and local obligations continue to range from 20 to 30 percent lower than the yields on other obligations of comparable quality, bank policy should generally emphasize state and local obligations as long as their marginal income is taxed at the 48 percent rate. When marginal income is not taxed or taxed at only the 22 percent rate, bank policy should usually emphasize taxable securities.

Scheduling maturities within the investment portfolio is undoubtedly the most difficult and exacting task of portfolio management. Other policies can be established, periodically reviewed, and occasionally adapted to new circumstances. Maturity policy, in contrast, requires constant review and decision-making as funds become available for investment or as opportunities to improve the income position present themselves. In addition to the procedures discussed in Appendix 3, there are three major philosophies for scheduling maturities — cyclical maturity determination, a spaced maturity structure, and a "barbell" maturity structure.

The ideal course of action in portfolio management would be to hold short-term securities when interest rates are likely to rise and move to longer maturities when rates are expected to decline. Under the flexible monetary policy followed by the Federal Reserve System since the Accord of 1951, this strategy is tantamount to shortening maturities when business conditions (and the demand for credit) are expected to improve and lengthening maturities when the first signs of a recession appear. Several problems arise when attempting to apply this investment strategy. First, even in textbooklike cyclical periods such as the 1950s, bank portfolio managers found themselves under heavy pressure to produce profits (and thereby encouraged to buy longer-term securities) when interest rates were low. When interest rates were high (and expected to decline), banks tended to have only limited funds to invest in any maturity. Second, business cycles do not always act as the textbooks indicate. For example, the 1960s might be described as ten years of growth without recession but with two credit crunches. In 1974 we experienced both a recession and rapid inflation which adversely affected the securities market. Third, maturity decisions can be seen to be closely integrated with economic forecasting, which remains more of an art than a science.

Because of the uncertainties involved in such an ideal approach, banks have frequently been counseled to solve the problem of maturity distribution by spacing maturities more or less evenly throughout their established maximum range. The proceeds from maturing securities are reinvested in securities of the longest maturity admitted into the account. In this way the bank will be assured that it is not gambling on changes in the level of rates or the state of the economy. As long as the yield curve is rising, the reinvestment of maturing assets at the longest end of the maturity schedule will assure the bank of higher than average income on a portfolio of which the exposure to interest rate risk is only moderate. Figure 5-5 illustrates a spaced portfolio in which the funds from maturing bonds are invested in seven-year maturity bonds. Note that the average maturity of this portfolio will be three-and-a-half years, but that the securities were earning the rates on seven-year issues at the time reinvestment was made.

Banks using the "barbell" maturity structure tend to strengthen their liquidity position by investing a part of their investment portfolio in very short-term liquid securities. The remainder of the typical barbell portfolio usually consists of high-yield, very long-term bonds. Figure 5-6 illustrates an example of the barbell portfolio. Advocates of this maturity philosophy reason that the greater liquidity and the higher returns more than compensate for any additional risks associated with the barbell portfolio. Barbell portfolios tend to be trading portfolios, and it is typical for the long-term proportion of the portfolio to be largest when interest rates are

Figure 5-5. Annual Maturity Distribution of a 7-Year Spaced Portfolio

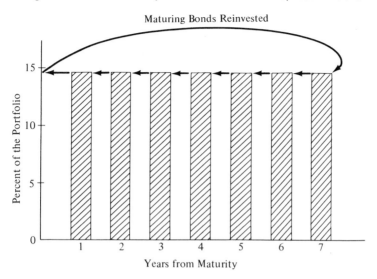

high and for the short-term portion of the portfolio to grow when rates are low. Managerial expertise is clearly a prerequisite for the barbell maturity structure.

Figure 5-6. An Illustrative Barbell Portfolio

For banks which lack the necessary managerial competence in the investment area, the average results obtained through regularly spaced maturities are undoubtedly better than what might result from a purely random or intuitive approach to the problem; however, the lack of liquidity from most spaced maturity portfolios is a source of concern. The barbell structure or other flexible approaches are generally preferable for banks with the necessary managerial competence and a willingness to exercise the proper judgment. As an example, it certainly does not make sense for such managers to invest the proceeds of maturing securities in the longest-term bonds permitted by the bank's policy at a time when the economy is obviously in a slack condition, when banks hold excess reserves, and when money rates are abnormally low.

Not even the most competent investment managers, of course, will be able to call every turn, nor do they need to. Alert and informed managers can take advantage of events that have already occurred; they do not need to gamble on the future. There is a vast difference between acting in accordance with the economic situation as it exists and blindly following a rigid policy of spaced maturities in every economic environment.

Finally, the investment policies of banks should provide the flexibility to use switching strategies which provide an opportunity for increased income and/or profits. The switching of maturities and the taking of profits and losses to best advantage is a technical aspect of bank investment management which must be left, in great part, to experts in the field. A few general principles, however, should be familiar to management responsible for investment policies in nearly all banks.

In periods of high loan demand, high interest rates, and monetary restraints, the price of securities will be depressed, causing many of the bonds in the investment portfolio of a bank to be priced below purchase price. This will be the time to take tax losses and to extend maturities in anticipation of lower interest rates and higher security prices. In such periods portfolio policy should flexibly encourage three actions: (1) investing any funds available in the investment portfolio at the longer end of the portfolio; (2) "refunding in advance" by selling short-term issues and reinvesting the proceeds of such sales in longer-term bonds; and, (3) switching from a security of a given maturity to one of comparable maturity to improve yields and long-term profit.

The first and second actions achieve the major portfolio objective of lengthening maturities when losses are taken in order to benefit from the expected easing of rates in a later period. The advantages of higher income and greater potential for gain in market price are obvious. The third action is more limited in objective but may contribute considerably to the long-run profitability of banks using a barbell type of portfolio policy. For example, assume that a bank owns some 20-year bonds which it bought at par a few years earlier and which are currently selling at 80. If the bank sells $1,000,000 worth of these bonds for $800,000, the $200,000 loss after taxes actually costs only $100,000. By reinvesting the $800,000 in similar bonds the bank will have a built-in future appreciation of $200,000, which after taxes will net $100,000 at maturity. This is not a break-even proposition, however, because the bank has $100,000 more in cash after the initial sale. This $100,000 is now invested and provides higher yields over the 20 years as well as the possibility of even greater price appreciation.

Banks with competent investment management may do even better. They might be able to switch into higher-yielding bonds of comparable quality and maturity. Table 5-6 demonstrates the earnings effect of an actual municipal bond switch by a bank in 1975. The bank sold 100 bonds of one A-1-rated general obligation yielding 5.75 percent and purchased 100 of another A-1-rated general obligation of similar maturity, returning 6.10 percent. By taking a $4,000 after-tax loss now, the bank purchased $535 of additional tax-exempt income per year for 11 years and over $6,000 in after-tax gains after 11 years — a 15.3 percent annual rate of return.

After studying this example, one may wonder why all banks do not sell most of their holdings at a loss in periods of high interest rates. The first consideration is how much of a reduction in reported net income the owners of the bank are willing to accept. Current accounting rules require that attention be focused on net income after securities' gains and losses rather than on net operating earnings. Explaining to shareholders that reductions in profits are advantageous is not easy. Second, there is the limitation of taxable income. Losses are valuable only to the extent that they can decrease the tax liability. Third, losses may reduce (or limit the increase in) bank capital, thereby encouraging supervisory authorities to ask for additional capital.

When the economy is clearly in a recessionary stage and interest rates are relatively low, bonds will be selling at above-average prices. Portfolio holdings, especially if acquired at comparatively low prices during a previous period of high interest rates, will show market appreciation. This is the time when banks generally should concentrate on short-term investments. They can largely offset the lower operating income by taking profits in the longer bonds.

Taking profits always seems more desirable than absorbing losses, but it can be dangerous merely to take profits and reinvest in comparable (or longer) maturities. To do so would leave the bank even more vulnerable to declines in prices which are bound to occur, since these declines will affect

TABLE 5-6   Earnings Effect of a Municipal Bond Switch

Sold	Cost	Sale Price	Loss	Coupon Income	Yield to Maturity
$100,000 Baytown, Texas (A-1)	$94,000	$86,000	$8,000	$4,100	5.75%

Purchase	Cost			Coupon Income	Yield to Maturity
$100,000 Denton, Texas (A-1)	$87,500			$4,500	6.10%
	$90,000*			$4,635*	

*Hypothetical amount to equalize investment ($86,000 sales price plus $4,000 in lower taxes).

booked profits rather than unbooked appreciation. The general rule therefore should be: do not take profits without shortening maturities (decreasing exposure to interest rate risk). The conviction that the economy is near the bottom of a recessionary period, which should lead a bank to take profits, is consistent with a policy of shortening maturities in anticipation of a future rise in rates.

Profits (after taxes) taken in times of low interest rates should not be viewed as permanent additions to the bank's capital funds. Rather, they should be carried as reserves against future security losses so they will be available to absorb losses when the next turn in interest rates provides new profit possibilities.

It should be noted that a flexible portfolio policy that takes full advantage of the swings in the business cycle will result in fairly wide variations in portfolio income on a year-to-year basis. If a bank stays short at times when money rates are low, it must make a considerable sacrifice of income. One must remember (and there is no reason not to explain to the stockholders of smaller banks) that flexible, sound management must be judged by the combination of income and profit over the period of a full business and/or credit cycle.

Capital

Capital is a difficult bank policy area because capital has numerous banking functions. It is a source of funds which a bank can use both directly to extend credit and indirectly as a base for attracting additional funds. Capital provides a cushion to protect depositors from a decline in a bank's assets and is an important factor in maintaining the confidence a bank must enjoy to grow and prosper. On the other hand, too much capital lowers a bank's rate of return on its capital and may inhibit the bank's ability to raise additional funds. Rational bank policies seek to balance the protection that more capital provides depositors and the public against the risks inherent in the banking business and the higher return when less capital is employed. In addition, bank management must also develop policies which indicate the composition of the total capital that should be raised in each of the various forms.

Figure 5-4 indicated the trends in four conventional capital ratios for all insured banks during the period from 1934 through 1974. These ratios provide some indication of how bank management (assisted by the appropriate supervisory authorities) chose to balance the risk–return conflicts of the capital position. In the postwar period capital has remained a relatively stable percentage of total assets and total deposits but has been a declining proportion of risk assets.

For each individual bank, it is essential that management understand the basis of the supervisory evaluation and know how to use one or more of the supervisory formulas, at least as a measusre of the trends in their capital positions. While not all banks will wish to go so far as to evaluate the risk in each and every bank asset, all banks should go further than rough groupings, such as those in the New York Federal Reserve formula. Within the logical framework of that formula, capital allocations ranging from perhaps 5 to 15 percent could be used to distinguish among types of loans that the bank considers prime and those in which it recognizes normal or greater risk. Different amounts of capital might be allocated to different groups of securities in order to reflect variations in maturity dates, credit risks, and marketability. Such an evaluation of the risks inherent in the loans and securities of a particular bank would be an instructive exercise and could provide an effective review of lending and investing policies.

Just how much capital is enough can perhaps never be fully determined in advance of the hour of need. The bank supervisor has substantial responsibility in the area of capital adequacy and tends to react accordingly. Some more aggressive bankers tend to keep the examiner somewhat less than completely happy without being antagonistic. However, from the viewpoint of both management and bank supervisors, the risks of having too little capital exceed the costs of a moderate success. In a review of the 1929–1934 experience, it is perhaps significant that the 19 banks that survived the Depression without having to raise additional capital had, in 1929, a capital ratio only 2.9 percent higher on average than the 31 banks that needed recapitalization.

Adequate capital is not, of course, a substitute for sound lending and investing policies; it cannot take the place of experienced and progressive management with a well-conceived program of planning and control. It can only provide assurance to the public, the stockholder, and the supervisor that the bank has the strength and the wherewithal to survive circumstances and conditions that even the best management can never foresee. In a real sense, the provision of adequate capital is the price of the private enterprise banking system in the United States.

The three principal forms of bank capital are long-term debt, preferred stock, and common equity. Of course, there are subclassifications within these broad categories—for example, there are several forms of long-term debt; some debts and preferred stock can be converted into common stock; or common equity may be raised externally or generated internally. However, these subclassifications share the basic characteristics of the three principal forms.

Long-term debt includes all forms of interest-bearing obligations that promise a fixed amount at some future time. The two major forms of long-term debt are *capital notes* and *debentures.* Some capital notes or relatively small debentures have been sold to the issuing bank's major correspondent banks. Large debenture issues with medium-term and long-term maturities have been privately placed or sold to the public through investment bankers (financial institutions such as life insurance companies and pension funds have been heavy purchasers). Nearly one-third of the total dollar value of debentures sold in recent years has been convertible into the bank's common stock at a predetermined price.

With *preferred stock,* the second major category of bank capital, the dividend and asset claims are fixed in amount and are subordinated to the claims of depositors and to all indebtedness of the bank. While preferred stocks do not mature, most preferred stocks may be called at a fixed price at the option of the issuing bank. A commercial bank may issue either straight (nonconvertible) preferred stock or preferred stock that is convertible into common stock at a predetermined price. Generally, long-term debt and preferred stock are referred to as senior capital, because their claims on assets and earnings are above those of common stock.

Common equity, the third form of capital, is composed of common stock, surplus, undivided profits, and the equity reserve accounts. Common equity has a residual claim on income and assets behind deposits, other liabilities, indebtedness, and preferred stock. It may be valued at either market value or book value. The total market value of a bank's common equity can be estimated by multiplying the per share market price by the number of shares outstanding. Although this measure has its shortcomings—some bank stocks are not traded in an active market—no feasible alternative has been proposed. The book value of the common equity of a commercial bank can be computed by the subtraction of deposits, other liabilities, and senior capital from the book value of total assets. This book value figure is also biased to the extent that market and book values differ for the bank's assets and liabilities.

The *common stock* consists primarily of the par or stated value of all outstanding shares of common stock. The *surplus* account contains funds generated both externally and internally—the accumulated premiums over par or stated value at which common stock was sold to the public (with one minor exception, discussed below) and whatever proportion of accumulated, undivided profits has been shifted to the surplus account. The primary reason for such a bookkeeping shift is that in the past the legal loan limit for all national banks and most state banks was computed as a percentage of the combined total of the common stock and surplus accounts. The Comptroller of the Currency now recognized undivided profits and equity reserves, as well as senior capital, as part of the lending base; however, many state banks are still subject to the older legal loan limit.

The *undivided profits* account is composed of accumulated retained earnings less any amounts that have been shifted to the surplus account. *Equity reserves* consist of retained earnings that have been set apart for some contingency or expected event, such as the retirement of preferred stock or an anticipated court settlement. The reserve for loan losses and the reserve for security losses are technically asset valuation reserves rather than equity reserves. They are considered to be expenses (even though the reserve for security losses is not deductible for tax purposes) in the determination of earnings. The Comptroller and some state regulators do include part of all of these reserves in a bank's lending base.

Table 5-7 indicates that as late as the early 1960s virtually all bank capital was generated from common equity (common stock, surplus, undivided profits and equity reserves). Long-term debt and preferred stock together accounted for less than 0.2 percent of all bank capital in 1960 and 1961. From Table 5-7 it is evident that this pattern changed markedly

TABLE 5-7   Capital Accounts of Insured Commercial Banks
(in $ millions)

As of Year-End	Total Capital	Long-Term Debt	Preferred Stock	Common Stock	Surplus	Undivided Profits	Equity Reserves
1950	$11,281.7	$ 20.3	$ 62.0	$ 3,436.6	$ 5,200.5	$ 2,093.5	$ 469.0
1955	15,009.4	29.8	20.3	4,517.7	7,208.5	2,776.5	456.6
1960	20,658.6	23.2	14.6	6,170.1	9,916.2	4,020.9	513.6
1961	22,123.0	22.1	14.7	6,584.7	10,798.4	4,156.8	546.3
1962	23,752.3	20.5	34.8	6,882.0	11,458.4	4,789.7	566.9
1963	25,322.7	130.0	37.8	7,283.0	12,163.5	5,113.4	595.0
1964	27,438.1	810.7	41.7	7,886.4	12,893.2	5,113.0	693.1
1965	29,905.0	1,652.7	39.9	8,507.8	13,464.8	5,437.6	802.2
1966	31,693.2	1,729.9	61.6	8,856.8	13,988.7	6,166.5	879.7
1967	34,005.9	1,984.4	87.1	9,253.4	14,983.4	6,610.7	1,086.7
1968	36,628.0	2,110.1	90.7	9,772.6	16,173.9	7,419.7	1,061.0
1969	39,576.2	1,998.3	103.4	10,529.3	17,460.8	8,426.8	1,057.6
1970	42,566.4	2,091.9	107.3	11,137.8	18,072.6	10,145.8	1,011.0
1971	46,905.0	2,956.2	91.9	11,811.1	19,895.8	11,135.1	1,014.9
1972	52,367.7	4,092.8	68.9	12,853.7	21,528.4	13,012.2	811.6
1973	57,838.6	4,117.4	65.7	13,846.1	23,593.3	15,361.9	854.4
1974	63,983.4	4,393.6	54.0	14,886.4	25,497.3	18,175.7	976.7
1975	69,464.3	4,578.1	53.9	15,678.5	26,886.0	21,381.2	886.5

Source: Annual Reports of the Federal Deposit Insurance Corporation, 1960-1975
(Washington, D.C.: FDIC, 1961-1976).

throughout the mid- and late 1960s and early 1970s. In the majority of these years, between 10 percent and 25 percent of the increases in total bank capital and over three-fourths of estimated externally raised bank capital came in the form of long-term debt and preferred stock.

In order to understand movements in the level of total capital and changes in the form used to raise bank capital, we must look at two distinct periods since the end of World War II. During the first period, 1950-1961, the deposits and assets of commercial banks grew slowly and the banks' market share, relative to other financial intermediaries, declined appreciably. For example, Table 5-8 indicates that bank assets and deposits grew at an average annual rate of between 4 and 5 percent from 1950 to 1961. During the same period, the aggregate assets of nonbank financial intermediaries grew at an annual rate of roughly 12 percent. This relatively slow bank growth did have a positive effect — it lessened the pressure for additional capital. Table 5-8 illustrates that bank capital grew considerably faster than bank assets and deposits. While part of the rapid growth in bank capital may be attributed to the shift from government securities to riskier assets, it is important to remember that the trend toward riskier assets continued through the 1960s and early 1970s, while the growth of bank capital declined relative to the growth in assets and deposits.

The form in which bank capital was raised during the early postwar

TABLE 5-8   Growth in Assets, Deposits and Capital of Commercial Banks
(in $ millions)

As of End of	Bank Assets	Bank Deposits	Bank Capital	Common Equity Capital	Senior Capital
1950	$168,932	$155,265	$11,590	$11,508	$ 82
1961	$278,561	$248,689	$22,459	$22,432	$ 27
Growth (1950–61):					
Dollar amount	$109,629	$ 93,424	$10,869	$10,924	$ (55)
Annual rate	4.7%	4.4%	6.3%	6.4%	. . . a
1962	$297,116	$262,122	$24,094	$24,039	$ 55
1975	$974,711	$792,882	$69,464	$64,886	$4,578
Growth (1962–75):					
Dollar amount	$677,595	$530,760	$45,370	$40,847	$4,523
Annual rate	9.7%	9.1%	8.5%	7.9%	. . .b
1969	$530,665	$435,517	$39,576	$37,574	$2,002
1975	$974,711	$792,882	$69,464	$64,886	$4,578
Growth (1969–75):					
Dollar amount	$444,046	$357,365	$29,888	$27,312	$2,576
Annual rate	10.9%	10.6%	9.8%	9.3%	14.8%

Sources: Selected *Federal Reserve Bulletins* (Washington, D.C.: Board of Governors of the Federal Reserve System, 1960–1975) and *Annual Reports of the Federal Deposit Insurance Corporation* (Washington, D.C.: Federal Deposit Insurance Corporation, 1960–1976).
aNegative annual compound rate of growth.
bLarge compound rate of growth because of small senior capital base.

period is also noteworthy. Outstanding senior capital (debt and preferred stock) actually declined from 1950 to 1961, primarily because none of the regulatory agencies would accept newly issued debt as part of a bank's capital. Moreover, the relatively rapid growth in equity capital during that period was accomplished almost entirely through retained earnings. The dollar amount of new external issues of common stock was minimal. In summary, banks financed nearly all of their capital growth in the 1950s from their internally generated funds.

In the early 1960s banks responded to the slow postwar growth in assets and deposits by (1) paying higher returns on their savings and time accounts, (2) aggressively offering certificates of deposit, savings certificates, and other liability forms, and (3) requiring their loan customers to retain larger demand deposit balances. The surge in asset and deposit growth was pronounced—rising at an average annual rate of nearly 10 percent from 1962 through 1975 (Table 5-8). By comparison, in the same period the assets of nonbank financial intermediaries grew at an average annual rate of slightly less than 7 percent. Among other things, this doubling in the rate of growth of bank deposits and assets meant that other sources of capital in addition to retained earnings had to be utilized.

Table 5-8 demonstrates that many commercial banks responded to this need by issuing senior securities, particularly long-term debt, in order to finance a high proportion of their external capital needs.[19] This decision was encouraged by regulatory acceptance of some senior capital, by pressures to maintain returns on common stock, and by changes in the banking structure. A review of the average levels of returns, marginal tax rates, and costs of preferred stock and long-term debt reveals the leverage benefits of senior capital. Banks found that they could increase their return on common equity by using the favorable leverage from long-term debt. As reflected in price-earnings multiples, this use of fixed cost financing did not seem to appreciably increase the risk exposure of the banks.

One additional observation can be made from the data in Table 5-8. The rate of growth in assets and deposits has increased to between 11 and 12 percent in the last five years; however, the rate of growth of bank capital increased to only 9.6 percent and was below 9 percent for equity capital. Thus, the rate of growth of bank assets and deposits has increased in recent years while the growth of total capital (especially equity capital) has not kept pace.

The key ingredient for predicting the form of future bank capital financing is forecasts of what will happen to environmental conditions and individual bank variables. Among the environmental conditions, the inadequacy of retained earnings as a means of financing all the capital needs of the growing commercial banking industry seems likely to continue. It also appears unlikely that the current capital adequacy rules of regulatory authorities will be further eased. Banks will, therefore, continue to be forced to choose among external sources of capital.

There will probably be some minor modifications in current regulatory acceptance of senior capital—perhaps smaller banks will be given some access to sources of senior capital and maturity and size of restrictions for larger issues of capital notes may be further tightened. It seems unlikely, however, that there will be substantial changes in the current level of regulatory acceptance of senior capital. While the nonpayment of the capital notes of the U.S. National Bank of San Diego and Franklin National Bank may cause lenders to examine bank debt issues more closely, there is no reason for this failure to lead to a tightening of regulatory acceptance of capital notes. Actually, recent happenings simply reaffirm that such notes are capital and clearly subordinated to all deposits.

On average, it seems likely that most banks will face continued pressure on profit margins. Increased volume will be necessary for the maintenance of adequate returns for owners, but this increase may necessitate a larger capital base and, therefore, result in a lower return on total capital. The marginal effective income tax rate of most banks will probably remain

---

[19]The dominance of long-term debt as an external source is clearly brought out in data on new issues. From 1966 to 1974, $795 million was raised through new issues of common stock, $49 million through preferred stock, and $7,439 million through new issues of debt. *Source:* Corporate Financial Counseling Department of Irving Trust Company, New York.

close to 50 percent. Over the next few years, the cost of long-term debt and preferred stock will probably average as high as or higher than the relatively high rates of the early 1970s. Finally, it seems probable that banks will become much more sophisticated in assessing the combined risks associated with their asset and liability holdings.

The net effect of these factors should be a continuation of outstanding increases in long-term bank indebtedness. Bank holding companies will probably issue higher proportions of debt because they face fewer restrictions on capital from regulatory authorities. Banks which currently have little or no debt outstanding will probably issue substantial amounts of debt (in addition to most smaller banks, some larger banks, for example, 21 of the largest 122 banks, have no senior capital outstanding). Continued high tax rates and lower earnings on total capital indicate that preferred stock will continue to be issued in only relatively small amounts and will continue to be issued in only relatively small amounts and will generally be convertible. Convertible debt will possibly grow to nearly half of new debt issues, because it is a form which will enable banks to lower the predicted high interest cost of debt and to add to the common equity base in a future period at a better common stock price than that obtainable when the convertible debt is originally issued.

Linear Programming: A Technique for Wealth-Maximization[20]

In this section, we indicate how linear programming can be used by commercial banks to achieve their financial management objective of wealth-maximization. This technique is presented in order to indicate how a model of bank resources allocation can be developed.

The objective of our linear programming model is to maximize shareholder wealth. This objective will be accomplished by maximizing the market value of the bank's common equity. The value of the bank's equity is determined by the residual value of assets over liabilities. With this in mind, the objective function becomes

$$\text{MAX } V_B = V_C X_C + V_G X_G + V_M X_M + V_L X_L - V_F X_F - V_{DD} D_{DD}$$
$$- V_{DD} X_{TD} - V_{CN} X_{CN} - V_{PS} X_{PS} - 0.0 B_e$$

where V_i is the market value of dollars expended for corresponding assets, or received in exchange for the respective liabilities; X_i represents dollars invested in the ith asset or obtained through the ith liability; and B_e is the book value of the bank's common equity. The book value is set equal to zero to simplify constraints in the model.

Once the objective function has been specified, linear constraints are constructed so as to model various regulations and behaviors that typify the banking environment.

---

[20]This section is adopted from a model constructed by William J. Marshall, Assistant Professor of Finance, Washington University, St. Louis.

One such constraint on bank activities is the reserve requirement for demand and time deposits. The progressive nature of the reserve requirement on demand deposits can be incorporated into the model by breaking demand deposits into five categories. Upper bounds are placed on these categories to get the model to evaluate this constraint at various levels of demand deposits. *Reserve requirement constraints* are modeled as

$$0 \leq X_C - 0.08X_{DD_1} - .105X_{DD_2} - .125X_{DD_3} - .135X_{DD_4} - 0.18X_{DD_5}$$

$$- 0.06X_{TD} \qquad X_{DD_1} \leq 2 \qquad X_{DD_2} \leq 8 \qquad X_{DD_3} \leq 90 \qquad X_{DD_4} \leq 300$$

Another constraint upon banks is the *capital adequacy constraint* which requires banks to have a sufficient level of capital given the risk and liquidity embodied in its asset structure and the level of volatility of bank deposits. To accomplish this within our model, weights are assigned to assets in order to reflect liquidity, and to deposits in order to reflect the risk of withdrawal, or volatility.

The illiquidity of assets is measured by A,

$$A = 0.00_J X_G + 0.10X_M + 0.10X_L.$$

The volatility of deposits and federal funds is denoted by D,

$$D = 0.47X_{DD} + 0.36X_{DD} + 1.0X_F.$$

The computation of the capital requirement depends on the types of assets (denoted by R_i) held against liabilities in D. The types hypothesized in this model are as follows:

$$R_1 = X_C + 0.8X_G$$
$$R_2 = R_1 + 0.18X_G$$
$$R_3 = R_2 + 0.20X_M$$

To develop the actual capital adequacy constraint, we make the following assumptions:

1. For every dollar that D exceeds R_i, 0.065 dollars of capital are needed.
2. For every dollar that D exceeds R_2, 0.040 dollars of capital are needed.
3. For every dollar that D exceeds R_3, 0.095 dollars of capital are necessary.

Taking all of the above assumptions into account, the capital adequacy constraint becomes

$$B_e + X_{CN} + X_{PS} \geq A + 0.065(D - R_1) + 0.04\ (D - R_2) + 0.095(D - R_3).$$

Other aspects of the banking environment can be included in the model. For example, there is a requirement that deposits of state and local political subdivisions must be matched dollar for dollar by securities. It has been found that these deposits in the past have made up about 4 percent of total demand deposits, and about 12 percent of total time deposits. Hence, this constraint is written as follows:

$$X_G + X_M \geq 0.04X_{DD} + 0.12X_{TD}.$$

Another example of a constraint would be to incorporate the fact that the use of capital notes to raise capital is limited in the banking industry. This *constraint on bank behavior* could be depicted linearly as

$$X_{CN} \leq 0.22B \quad \text{or} \quad X_{CN} \leq 0.25(X_{PS} + B_e).$$

Two other constraints must be added. One is the *balance sheet identity constraint*:

$$B_e + X_{PS} + X_{CN} \, X_F + X_{TD} + X_{DD} - X_L - X_M - X_G - X_C = 0.$$

Another is the *nonnegativity constraint*:

$$X_i = 0 \qquad \text{for all } i.$$

Any number of linear constraints can be added to better reflect the bank's environment. We have only included a few to indicate how the bank's environment can be depicted in a linear programming model which maximizes the wealth of the stockholders as the objective function.

Chapter 5

Review Questions

1. What are the four forms of control that have had the greatest influence on the banking industry in recent years?
2. We considered an example of the wealth-maximization principle applied to commercial banks (Third National Bank example). What three basic points were illustrated by this example?
3. How can a bank's liquidity needs be estimated? What are the two major approaches to meeting these needs? Which is the most risky? What types of benefit/cost decisions must be made in order to choose between the two ways?
4. What is the basic procedure behind managing a bank's liquidity position? How should a bank choose the short-term assets to meet its short-term liquidity needs?
5. In what three ways do a bank's loan portfolio differ from its investment portfolio?
6. What are the three broad areas of a bank's lending policy? List some examples

of problems facing banks when they attempt to determine the composition of their loan portfolio.

7. In recent times, loan pricing has become a major concern of bank managers. What are the major determinants of bank lending terms? What three costs must be considered when loan rates are set? Which of these costs explains most of the rate differences between banks?

8. Why is a bank's investment portfolio important? Name some of the factors that determine the investment media and quality in the portfolio.

9. What is the ideal course of action in bank portfolio management? What are the problems associated with this approach? Discuss a couple of the alternatives to the ideal approach which are followed by bank portfolio managers.

10. In periods of high interest rates, security prices are depressed. You are a bank portfolio manager in a period of high rate and high loan demand. Outline the investment policy you would recommend in this situation. Assume that the yield curve is downward sloping.

Selected References

American Bankers Association. *The Commercial Banking Industry.* Englewood Cliffs, N.J.: Prentice-Hall, 1962.

American Institute of Banking. *Savings and Time Deposit Banking.* New York: American Bankers Association, 1968.

"Bank Holding Companies: An Overview." Federal Reserve Bank of Chicago. *Business Conditions,* August 1973, pp. 3-13.

Barger, Harold. *Money, Banking, and Public Policy.* 2d ed. Chicago: Rand McNally, 1968.

Bradley, Stephen P. and Crane, Dwight B. *Management of Bank Portfolios.* New York: Wiley, 1975.

Christopher, Cleveland A. "Competition in Financial Services." New York: First National City Corporation, 1974.

Crosse, Howard and Hempel, George A. *Management Policies for Commercial Banks.* Englewood Cliffs, N.J.: Prentice-Hall, 1973.

Hayes, Douglas A. *Banking Lending Policies—Issues and Practices.* Ann Arbor, Mich.: University of Michigan Press, 1964.

Hempel, George H. "Bank Capital: Issues and Answers." *The Magazine of Bank Administration* (in 4 parts), November 1974-March 1975.

————, "Basic Ingredients of Commercial Banks' Investment Policies." *The Bankers Magazine,* Autumn 1972.

Hempel, George H. and Yawitz, Jess B. "Maximizing Bond Returns." *The Bankers' Magazine,* Summer 1974.

Innovations in Bank Management: Selected Readings. Jessup, Paul F., ed. New York: Holt, Rinehart & Winston, 1969.

Lyon, Roger A. *Investment Portfolio Management in the Commercial Banks.* New Brunswick, N.J.: Rutgers University Press, 1960.

Mayne, L. S. "Supervisory Influence on Bank Capital." *Journal of Finance,* June 1972, pp. 637-651.

Nadler, Paul S. *Commercial Banking in the Economy.* New York: Random House, 1968.

Robinson, Roland I. *Management of Bank Funds.* 2d ed. New York: McGraw-Hill, 1962.

Smith, Harlan M. *The Essential of Money and Banking.* New York: Random House, 1968.

"The New Banking." *Business Week,* September 15, 1963.

Van Horne, James C. *Fundamentals of Financial Management.* 2d ed. Englewood Cliffs, N.J.: Prentice-Hall, 1974.

For current information see the *Federal Reserve Bulletins* (monthly) and the *Annual Reports of the Federal Deposit Insurance Corporation.*

```
66666666666666666666666666666666666666666666666666666666666666666666666666666666666666
66666666666666666666666666666666666666666666666666666666666666666666666666666666666666666
666666666666666666666666666666666    6666666666    666    66666666666666666666666666666666
666666666666666666666666666666666    6666666666    6666    66666666666666666666666666666666
66666666666666666666666666666666666    666666666    66666    66666666666666666666666666666666
66666666666666666666666666666666666    6666666    666666    66666666666666666666666666666666
6666666666666666666666666666666666666    66666    6666666    66666666666666666666666666666666
666666666666666666666666666666666666666    666    6666666    66666666666666666666666666666666
6666666666666666666666666666666666666666    6    666666666    66666666666666666666666666666666
66666666666666666666666666666666666666666        6666666666    66666666666666666666666666666666
666666666666666666666666666666666666666666666    6666666666    66666666666666666666666666666666
66666666666666666666666666666666666666666666666666666666666666666666666666666666666666666
66666666666666666666666666666666666666666666666666666666666666666666666666666666666666666
```

Financial Management
of Thrift Institutions

THRIFT institutions include savings and loan associations, mutual savings banks, and credit unions. The main characteristic allowing us to group these three financial institutions is the similarity of liabilities they use to attract funds. At the present time, these institutions employ time and savings deposits to obtain the majority of their financial resources. In employing these resources they emphasize intermediate and long-term loans to consumers. The other assets they acquire differ considerably among the three institutions because of legal and regulatory constraints. There are, however, sufficient similarities to group these institutions together for the purposes of this chapter. Specifically, we will (1) consider the environmental and regulatory characteristics affecting each thrift institution; (2) demonstrate how our wealth-maximization model can be applied to a thrift institution; (3) examine the historical pattern of their performance; and (4) discuss some specific financial management decisions for wealth-maximization.

Financial Decisions of Thrift Institutions

Savings and Loan Associations

At the beginning of 1975 there were 673 stockholder-owned savings and loan associations (S&L's) under the corporate form and 4,429 mutually owned associations without stockholders. The total number of savings and loan offices, including branches, was 13,922. Depositors and borrowers ostensibly elect the board of directors of the mutual associations; however, control is easily maintained by the existing directors through proxies obtained at the start of the savings or borrowing relationship. Savings and loan associations can be organized under either federal or state charters. In early 1975 there were 2,060 federally chartered associations[1] with assets of $167.7 billion and 3,042 state- chartered associations with assets of $127.9 billion.[2]

Most regulation of savings and loan activities is centralized in the Federal Home Loan Bank system (FHLB). This system is composed of the Federal Home Loan Bank Board, the 12 regional Federal Home Loan Banks, and member associations. Member associations—of which all federal associations and most state associations are members—hold approximately 98 percent of the assets of the industry. In addition, the time and savings accounts of all federal and most state associations are insured (to $40,000 for the accounts of individuals, partnerships, and corporations and to $100,000 for the accounts of public units) by the Federal Savings and Loan Insurance Corporation (FSLIC). Members of the FSLIC hold slightly over 97 percent of the total assets of the industry. State regulations and state regulatory departments also affect savings and loan activities within a particular state.[3]

The constraints placed on savings and loan activities by the environment and by regulation are divided into two categories: methods for attracting funds and methods for employing funds. Savings and loan associations are limited primarily to time and savings deposits as the media for obtaining funds from surplus units. Their competitive position vis a vis commercial banks and other thrift institutions was enhanced in the late 1960s and early 1970s when they were permitted to pay varying rates on different kinds of passbook savings accounts and to issue numerous maturities of certificates of deposits. The maximum interest rate payable (which varies by type of account and maturity) by an association is set by the Federal Home Loan Bank Board. Associations that are members of the Federal Home Loan Bank System have the privilege of borrowing, from their regional Federal Home Bank, up to 25 percent of their total withdrawable deposits. Such advances are available at various maturities (generally short-term) and at rates set by the Board which are consistent with economic and capital market conditions. While the primary source of

---

[1]All federally chartered associations were organized as mutuals, however, 30 federally chartered associations have been allowed to convert to the corporate form. Legislation and regulatory rules pertaining to conversion of federally chartered associations to the corporate form are currently being reviewed.

[2]The number of state-chartered associations has declined by approximately 1,300 since 1960, while there has been a net increase of roughly 170 federally chartered associations during the same period. A near halt in chartering by most states, mergers, liquidations, and conversions by some state-chartered association to federal associations are the primary causes of these changes.

[3]The Federal Home Loan Bank System, Federal Savings and Loan Insurance Corporation, and other government agencies are described in detail in the *Savings and Loan Factbook, 1975*, (Chicago: U.S. League of Savings Associations, 1975).

capital for mutual associations is retained earnings (some can sell long-term debt), stock associations can raise external long- term capital by issuing additional debt or stock. Most savings and loan associations are continually seeking ways of enhancing their ability to attract additional funds, for example, the use of off-premises automated deposit terminals, the ability to have interest-receiving demand accounts, and the ability to raise long-term capital.

As we described briefly in Chapter 3, from their very beginning savings and loan associations had the objective of assimilating savings in a geographic area to finance housing in that same area. While some liberalization of this emphasis on local mortgage financing has occurred (geographic areas have been widened, larger amounts can be placed outside local areas, and loans secured by deposits or for home improvement are permitted), savings and loans continue to be restricted to mortgages as their primary method of employing funds. These restrictions have both positive and negative effects. Investment alternatives are severely limited; for example, nearly all associations are prohibited from making consumer installment loans and from buying corporate stocks or bonds. Political pressures, state laws, and Federal Home Loan rules tend to support continued emphasis on mortgages. Savings and loan associations are also required to hold a minimum percentage of their resources in the form of cash and investments eligible for liquidity (the FHLB can vary this percentage between 4 and 10 percent; it is 6.5 percent at this time). Eligible investments include U.S. government securities, federal agency issues with maturities of five years or less, municipal securities with maturities of two years or less, and commerical bank time deposits with maturities of one year or less. Most associations are continually seeking to broaden the spectrum of assets that they can purchase and to increase their flexibility in choosing among alternative assets.

Finally, the environmental and regulatory characteristics would be incomplete without mentioning the relatively low but increasing (in the last few years) level of income taxes paid by both mutual and stock savings and loan associations. Income tax rates remain low enough to discourage aggressive acquisition of taxfree state and local securities. The possibility of a further removal of their favorable tax status has been responsible for the continued emphasis on mortgages and less aggressive demands for broader fund acquisition or employment powers by savings and loan associations.

Mutual Savings Banks

At the beginning of 1975 there were 480 mutual savings banks. While there are no provisions for federal chartering, state charters can be obtained in 17 states (primarily New England and mid-Atlantic states). Nearly three-fourths of all savings banks and roughly four-fifths of savings bank assets are concentrated in banks located in Connecticut, New York, and Massachusetts. All savings banks are owned by depositors who receive all earnings after provision for adequate reserves. These depositors elect, usually by proxies obtained at the beginning of their depositor relationship, a board of trustees who appoint management. In practice, the board and management are virtually self-sustaining.

Regulatory departments or agencies in each state have primary regulatory authority over mutual savings banks. Thus, regulation over mutual savings banks is as diversified as savings and loan regulation is centralized. All state regulatory authorities, however, seem firmly committed to the safety of the thrift accounts of bank members and seem to prefer low-risk alternatives among the menu of available risk–return options. Savings account insurance is available from the FDIC (to a maximum of $40,000 for each private account and $100,000 for public accounts) or from state funds in some states. There are currently 320 savings banks which are members of the FDIC and all but one of the remaining banks are affiliated with a state-sponsored insurance fund. In some states, mutual savings banks may belong to the Federal Home Loan Bank if they so desire. At the present time, 47 savings banks are members of the FHLB.

Methods for attracting funds by mutual savings banks are even more limited than those available to savings and loan associations. Savings banks are limited pirmarily to time and savings deposits as a media for obtaining funds from surplus units. They are able to pay different rates for different types of accounts and can issue various maturity certificates of deposits. They are also permitted to sell life insurance in Massachusetts, New York, and Connecticut. The maximum rates paid for most of the various categories of deposits are set by the Federal Reserve. Prior to 1974 these rates were approximately equal to those paid by savings and loan associations and have averaged 0.5 percent above the comparable rates paid by commercial banks. At the present time the maximum ratio payable on restricted time deposits is equal for all these institutions; however, savings and loans and mutual savings banks are still permitted to pay 0.5 percent higher on passbook savings. Most mutual savings banks (excluding a few which have joined the FHLB), however, do not have the privilege of borrowing as in the case of the FHLB advances available to savings and loan associations or the discounts and advances available to commercial bank members of the Federal Reserve System. Since all savings banks are mutually-owned, they are unable to issue common stock and are often limited in their ability to issue long-term debt. Such severe restrictions on attracting funds have encouraged mutual banks to seek liberalization of state regulation. *NOW* accounts — interest-bearing savings accounts with *negotiable order of withdrawal* provisions — are currently being offered in Massachusetts, New Hampshire, and New York. Legislation permitting these accounts, which resemble   commercial bank demand deposits that pay interest, has passed or been proposed in most other mutual savings bank states.

Constraints on the employment of funds are much less restrictive than those for savings and loans and vary widely from state to state. In most states, mutual savings banks can purchase most forms of debt instruments as well as common and preferred stock. Savings banks can make mortgage loans but are usually prohibited from making most other forms of consumer loans with the notable exception of loans secured by deposits in the savings bank. Restrictions often limit the proportion of out-of-state mortgages but these restrictions tend to be much less rigorous than the geographic limits applied to savings and loans. The main message in regulations in most states seems to be that savings banks are to emphasize safety rather than return. Most states list eligible types of securities (which tend to be broad) and the minimum quality standards or categories of the securities purchased. In two states (Delaware and Maryland) the prudent-man rule is applied to savings banks. Savings banks have been lobbying for even more liberalized regulations on employing their funds. The ability to make consumer installment loans has been a recent target because such loans would enhance savings banks' ability to provide a complete line of consumer financial services.

Mutual savings banks are able to use additions to reserves and other methods to reduce their effective income tax rate; however, the average income tax rate that mutual savings banks pay has climbed sharply in recent years. Their marginal income tax rate remains low enough to discourage purchasing tax-free state and local bonds or overzealous pushing for rapid regulatory changes (*e.g.*, permission to make short-term business loans) which might terminate some preferred tax treatment.

Credit Unions

In early 1975 there were approximately 23,000 credit unions. Currently, credit unions can be chartered under both federal and state law.[4] The powers and regulation of credit unions vary widely according to the chartering agency. At the federal level, the National Credit Union Administration examines, supervises, and insures all federally chartered credit unions. At the state level, these powers are generally found in the office of the state bank regulator. At both levels, credit union membership is limited to groups sharing a common bond of occupation, association, or well-defined residential ties. Members elect a board which appoints management. Because of the "common bond" restriction, most credit unions are small in size and many of them are forced to depend on volunteer and part-time employees. For this reason, most credit unions have voluntarily joined the credit union leagues in their state and these leagues have joined together in the Credit Union National Association (CUNA). The state leagues typically provide financial advice, centralized purchasing, and interlending among member unions. Through its various agencies, CUNA provides services such as saver and borrower life insurance, broader interlending and capital market services, computerized accounting services, and the potential for a national electronic monetary transfer system. Accounts in all federal credit unions and any state-

---

[4]Five states—Alaska, Delaware, Nevada, South Dakota, and Wyoming—do not provide for state-chartered institutions.

chartered institutions that choose the service are insured up to $40,000 by the National Credit Union Share Insurance Fund under the control of the administrator of the Credit Union National Association.[5]

All federal and many state credit unions are limited to shares of qualifying members as their primary method for attracting funds. Legally, these shares are analogous to a corporation's equity capital because there can be no guarantee of dividends or repayment of principal. Practically, these shares tend to resemble time and savings deposits yielding fixed interest payments. The maximum allowable dividend rate on shares for federally chartered credit unions is 6 percent per year, the most common ceiling for state-chartered unions, but state provisions vary from a low ceiling of 4 percent (in New Hampshire) to no limit (in eight states). There are, however, approximately 30 states in which time deposits may be accepted from members of state-chartered credit unions. In these states, credit unions are able to pay higher rates of interest than they are permitted by law to pay in the form of dividends. The other two potential sources of funds are reserves and borrowings. In most states credit unions are required to set aside 20 percent of net earnings (before dividends on shares) as reserves until these reserves accumulate to 10 percent of the federally chartered union's risk assets or to 10 percent of shareholdings. All federal and most state credit unions are permitted to borrow from other credit unions or other sources up to 50 percent of capital and surplus.

Credit unions are limited in employing their funds to members and acceptable securities. Loans to members tend to produce higher returns and there are political pressures to emphasize such loans; however, these loans are usually restricted as to rate, size, and maturity. There is a nearly universal interest ceiling of 1 percent per month on the unpaid balance of loans. Unsecured loan limits vary (by state) from $1,000 to $5,000 and secured personal loans usually may not exceed 10 percent of capital and surplus. The maturity of loans made by federal credit unions may not exceed 10 years. State laws are generally silent on the subject, leaving the issue to be dealt with by an individual union's bylaws. The result is that some credit unions make mortgage loans while others restrict mortgages by setting low maximum maturities for their loan portfolio. Regulations on investments — which should be the imbalance between funds supplied and demanded by members — vary widely from state to state. The most common investments allowed are deposits in insured banks or savings and loans, loans to other credit unions, and government securities.

Credit unions enjoy tax advantages superior to those enjoyed by the other two thrift institutions. No federal credit union may be taxed on either its income or its financial assets by any level of government. State laws vary widely, with the most common practice being to tax credit unions in the same fashion as that particular state taxes mutual savings banks or

---

[5]For detailed information on NCUA, CUNA, and other organizational aspects of credit unions see Mark J. Flannery, *An Economic Evaluation of Credit Unions in the United States* (Boston: Federal Reserve Bank of Boston Research Report No. 54, 1974).

savings and loans. The desire to retain their favored tax status may discourage the industry from taking more aggressive actions in their asset and liability management decisions.

The Wealth-Maximization Model and Thrift Institutions

While the environmental and regulatory characteristics of savings and loan associations, mutual savings banks, and credit unions make minor adjustments necessary, we believe our basic conceptual model developed in Chapter 2 can be applicable to these thrift institutions. To keep our example simple, we apply equation (4a)

$$W = \frac{R - (C + O + T)}{i + p} \qquad (4a)$$

The equation was applied to a hypothetical mutual thrift institution where we assumed constant average returns and costs. Let us briefly examine the effect on our hypothetical thrift institution if interest rates change.

It is assumed that Suburban Thrift Association has $50 million in assets that can be distributed between: A_1, short-term securities with low risks (both credit and interest rate risks) and low returns, and A_2, longer-term securities with higher risks (particularly from interest rate fluctuations) and higher returns. These assets are financed by $45 million in deposits, distributed between D_1, passbook savings with lower costs but greater risks of withdrawal or rate increase, and D_2, time deposits that cost more but cannot change in rate or be withdrawn prior to maturity without penalty. The Association has $700,000 of other expenses (for overhead, the $1 million of other liabilities, etc.) and has accumulated reserves of $4 million. The returns and costs of these assets and deposits, the amount for other expenses, the income tax rate, and the capitalization rate applied to various risk streams of benefits appear in Table 6-1. Given the alternatives available, we can make inferences about the optimal asset and deposit allocation decisions for the mutually owned Suburban Thrift Association.

Four possible situations are reviewed in Table 6-2. In the first case, it is assumed that Suburban chose to obtain $30 million in passbook savings and $15 million in time deposits and chose to invest $5 million in short-term securities and $45 million in long-term consumer loans. These deposit and asset decisions produced net benefits after expenses and taxes of $600,000. These benefits are assumed to be capitalized at a 13 percent rate, which reflects the combined risk of the portfolios of assets, deposits, liabilities, and reserves, and produces a wealth position of $4.6 million for the Association's members. The same deposit mix was assumed for case 2; however, the Association was considerably less aggressive in its asset management by employing $15 million in short-term assets and $35 million in long-term assets. Even if one assumes that the capitalization rate falls to 10 percent because of the lower overall risk, the net benefits pro-

TABLE 6-1   Assumptions About Suburban Thrift Association

Balance Sheet Totals:

Assets	$50,000,000	Time and savings deposits	$45,000,000
		Other liabilities	1,000,000
		Accumulated reserves	4,000,000

Available Asset Returns:

A_1 (short-term securities) = 5%
A_2 (long-term consumer loans) = 8%

Cost of Acquiring Funds, Overhead, and Taxes:

D_1 (passbook savings) = 5%
D_2 (time deposits) = 6%
L (cost of other liabilities and reserves) = $100,000
O (overhead per period) = $600,000
t (income tax rate) = 40%
$T = 0.5t(R - (C + O))$

Capitalization Rates:

i (riskless rate)	= 8%
P_1 (low-risk premium)	= 2%
P_2 (medium-risk premium)	= 5%
P_3 (high-risk premium)	= 8%

duce a lower wealth position of $3.6 million for the Association's members. Given the capitalization and interest rate assumptions, Suburban Thrift would be hurt by not taking the additional risk of the higher-return, long-term assets (as in case 1).

TABLE 6-2   Alternative Decisions by Suburban Thrift Association

Balance Sheet	Case 1	Case 2	Case 3	Case 4
A_1	$ 5,000,000	$15,000,000	$ 3,000,000	$ 7,000,000
A_2	45,000,000	35,000,000	47,000,000	43,000,000
D_1	30,000,000	30,000,000	35,000,000	20,000,000
D_2	15,000,000	15,000,000	10,000,000	25,000,000
L	1,000,000	1,000,000	1,000,000	1,000,000
C	$ 4,000,000	$ 4,000,000	$ 4,000,000	$ 4,000,000
Returns and Costs				
R	$3,850,000	$3,550,000	$3,910,000	$3,790,000
C	2,500,000	2,500,000	2,450,000	2,600,000
O	600,000	600,000	600,000	600,000
T	150,000	90,000	172,000	118,000
B	$ 600,000	$ 360,000	$ 688,000	$ 427,000
Capitalization Rate and Wealth				
i	8%	8%	8%	8%
p	5%	2%	8%	2%
W	$600,000	$360,000	$688,000	$472,000
	0.13%	0.10%	0.16%	0.10%
	or $4,615,000	or $3,600,000	or $4,300,000	or $4,720,000

The mixture of deposits is allowed to shift in cases 3 and 4. In case 3 the Association obtained $35 million in passbook savings and $10 million in time deposits. In this case, Suburban Thrift chose an aggressive asset structure of $3 million in short-term assets and $47 million in long-term assets. The resulting wealth position of the Association's members is $4.3 million if one assumes the net benefits of $698,000 is capitalized at a 16 percent (high risk) rate. Thus, when compared with case 1, Suburban's position deteriorated slightly since the higher returns were not sufficient to compensate for the higher risk exposure. A different strategy is chosen for case 4. Suburban Thrift attracted $20 million in passbook savings and $25 million with time deposits. The asset structure of $7 million in short-term securities and $43 million in long-term consumer loans seems reasonably conservative given the liability structure. This strategy produces net benefits after interest and taxes of $472,000 and a wealth position of $4.7 million when capitalized at a 10 percent (low risk) rate. Given our assumptions, case 4 is preferable among the four alternatives. The slightly lower net benefits from buying more expensive, but safer funds and from having adequate short-term securities produced the highest capitalized value.

The conclusions reached for each of these situations are dependent on the environment (assumptions made); furthermore, numerous other situations could be presented for even the rudimentary asset and deposit decisions facing Suburban Thrift Association. After admitting these limitations, we believe it is more important to examine four additional considerations rather than to make our model more sophisticated. These considerations are: (1) the effects of change in the level of interest rates; (2) the use of wealth as a measure of performance for a mutually owned financial institution; (3) how the constraints on each of the three thrift institutions would affect the results; and (4) how the analysis of the thrift institution differs from the commercial bank situations discussed in Chapter 5.

Interest Rates

Table 6-3 demonstrates a problem that has been very harmful to thrift institutions in the last decade or so—the upward trend in interest rates. The majority of the assets held by thrift institutions are fixed-return, long-term loans, while their liabilities are primarily short-term. When rates increase, the income generated from long-term loans previously acquired remains constant while the cost of the short-term deposits increases with the rate change. Table 6-3 illustrates the effect of a 2 percent increase in interest rates. The rates on short-term securities and all passbook savings increase immediately while the income on outstanding loans and the cost of time deposits will change more slowly as loans mature, new loans are made, deposits mature, and new time deposits are attracted. As expected in case 4, the net benefits for the highest wealth (and low risk) declined less than in the other cases. The Suburban Thrift Assocation has hedged itself

TABLE 6-3 Effects on Net Benefits of a 2 Percent Increase In Short-Term Securities and Passbook Savings on Suburban Thrift Association

Balance Sheet	Case 1	Case 2	Case 3	Case 4
A_1	$ 5,000,000	$15,000,000	$ 3,000,000	$ 7,000,000
A_2	45,000,000	35,000,000	47,000,000	43,000,000
D_1	30,000,000	30,000,000	35,000,000	20,000,000
D_2	15,000,000	15,000,000	10,000,000	25,000,000
L	1,000,000	1,000,000	1,000,000	1,000,000
C	$ 4,000,000	$ 4,000,000	$ 4,000,000	$ 4,000,000
Returns and Costs				
R	$ 3,950,000	$ 3,850,000	$ 3,960,000	$ 3,930,000
C	3,100,000	3,100,000	3,150,000	3,000,000
O	600,000	600,000	600,000	600,000
T	50,000	30,000	32,000	66,000
B	$ 200,000	$ 170,000	$ 178,000	$ 264,000

better against the erosion in income which accompanies rising interest rates by having more fixed cost liabilities relative to fixed return assets.

The reverse would, of course, be true if rates fell — the lowest increase in net benefits is seen in case 4 and the highest increase in case 3. The lower sensitivity of profit to interest rate changes is one factor which is responsible for the lower capitalization rate in case 4.

Several additional inferences can be made about conditions when rates increase. First, the variability of earnings is higher the greater the proportion of fixed return assets relative to fixed cost liabilities. Case 3 has the highest variability in earnings and case 4 has the lowest variability for this reason. Second, this variability in earnings is accentuated by fluctuations in net asset values when assets and liabilities are valued at market price. For example, when rates increase, the large decrease in the value of the portfolio of fixed-return, long-term assets in case 3 would be much in excess of the small reduction in the value of the Association's liabilities. Third, estimation of the wealth position after a rise in interest rates is not presented for the four cases because estimations have not been made for the decreases in the market value of outstanding long-term assets and liabilities. Nevertheless, we believe we can correctly conclude that the declining net benefits, higher variability of benefits, and larger relative declines in the market value of assets less liabilities that occur as rates increase are among the major problems facing managers of thrift institutions.

Wealth-Maximization

The use of wealth-maximization as the criterion for decision-making by a mutual association has been questioned. Since the beneficiaries of higher wealth are usually the depositor-owners, one might ask why all net income should not be paid as dividends rather than accumulated as residual in general reserve accounts. Our opinion is that mutual associations should generally pay depositors a rate high enough to attract funds that can profitably be employed at a rate sufficiently low to attract borrowers. Competition among thrift associations and with other financial institutions should assure that the spread between rates does not exceed that which is commensurate with the risk exposure incurred. It is acceptable for any excesses of returns over interest paid and operating expenses to go to reserve accounts because such an account (and the earnings on the additional asset investment it finances) provides a cushion against decline in the depositors' principal and the subsequent return. Believing this, we are concerned with the rights of depositors who have withdrawn their funds from the thrift association, the tax advantages thrift institutions continue to enjoy, and the borrowers' rights, if any, to the excess of returns over all total expenses. Nevertheless, such concerns do not seriously weaken our opinion that wealth-maximization is the appropriate criteria for management decisions of thrift institutions.

Constraints

Different constraints will modify slightly our wealth-maximizing example for the hypothetical Suburban Thrift Association. The more significant constraints are briefly reviewed. Savings and loans must hold a minimum percentage of their assets (set by regulation) in cash and eligible securities and have FHLB advances at varying rates and maturities as another possible source of funds. Mutual savings banks have a broader menu of available assets, no requirements for a minimum percentage in cash, in securities, or any other assets, and generally no lender of last resort such as the FHLB. Savings banks must, therefore, be more careful in assessing their liquidity needs before they choose among the wide variety of available assets. Credit unions have restrictive membership requirements for depositors and borrowers, which severely restrict their fund inflows and allocations. They can borrow or lend from each other through their national and state associations. Loans to their members are subject to numerous restrictions and since borrowers are members they often receive rebates if net income exceeds a certain size.

Analysis

Finally, it is interesting to compare the results obtained from the same wealth-maximization model when applied to Third National Bank and Suburban Thrift Association. The commercial bank was required to hold a given percentage of its assets in the form of nonearning reserves, while the thrift association did not have reserve requirements. The commercial bank had broad choices among maturity, credit risk, and type of assets that could be acquired, while the thrift association was forced by its environment and regulations to emphasize long-term consumer loans. The bank had the option of raising capital externally and its capital position was scrutinized by regulators and management. The capital (reserve) position of the (mutual) thrift association tended to be the passive result of net income the association was able to retain. Both the commercial bank and the thrift association had to contend with maximum rates on at least some of their deposits. The commercial bank had access to the Federal Reserve for obtaining emergency liquidity, while our model thrift association lacked this emergency source of funds. (In practice savings and loans can use advances from the FHLB as an emergency source of liquidity but mutual savings banks and credit unions do not have an effective source.) The commercial bank was required to pay a higher effective income tax rate than the thrift association.

As with commercial banks, the key variables affecting the wealth-maximization of thrift institutions can be divided into four categories: spread management, control of overhead, liquidity management, and capital management. With the possible exception of capital management, the conceptual presentation in Chapter 2 is relevant for thrift institutions. Rather than repeat these ideas, we will demonstrate how thrift institutions have applied these techniques in the past and will then discuss some detailed applications for thrift institutions.

Historical Patterns of Performance by Thrift Institutions

Knowing the environmental and regulatory constraints and possessing a basic normative management model, we can now turn to a review of the past performances of thrift institutions. The most common problem, attracting deposits, is treated jointly; then fund employment and other problems are considered separately.

Table 6-4 contains the annual net change in over-the-counter savings at saving and loans, mutual savings banks, credit unions, commercial banks, and the combined savings from 1950 through 1975. Table 6-5 contains data for the average annual interest rates paid by savings and loans, mutual savings banks, and commercial banks (comparable figures are not available for credit unions) and average annual yields on selected types of bonds over the same period.

Analysis of these tables and knowledge of the maximum rates the various institutions were permitted to pay reveals the actual and potential vulnerability of the primary net source of funds for the three thrift institutions. Total over-the-counter savings from these four institutions appears highly vulnerable to the differential between the rates they pay and the rates available on open market securities. The annual rate of increase in these deposits declined noticeably in each period in which the rates on these securities exceeded the average rates paid on deposits. This decline in deposit inflows is particularly noticeable in 1966, 1969, and 1974. The process of losing deposits to direct market instruments, called *disintermediation,* was then followed by rapid deposit inflows (*reintermediation*) when interest rates on open market securities fell relative to the rates paid on over-the-counter savings. Since these large fluctuations in savings inflows obviously caused severe strains on liquidity and asset management, it

TABLE 6-4   Annual Changes in Over-the-Counter Savings,
1950-1975 (in $ billions)

Year	Savings Associations[1]	Mutual Savings Banks[2]	Credit Unions[3]	Commercial Banks[4]	Total
1950	$ 1.5	$ 0.7	$0.2	$ 0.1	$ 2.5
1951	2.1	0.9	0.2	1.4	4.6
1952	3.1	1.7	0.3	2.7	7.8
1953	3.6	1.8	0.3	2.7	8.4
1954	4.5	2.0	0.4	2.7	9.6
1955	4.9	1.8	0.4	1.6	8.6
1956	5.0	1.8	0.5	2.2	9.5
1957	4.8	1.7	0.5	5.2	12.2
1958	6.1	2.3	0.5	6.2	15.1
1959	6.6	1.2	0.5	3.1	11.0
1960	7.6	1.4	0.6	4.1	13.7
1961	8.7	1.9	0.6	9.9	21.1
1962	9.4	3.1	0.7	14.3	27.6
1963	11.1	3.3	0.9	11.9	27.1
1964	10.6	4.2	1.0	13.7	29.4
1965	8.5	3.6	1.0	17.6	30.7
1966	3.6	2.6	0.8	12.1	19.1
1967	10.6	5.1	1.2	21.3	38.1
1968	7.5	4.2	1.1	17.3	29.9
1969	4.1	2.5	1.3	- 3.5	4.3
1970	11.0	4.6	1.7	28.8	46.0
1971	28.0	9.9	2.9	33.4	73.9
1972	32.7	10.2	3.4	34.3	80.5
1973	20.2	4.9	2.9	40.9	68.9
1974	16.1	3.0	3.0	46.3	67.4
1975	$43.0	$11.1	$5.5	$25.4	$85.0

Source: Savings and Loan Fact Book, 1975 and 1976 (Chicago: U.S. League of Savings Associations, 1975 and 1976).

[1] All types of savings.
[2] Regular and special savings accounts.
[3] Shares and member deposits.
[4] Time and savings deposits of individuals, partnerships, and corporations.

is natural to ask why these institutions did not pay sufficiently high rates to halt the disintermediation process. These are two related explanations. First, the returns on the asset portfolios of these institutions are much less flexible than are the costs of attracting deposits (in particular, the asset returns on savings and loans and savings banks are nearly fixed in the short run). Second, maximum rates on most deposits were set by the Federal Reserve and the Federal Home Loan Board, at least partially because of these inflexible asset returns. Thus, even if a financial institution could afford to raise rates, it was legally restricted from doing so.

TABLE 6-5   Average Annual Yield on Selected Types of Investments, 1950–1975

Year	Savings Accounts in Savings Associations	Savings Deposits in Mutual Savings Banks	Time and Savings Deposits in Commercial Banks	United States Government Bonds	State and Local Bonds	Corporate (Aaa) Bonds
1950	2.5%	1.9%	0.9%	2.3%	1.9%	2.6%
1951	2.6	2.0	1.1	2.6	2.0	2.9
1952	2.7	2.3	1.2	2.7	2.2	3.0
1953	2.8	2.4	1.2	2.9	2.8	3.2
1954	2.9	2.5	1.3	2.6	2.5	2.9
1955	2.9	2.6	1.4	2.8	2.6	3.1
1956	3.0	2.8	1.6	3.1	2.9	3.4
1957	3.3	2.9	2.1	3.5	3.6	3.9
1958	3.38	3.07	2.21	3.43	3.36	3.79
1959	3.53	3.19	2.36	4.07	3.74	4.38
1960	3.86	3.47	2.56	4.01	3.69	4.41
1961	3.90	3.55	2.71	3.90	3.60	4.35
1962	4.08	3.85	3.18	3.95	3.30	4.33
1963	4.17	3.96	3.31	4.00	3.28	4.26
1964	4.19	4.06	3.42	4.15	3.28	4.40
1965	4.23	4.11	3.69	4.21	3.34	4.49
1966	4.45	4.45	4.04	4.66	3.90	5.13
1967	4.67	4.74	4.24	4.85	3.99	5.51
1968	4.68	4.76	4.48	5.25	4.48	6.18
1969	4.80	4.89	4.87	6.10	5.73	7.03
1970	5.06	5.01	4.95	6.59	6.42	8.04
1971	5.33	5.14	4.78	5.74	5.62	7.39
1972	5.39	5.23	4.66	5.63	5.30	7.21
1973	5.55	5.45	5.71	6.30	5.22	7.44
1974	5.98	5.76	6.93	6.99	6.19	8.57
1975	6.22%	5.89%	5.90%	6.98%	7.05%	8.83%

Sources: Federal Deposit Insurance Corporation; Federal Home Loan Bank Board: Federal Reserve Board: Moody's Investors Service; National Association of Mutual Savings Banks; United States League of Savings Associations.

Analysis of the changes in over-the-counter savings among the different types of institutions verifies the importance of relative rates and the exacerbating influence of rate ceilings. Credit unions, whose dividend rates have typically exceeded the savings rates of other institutions and whose legal maximum rates are generally highest among the savings rates of the four institutions, have had relatively stable savings inflows. While commercial banks suffered in all three periods they were particularly hard hit by disintermediation in 1969. Their vulnerability to time and savings deposit outflows has decreased since 1969 as banks have tied more of their loan rates to fluctuations in money market interest rates. Also, bank regulatory authorities have removed Regulation Q interest ceilings from many maturities of large bank time deposits, in part because of the pressures placed on municipal bond prices when banks were unable to add to their municipal portfolios in 1969.

Savings and loan associations and mutual savings banks did not fare as well. Their rates of deposit growth tended to slow as banks became more competitive ratewise and they suffered painful slowdowns in deposit growth in 1966, 1969, and 1974. The highly vulnerable position of savings and loans was eased somewhat in the early 1970s when they were permitted to pay varying rates on deposit accounts and to issue intermediate-term savings certificates. In summary, one can conclude that the high proportions of assets having fixed returns in conjunction with rate ceilings on most deposits have been a major source of instability for thrift institutions. As described in the following paragraphs, this vulnerability has affected the management of thrift institution assets and other sources of funds.

Savings and Loan Associations

Table 6-6 contains the major asset and liability accounts of all savings and loan associations in selected years from 1950 to 1975. Table 6-7 reviews the major sources and uses of funds for savings and loans from 1965 through 1975. These two tables generally reflect the environmental and regulatory contraints on and the potential variability of savings and loan deposits.

Three other sources of funds, in addition to deposits (previously discussed), seem worthy of analysis. The reserve and net worth accounts of savings and loan associations have remained relatively constant, averaging about 7 percent over the postwar period. Nearly all of the increases in the reserve and net worth accounts have been internally generated, that is, net income after expenses and interest rather than by the sale of new debt or equity by stock savings and loan associations. Debt and equity (for stock associations) remain a relatively untapped potential source for savings and loans. Mortgage portfolio payments have exceeded net savings inflows in all of the postwar years with the exceptions of 1971 and 1972. These inflows tend to increase when rates fall (higher prepayment) and decline when rates rise (few prepayments), adding slightly to deposit volatility; nevertheless, the more stable nature of this large account helps lower the percentage fluctuations from the disintermediation–reintermediation cycle savings and loans face. Borrowings (advances) from the Federal Home Loan Bank are then employed in conjunction with changes in investments in order to smooth the differences between the other inflows and new loans made. From Table 6-6 it is evident that the proportionate amount of advances has been increasing and Table 6-7 illustrates the sizeable net fluctuations of this account. It is important to realize that these advances can vary in maturity and that reasonable amounts of advances outstanding are acceptable to the Federal Home Loan Banks. As discussed later, the difference between an association's advances outstanding and its advance potential (25 percent of deposits at the present time) represents a source of potential liquidity.

TABLE 6-6 Primary Assets and Liabilities of All Savings and Loan Associations, Selected Years, 1950–1975
(in $ billions)

	1950 $	1950 %	1960 $	1960 %	1965 $	1965 %	1970 $	1970 %	1975 $	1975 %
Assets										
Cash	$ 1.0	5.9	$ 2.7	3.8	$ 3.9	3.0	$ 3.5	2.0	$ 4.0	1.2
Securities and liquid investments	1.5	8.9	5.2	7.2	8.1	6.3	9.0	5.1	26.9	7.9
Mortgages:										
Home	13.1	77.5	55.4	77.5	94.2	72.7	125.0	70.9	225.3	66.6
Other	0.6	3.6	4.7	6.6	16.1	12.4	25.3	14.4	53.4	15.8
Other assets	0.7	4.1	3.5	4.9	7.2	5.6	13.4	7.6	28.8	8.5
Total	$16.9	100.0%	$71.5	100.0%	$129.6	100.0%	$176.2	100.0%	$338.4	100.0%
Liabilities and Net Worth										
Savings accounts	$14.0	82.8	$62.1	86.9	$110.4	85.2	$146.4	83.1	$286.0	84.5
Borrowings (FHLB)	0.9	5.3	2.2	3.1	6.4	4.9	10.9	6.2	20.7	6.1
Loans in process	0.4	2.4	1.2	1.7	2.2	1.7	3.1	1.8	5.2	1.5
Other liabilities	0.3	1.8	1.0	1.4	1.8	1.4	3.4	1.9	6.7	2.0
Reserves and net worth	1.3	7.7	5.0	7.0	8.8	6.8	12.4	7.0	19.8	5.9
Total	$16.9	100.0%	$71.5	100.0%	$129.6	100.0%	$176.2	100.0%	$338.4	100.0%

Source: Savings and Loan Fact Book, 1976 (Chicago: U.S. League of Savings Associations, 1976).

TABLE 6-7 Major Sources and Uses of Funds for Savings and Loan Associations, 1964–1975
(in $ billions)

	1964	1965	1966	1967	1968	1969	1970	1971	1972	1973	1974	1975
Major sources:												
Net savings receipts	$10.6	$ 8.5	$ 3.6	$10.6	$ 7.5	$ 4.1	$11.0	$28.0	$32.7	$20.2	$16.1	$43.1
Mortgage portfolio inflows[1]	16.1	17.0	14.3	14.6	15.0	14.5	14.8	23.0	30.1	30.9	27.4	34.2
Net income[2]	0.8	0.8	0.7	0.6	0.9	1.0	0.9	1.3	1.7	1.9	1.5	1.5
Total	$27.4	$26.3	$18.6	$25.8	$23.4	$19.6	$26.7	$52.3	$64.5	$53.0	$45.0	$78.8
Primary use:												
New loans made	$27.2	$26.7	$18.2	$22.3	$24.4	$24.3	$25.3	$47.2	$62.3	$56.8	$45.0	$63.8
Excess of sources over primary use	0.3	− 0.4	0.4	3.5	− 1.0	− 4.7	1.4	5.1	2.2	− 3.8	0.0	15.0
Other uses of funds:												
Increase in securities and cash	0.5	0.4	− 0.1	1.9	0.2	− 0.8	3.2	4.5	2.3	− 3.3	2.2	7.7
Increase in other assets (net)	0.4	0.0	1.5	− 1.1	− 0.2	0.1	− 0.6	− 1.3	− 0.3	6.9	5.4	3.3
Residual source of funds:												
Net borrowings from FHLB	$0.6	$0.8	$1.0	$ − 2.7	$1.0	$4.0	$1.2	$ − 1.9	$0.8	$7.4	$7.6	− 0.4

Source: Savings and Loan Fact Book, 1976 (Chicago: U.S. League of Savings Associations, 1976).

[1] Includes payments on amortized principal, prepayments, and loan liquidations.
[2] Revenues less all expenses and interest paid on all deposits.

The employment of funds has also been strongly affected by the environmental and regulatory constraints on savings and loans. Table 6-6 illustrates that mortgages have been above 80 percent of all savings and loan assets throughout the postwar period. Furthermore, while home mortgages continue to dominate savings and loan portfolios, mortgages on multifamily units and on income properties have been a growing proportion of total mortgages in the late 1960s and early 1970s. Mortgages other than home mortgages had reached 15.8 percent of savings and loans' assets by the end of 1975. Table 6-8, which presents a more detailed statement of conditions for 1975, indicates that all loans other than mortgage loans—mobile loans, home improvement loans, loans on savings accounts, educational loans, and other consumer loans—composed only about 2 percent of savings and loan assets at the end of 1975.

The composition and level of cash and securities is strongly affected by the required liquidity ratio and by the list of eligible securities as determined by the FHLB. Other factors which affected the type and level of

TABLE 6-8   Statement of Condition of All Savings and Loan Associations, December 31, 1975

	Amount (in $ millions)	Percentage of Total
Assets		
Cash and investments eligible for liquidity	$ 27,305	8.1%
Other investments	3,330	1.0
Insured mortgages and mortgage-backed securities	9,326	2.8
Mortgage loans outstanding	278,693	82.4
Mobile home loans	2,298	0.7
Home improvement loans	2,281	0.7
Loans on savings accounts	1,685	0.5
Education loans	501	0.1
Other consumer loans	280	0.1
Federal Home Loan Bank stock	2,600	0.8
Investment in service corporations	1,123	0.3
Building and equipment	5,066	1.5
Real estate owned	1,555	0.5
All other assets	2,357	0.7
Total	$338,395	100.0%
Liabilities and Net Worth		
Savings Deposits:		
Earning regular rate or below	$122,152	36.1%
Earning in excess of regular rate	162,891	48.4
Federal Home Loan Bank advances	17,545	5.2
Other borrowed money	3,185	0.9
Loans in process	5,187	1.5
All other liabilities	6,659	2.0
Net worth	19,776	5.8
Total	$338,395	100.0%

Source: Savings and Loan Fact Book, 1976 (Chicago: U.S. League of Savings Associations, 1976).

these assets included the relative returns on eligible securities, the cost of advances, the volatility of cash inflows and outflows, and the increasing income tax burdens of many associations. For example, over the last decade associations have reduced the absolute amount of U.S. government securities they hold and have increased the absolute and relative amounts of their government agency securities and bank time deposits because of the significant yield differential in favor of the latter two securities. Table 6-7 indicates that in years when fund inflows were large, savings and loans often attempted to build up liquidity in their security portfolios. The most important assets held by savings and loan associations after accounting for mortgages, other loans, and cash and securities are Federal Home Loan Bank stock (0.8 percent of assets) and building and equipment (1.5 percent of assets).

As the final topic in our historical review of savings and loan associations, we briefly examine the operating results of the savings and loan industry. Table 6-9 presents annual summary statements of operations for savings and loans from 1960 through 1975. During this period the proportion of operating income associated with operating expenses had a slow but continual downward trend while interest on time and savings deposits and on borrowed money had a steady upward trend. The net result was that net income as a percentage of total operating income declined noticeably during the period. This increasing tax burden meant that net income after taxes declined even more over the same period.

Mutual Savings Banks

Savings banks are even more restricted in their ability to obtain funds than are savings and loan associations. Table 6-10 indicates that mutual savings banks have, in recent years, obtained approximately 90 percent of their funds from savings and time deposits. The data in Tables 6-4 and 6-5 demonstrated that the time and savings deposits of mutual savings banks are highly vulnerable to disintermediation and the rates paid by commercial banks. Savings banks have had only modest success in expanding their deposit base. Furthermore, when compared with savings and loan associations and commercial banks, mutual savings banks have the lowest percentage of their deposits in time and special accounts. Interest-bearing savings accounts, from which withdrawals may be made by negotiable orders of withdrawal, were a minute $0.3 billion at the end of 1975 (Table 6-11); however, such accounts seem likely to grow rapidly in the next few years.

The three other potential sources of funds for savings banks are mortgage principal payments, net income after interest, and other liabilities. From Table 6-12 it is evident that principal payments on mortgages have averaged roughly $7 billion in the last two or three years. New income (additions to general reserves) for the industry has increased fund inflows between $0.1 and $0.6 billion per year over the last decade. All other liabilities (borrowings, mortgage warehousing, capital notes and deben-

TABLE 6-9 Statement of Operations of All Savings and Loan Associations, 1960–1975

Year	Operating Income	Operating Expense	Net Operating Income	Interest on Savings Deposits	Interest on Borrowed Money	Net Income Before Taxes	Taxes	Net Income After Taxes
				(in $ millions)				
1960	$ 3,711	$ 811	$ 2,900	$ 2,250	$ 81	$ 581	$ 4	$ 577
1961	4,282	919	3,363	2,606	67	706	4	702
1962	5,041	1,024	4,017	3,077	93	891	3	888
1963	5,716	1,223	4,493	3,575	134	792	96	696
1964	6,476	1,291	5,185	4,032	195	952	135	817
1965	7,081	1,366	5,715	4,486	247	978	157	821
1966	7,566	1,417	6,149	4,986	380	771	117	654
1967	8,066	1,471	6,595	5,585	290	725	111	614
1968	8,913	1,602	7,311	6,013	290	1,041	170	871
1969	9,941	1,773	8,168	6,450	466	1,273	227	1,046
1970	11,039	1,967	9,072	7,187	785	1,152	248	904
1971	13,073	2,180	10,893	8,604	623	1,739	448	1,291
1972	15,572	2,524	13,048	10,266	493	2,378	649	1,729
1973	18,692	3,026	15,666	12,012	942	2,729	779	1,950
1974	21,477	3,490	17,987	14,015	1,731	2,213	681	1,532
1975	24,354	4,112	20,242	16,460	1,569	2,145	634	1,511
				(percentage distribution)				
1960	100.0	21.9	78.1	60.6	2.2	15.7	0.1	15.5
1961	100.0	21.5	78.5	60.9	1.6	16.5	0.1	16.4
1962	100.0	20.3	79.7	61.0	1.8	17.7	0.1	17.6
1963	100.0	21.4	78.6	62.5	2.3	13.9	1.7	12.2
1964	100.0	19.9	80.1	62.3	3.0	14.7	2.1	12.6
1965	100.0	19.3	80.7	63.4	3.5	13.8	2.2	11.6
1966	100.0	18.7	81.3	65.9	5.0	10.2	1.5	8.6
1967	100.0	18.2	81.8	69.2	3.6	9.0	1.4	7.6
1968	100.0	18.0	82.0	67.5	3.3	11.7	1.9	9.8
1969	100.0	17.8	82.2	64.9	4.7	12.8	2.3	10.5
1970	100.0	17.8	82.2	65.1	7.1	10.4	2.2	8.2
1971	100.0	16.7	83.3	65.8	4.8	13.3	3.4	9.9
1972	100.0	16.2	83.8	65.9	3.2	15.3	4.2	11.1
1973	100.0	16.2	83.8	64.3	5.0	14.6	4.2	10.4
1974	100.0	16.2	83.8	65.3	8.1	10.3	3.2	7.1
1975	100.0	16.9	83.1	67.6	6.4	8.8	2.6	6.2

Source: *Savings and Loan Fact Book, 1976* (Chicago: U.S. League of Savings Associations, 1976).

Note: Components do not add to totals because of the exclusion of some minor nonoperating income and expense items.

TABLE 6-10 Primary Assets and Liabilities of All Mutual Savings Banks, Selected Years, 1950–1975
(in $ billions)

	1950 $	1950 %	1960 $	1960 %	1965 $	1965 %	1970 $	1970 %	1975 $	1975 %
Assets										
Cash	$ 0.8	3.5%	$ 0.9	2.2%	$ 1.0	1.7%	$ 1.3	1.6%	$ 2.3	1.9%
Securities:										
U.S. government and agencies	10.9	48.4	6.2	15.4	5.5	9.4	3.2	4.0	7.5	6.2
State and local governments	0.1	0.4	0.7	1.7	0.3	0.5	0.2	0.2	1.5	1.3
Corporations and other bonds	2.3	10.1	4.2	10.5	3.7	6.4	10.4	13.2	20.9	17.3
Preferred stock	–	–	0.3	0.7	0.4	0.7	0.7	0.9	1.5	1.2
Common stock	0.2	0.9	0.6	1.5	1.0	1.8	1.8	2.3	2.9	2.4
Mortgages:										
Conventional	4.9	35.7	10.9	65.8	19.4	76.3	29.8	73.1	50.1	63.8
FHA	1.6		7.0		13.8		16.1		14.5	
VA	1.5		9.0		11.4		12.0		12.6	
Other assets	0.4	2.1	1.0	2.5	1.8	3.1	3.7	4.7	7.2	6.0
Total	$22.4	100.0%	$40.6	100.0%	$58.2	100.0%	$79.0	100.0%	$121.1	100.0%
Liabilities and Reserves										
Deposits	$20.0	89.2%	$36.3	89.6%	$52.4	90.1%	$71.6	90.6%	$109.9	90.8%
Other liabilities	0.1	0.6	0.7	1.7	1.1	1.9	1.7	2.1	2.8	2.3
General reserves	2.3	10.3	3.6	8.8	4.7	8.0	5.7	7.2	8.4	7.0
Total	$22.4	100.0%	$40.6	100.0%	$58.2	100.0%	$79.0	100.0%	$121.1	100.0%

Source: 1976 National Fact Book of Mutual Savings Banking (New York: National Association of Mutual Savings Banks, 1976).

TABLE 6-11   Statement of Condition of Mutual Savings Banks,
December 31, 1975

	Amount (in $ millions)	Percentage of Total
Assets		
Cash and due from banks	$ 2,330	1.9%
U.S. government obligations	4,740	3.9
Federal agency obligations	2,767	2.3
State and local obligations	1,545	1.3
Mortgage-backed securities	3,367	2.8
Corporate and other bonds	17,536	14.5
Preferred stock	1,471	1.2
Common stock	2,851	2.4
Mortgages:		
FHA and VA residential	27,128	22.4
Conventional residential	35,967	29.7
Nonresidential and other	14,126	11.7
Other loans:		
Federal funds	1,110	.9
Passbook loans	615	.5
All other loans	2,298	1.9
Bank premises owned	1,075	.9
Other real estate	426	.4
Other assets	1,703	1.4
Total	$121,056	100.0%
Liabilities		
Regular deposits:	$109,056	90.3%
Ordinary savings	69,652	57.5
Time and other	39,639	32.7
School and club deposits	199	.2
Other deposits	383	.3
Borrowings	555	.5
Other liabilities	2,200	1.8
Capital notes and debentures	185	.2
General reserve accounts	8,243	6.8
Total	$121,056	100.0%

Source: 1976 National Fact Book of Mutual Savings Banking (New York: National Association of Mutual Savings Banks, 1976).

tures, accruals, etc.) remain a relatively insignificant source of funds for mutual savings banks. We conclude that savings banks are dependent on attracting deposits (which have been volatile in recent years) and that they do not have access to an emergency liability source of liquidity, such as advances to savings and loans from the FHLB.

Mutual savings banks, however, do have considerably greater flexibility in choosing among assets than do savings and loans and most other financial institutions. Tables 6-10 and 6-11 illustrated the breadth of potential asset selection available to savings banks. From the early postwar years through the mid-1960s, savings banks shifted from an emphasis on government securities to mortgages as their principal assets. Over half of these

TABLE 6-12 Major Sources and Uses of Funds for Mutual Savings Banks, 1964–1975
(in $ billions)

	1964	1965	1966	1967	1968	1969	1970	1971	1972	1973	1974	1975
Major sources:												
Net savings receipts												
Major sources:												
Net savings receipts	$4.2	$3.6	$2.6	$5.1	$4.2	$2.5	$4.5	$ 9.7	$10.1	$ 4.9	$ 3.0	$11.2
Mortgage repayments	4.2	4.6	4.4	4.3	4.2	4.2	4.0	5.7	7.4	7.6	6.6	7.1
Net income	0.2	0.3	0.2	0.1	0.3	0.3	0.2	0.4	0.6	0.6	0.4	0.4
Total	$8.6	$8.5	$7.2	$9.5	$8.7	$7.0	$8.7	$15.8	$18.1	$13.1	$10.0	$18.7
Major uses:												
Mortgage loans acquired	$8.5	$8.7	$7.1	$7.4	$7.0	$6.7	$5.9	$ 9.9	$12.9	$13.3	$ 8.7	$ 9.4
Net investment in:												
U.S. government	−0.1	−0.3	−0.7	−0.6	−0.4	−0.5	−0.2	0.2	0.2	−0.6	−0.4	2.2
Federal agency securities	0.1	0	0.2	0.3	0.3	0	0.5	0.3	0.5	−0.5	−0.1	0.6
Corporate bonds	−0.2	−0.2	0.3	2.0	1.3	0.4	1.3	3.5	2.1	−0.9	0.8	3.5
Corporate stock	0.1	0.1	0	0.1	0.2	0.2	0.3	0.5	0.6	0.4	0.3	0.2
GNMA-backed securities	0	0	0	0	0	0	0.1	0.7	0.6	0.5	0.4	1.1
All other uses (net)	0.2	0.2	0.3	0.3	0.3	0.2	0.8	0.7	1.2	0.9	0.3	1.7
Total	$8.6	$8.5	$7.2	$9.5	$8.7	$7.0	$8.7	$15.8	$18.1	$13.1	$10.0	$18.7

Source: 1976 National Fact Book of Mutual Savings Banking (New York: National Association of Mutual Savings Banks, 1976).

mortgages were either insured or guaranteed by the federal government. The credit crunch of 1966 seemed to indicate that, despite the lack of credit risk, the fixed returns and price fluctuations accompanying interest rate fluctuations made even guaranteed or insured mortgages less than perfectly safe. The reduction in government securities continued; however, as Table 6-12 demonstrates, fund inflows were more likely to be invested in corporate bonds, federal agency bonds, conventional mortgages, or even common stock. One goal of management appeared to be to raise returns on assets. State and local securities and preferred stock represented a small portion of mutual savings bank assets because of their low income tax rate. The composite portfolio of mutual savings banks continues to be dominated by longer-term securities—mortgages and corporate bonds. However, since cash, U.S. government securities, and federal agency securities accounts included nearly $5 billion of assets maturing in less than a year, the need for asset liquidity was not being ignored.

Table 6-13 presents an annual operating statement for all mutual savings banks from 1960 to 1975. From 1960 to 1968 the proportion of operating income spent on interest steadily increased, while the proportion of total operating expenses and taxes declined. Tax revisions in 1969 caused total operating expenses and taxes to begin rising again, while the proportion of operating income spent on interest declined. Table 6-2 and Figure 6-1 provide some comparison of mutual savings bank operations with those of savings and loan associations and commercial banks. Mutual savings banks have been more successful than savings and loan associations in increasing the rates of return on their total assets (from a lower base). The greater asset flexibility of savings banks has obviously helped; however, one must be concerned with the fact that mutual savings banks do not have a lender of last resort such as the Federal Reserve or Federal Home Loan Bank. In addition, mutual savings banks do not have the ability to maintain a yield spread over time—note how commercial bank rates of return and costs of deposits have fluctuated together—and savings bank costs of funds and tax expenses have both increased faster than have their rates of return.

Credit Unions

Table 6-14 indicates the principal assets and liabilities of credit unions in selected years from 1950 through 1975. It is evident that credit unions were relatively small in the early 1950s and that they have grown rapidly in recent years. While detailed information on sources and uses of funds and operations is not available for credit unions as a group, several conclusions about their performance can be derived from Tables 6-4 and 6-14 and from our knowledge of their environmental and regulatory constraints.

Table 6-14 illustrates that credit unions are highly dependent on time and savings deposits (technically called *shares*) as a source for attracting funds. Table 6-4 indicated that credit union deposits have not been as volatile as those of savings and loan associations and mutual savings banks.

TABLE 6-13   Income and Expenses of Mutual Savings Banks, 1960–1975

Year	Total Operating Income	Total Operating Expenses and Taxes	Net Operating Income After Expenses and Taxes	Interest	Net Operating Income After Expenses, Taxes, and Interest	Net Realized Losses on Asset Transactions	Retained Earnings
				(in $ millions)			
1960	$1,687.2	$ 277.3	$1,409.9	$1,233.7	$176.2	$ 27.5	$148.7
1961	1,835.1	297.8	1,537.3	1,326.3	211.0	.4	210.6
1962	2,022.3	313.7	1,708.6	1,530.5	178.1	6.0*	184.1
1963	2,240.7	344.1	1,896.6	1,700.0	196.6	13.5*	210.1
1964	2,484.9	266.3	2,118.6	1,895.1	223.5	5.4*	228.9
1965	2,745.1	394.7	2,350.4	2,076.0	274.4	18.1	256.3
1966	2,990.9	429.3	2,561.6	2,383.0	178.6	16.0*	194.6
1967	3,301.5	454.1	2,847.4	2,712.8	134.6	6.2	128.4
1968	3,701.5	505.9	3,195.6	2,967.0	228.5	26.2*	254.7
1969	4,110.5	580.8	3,529.6	3,218.9	310.7	56.1	254.6
1970	4,487.3	685.1	3,802.3	3,451.8	350.5	142.8	207.7
1971	5,221.9	810.8	4,411.0	3,936.3	474.7	66.7	408.0
1972	6,081.1	979.5	5,101.6	4,516.7	584.9	15.3	569.6
1973	6,977.5	1,165.5	5,812.0	5,138.9	673.1	112.3	560.8
1974	7,471.4	1,275.2	6,196.3	5,620.4	575.8	198.5	377.4
1975	8,116.7	1,421.6	6,695.1	6,165.2	529.9	88.6	441.3
				(percentage distribution)			
1960	100.0	16.4	83.6	73.1	10.4	1.6	8.8
1961	100.0	16.2	83.8	72.3	11.5	.0	11.5
1962	100.0	15.5	84.5	75.7	8.8	.3*	9.1
1963	100.0	15.4	84.6	75.9	8.8	.6*	9.4
1964	100.0	14.7	85.3	76.3	9.0	.2*	9.2
1965	100.0	14.4	85.6	75.6	10.0	.7	9.3
1966	100.0	14.4	85.6	79.7	6.0	.5*	6.5
1967	100.0	13.8	86.2	82.2	4.1	.2	3.9
1968	100.0	13.7	86.3	80.2	6.2	.7*	6.9
1969	100.0	14.1	85.9	78.3	7.6	1.4	6.2
1970	100.0	15.3	84.7	76.9	7.8	3.2	4.6
1971	100.0	15.5	84.5	75.4	9.1	1.3	7.8
1972	100.0	16.1	83.9	74.3	9.6	.2	9.4
1973	100.0	16.7	83.3	73.6	9.6	1.6	8.0
1974	100.0	17.1	82.9	75.2	7.7	2.7	5.0
1975	100.0	17.5	83.5	76.0	6.5	1.1	5.4

Source: *1976 National Fact Book of Mutual Savings Banking* (New York: National Association of Mutual Savings Banks, 1976).
*Net realized gain.
Note: Data for 1971–1973 were compiled on a somewhat different basis than in earlier years. The differences are small in most cases, except for net realized losses on asset transactions.

TABLE 6-14 Primary Assets and Liabilities of All Credit Unions, Selected Years, 1950-1975
(in $ billions)

	1950		1960		1965		1970		1975	
	$	%	$	%	$	%	$	%	$	%
Assets										
Cash and deposits	$0.1	10.0%	$0.2	3.5%	$ 0.4	3.8%	$ 0.8	4.5%	$ 1.7	4.4%
Securities and other assets	0.2	20.0	1.1	19.3	2.1	19.8	2.9	16.3	7.9	20.5
Loans outstanding	0.7	70.0	4.4	77.2	8.1	76.4	14.1	79.2	28.9	75.1
Total	$1.0	100.0%	$5.7	100.0%	$10.6	100.0%	$17.8	100.0%	$38.5	100.0%
Liabilities										
Savings deposits	$0.8	80.0%	$5.0	87.7%	$ 9.2	86.8%	$15.5	87.1%	$33.6	87.2%
Other liabilities	0.1	10.0	0.4	7.0	0.8	7.5	1.2	6.7	2.9	7.4
Reserves	0.1	10.0	0.3	5.3	0.6	5.7	1.1	6.2	2.1	5.4
Total	$1.0	100.0%	$5.7	100.0%	$10.6	100.0%	$17.8	100.0%	$38.5	100.0%

Source: CUNA Yearbook, 1976 (Madison, Wis.: Credit Union National Association, Inc., 1976).

Figure 6-1. Rates or Return on Total Assets Held by Selected
Types of Financial Institutions, 1951–1975

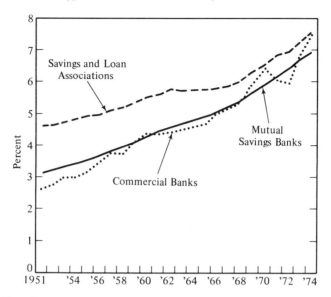

Note: Data are operating income as a percent of average total assets for in-sured commercial banks and all mutual savings banks, member savings and loan associations of the Federal Home Loan Bank System, 1951–1970, and all savings and loan associations beginning in 1971.

Source: Federal Deposit Insurance Corporation, Federal Home Loan Bank Board, National Association of Mutual Savings Banks and United States League of Savings Associations.

The reason for the relative stability in credit unions net savings inflows is that they have not been affected by maximum rates as much as the other thrift institutions. Allowable dividend rates have generally exceeded rates on competitive types of savings accounts, but this situation may change in the future. If Regulation Q and FHLB ceilings are finally removed, credit unions may find themselves severely limited by their legislated dividend ceilings and by their emphasis on passbook-type share accounts rather than on the longer-maturity time accounts. Net earnings retained as reserves have been a small but stable source of funds. In the case of credit unions, repayments of loans are a much larger source of funds for new loans than for other thrift institutions because about one-fourth of the credit union loans outstanding are repaid each year, compared with 10 to 15 percent for savings and loans and mutual savings banks. While other liabilities — the majority of which are borrowings from credit unions with excess funds — remain relatively small, they can be an important source of funds for credit unions facing heavy borrowing demands. Also, ICU Services Corporation has the potential to borrow from the capital market and relend such funds to individual credit unions.

In spite of these secondary sources of liquidity, the average credit union has tended to maintain a relatively liquid portfolio of assets. Rapidly amortizing loans are made to members who, because of the bonds of association, are usually very good credit risks. Investments have been dominated by short-term loans to other credit unions and short-term U.S. government or federal agency securities. The low rate of income taxes tends to discourage purchase of state and municipal securities, and purchase of corporate bonds is often prohibited.

Specific Management Policies for Maximizing Owner Wealth

We now turn to specific management policies and actions which we believe are consistent with the maximization of the wealth position of the owners (generally depositors) of thrift institutions. Policies in the area of control of overhead are similar for banks and thrift institutions. This is an important area that has severely hurt several thrift institutions, and the general statements in Chapter 2 are appropriate for thrift institutions. A few credit unions may have carried control of overhead to the opposite extreme. The use of an employer's space and volunteer workers may lower efficiency more than it lowers cost.

Capital (reserve) management is considerably different for all thrift institutions except stock savings and loan associations when compared with commercial banks (basically the strategies for capital management of commercial banks are appropriate for stock savings and loans). Mutual thrift institutions are often restricted to internally-generated funds, and cannot raise capital externally.[6] There is often a potential conflict between the payment of a higher interest rate to depositors and allowing the funds to accumulate in a reserve (capital) account. While the problem disappears in periods when thrift institutions are paying maximum regulatory-allowed rates and desire all the funds they can obtain, it is most serious when there is rate flexibility or when institutions are having a difficult time profitably employing all of the funds they are attracting. The appropriate policy would seem to be the payment of sufficiently high rates on deposits to attract needed funds, and to lend and buy securities at the highest rate allowed by quality and competitive constraints. Such a policy means that accumulation of reserves is a passive residual rather than an active source of funds, as it may be for stock institutions. Depositor-owners gain a lower risk from higher reserves because of the higher asset coverage of their liabilities and because of higher earnings on larger amounts of assets. Potential drawbacks include the possibility of overaccumulation of reserves (competition should usually prevent this) or the possibility of underaccumulation permitting too high a level of risk. An easing of regulatory con-

---

[6]Mutual thrift institutions do not have equity capital; however, long-term debt is often considered a part of capital. Some states have recently passed legislation which allows mutual institutions to issue long-term debt, and a few institutions in these states have already issued such securities.

straints on raising external capital would permit greater flexibility in capital management.

The policy areas of liquidity management and spread management represent unique problems and opportunities for thrift institutions. There are two primary causes for such problems. First, the lack of flexibility in the payment of rates to attract deposits has led to significant instability in the amount of funds attracted. The major causes of this instability are long-term assets earning returns significantly below current market returns and regulatory maximums on rates. The liquidity pressures from deposit instability have been intensified by heavy loan demand when deposit inflows are low or negative. Second, spread management is difficult because longer-maturity assets are acquired with shorter-maturity loans. The manager faces the problem of deciding, for example, if an 8 percent return is a sufficiently high incremental return on a mortgage when the cost of short-term deposits is 6 percent. If rates fall the spread will improve, but if rates increase the spread will not likely decrease significantly. We suggest two basic management techniques that can be used to improve thrift performance in attaining resources and in maintaining an adequate spread on the resources attracted. First, we favor using intermediate-maturity deposits both to attract funds and to enable management to estimate its cost of funds for a longer period. Second, we believe thrift institutions should encourage variable rate loans.

The use of intermediate-maturity deposits broadens the menu of available liabilities offered by thrift institutions. Used in conjunction with aggressive marketing policies, an increased use of these deposits should increase the size and stability of thrift liabilities. While the average cost will probably increase, returns should also increase because the institution will need less investment in short-term securities since its deposit liquidity risk is lower and because the increase in the ability to plan should increase returns.

Table 6-15 indicates that mutual savings banks and savings and loan associations have steadily increased the proportion of deposits other than savings deposits that are ordinarily withdrawable at any time. Most of these time and other special accounts have maturities exceeding 90 days. These time and other special deposit accounts have grown more rapidly for thrift institutions than for commercial banks and now compose 55.9 percent of all savings and loan deposits.

We recommend continued rational expansion in the use of longer-maturity deposits. Maturities generally should be lengthened to better match the maturity of thrift institution assets. The interest rate risk from paying a fixed interest rate for six years is not high if there is a sufficient spread between this fixed return (cost to the thrift institution) and some eight-year average maturity mortgages financed with the proceeds. Two potential dangers can be controlled with competent management policies. First, the institution should protect itself against rapid refinancing of its assets if interest rates decline. This can be accomplished on traditional

TABLE 6-15   Time and Savings Accounts in Selected Types of Financial Institutions by Types of Account, 1971-1974

	Total	Ordinary	Time and Other Special	Time and Other Special (as percent of total)
Mutual Savings Banks:				
1971	$ 81,440	$ 64,535	$ 16,904	20.8%
1972	91,613	68,637	22,976	25.1
1973	96,496	65,660	30,836	32.0
1974	98,701	64,766	33,935	34.4
Savings and loans associations:				
1971	169,045	92,310	76,735	45.4
1972	200,970	101,634	99,337	49.4
1973	220,893	103,321	117,633	53.3
1974	236,685	104,403	132,286	55.9
Commercial banks:				
1971	200,055	110,931	89,124	44.5
1972	221,733	121,453	100,280	45.2
1973	236,066	126,175	109,891	46.6
1974	253,900	135,900	118,000	46.5

Sources: Board of Governors of the Federal Reserve System, Federal Deposit Insurance Corporation, Federal Home Loan Bank Board, and National Association of Mutual Savings Banks.

Note: Commercial bank data refers to ordinary passbook savings deposits and time deposits in denominations of less than $100,000 at insured institutions. Data for savings and loan associations refer to FSLIC-insured institutions.

mortgages by requiring a reasonable prepayment penalty—enough to keep the return on the mortgages near its current level for the maturity of the deposits. Second, the institution should be aware of the interest-sensitive nature of longer-maturity deposits. It should schedule maturities to prevent a concentration of maturities at any one point in time and to provide sufficient flexibility in fund inflows for an institution to be able to finance additional assets at a sufficient spread at any level of interest rates.[7]

Our second recommendation is that thrift institutions encourage variable rate loans. The reasons for this are obvious. Thrift institutions will still obtain significant proportions of their lendable funds from deposits on which rates may vary as money and capital market conditions change. Flexibility in lending rates will help the institutions maintain an adequate spread on their longer-term assets (primarily mortgages). Commercial banks have used variable rates on intermediate-term commercial loans to maintain their spreads on such loans.

[7]We assume that Regulation Q will be further eased or lifted so that it will not restrict thrift institutions' ability to compete.

There are several potential problems with charging consumers variable rates on longer-term loans. Consumers in the United States are accustomed to paying fixed rates on mortgages and may be reluctant to change to variable rates on such commitments. Consumers are generally unable to pass on higher interest costs, so most consumer budgets cannot absorb the fluctuations in interest rates as well as business. These and similar concerns can be lessened by charging slightly lower rates on variable versus fixed rate mortgages; by allowing the maturities of long-term loans to shift rather that rates (*e.g.*, if rates increased, total payments might remain the same but maturity would increase because a greater proportion of the payment would be for interest); and by limiting the amount of fluctuation in interest cost in a given time period.

The combination of increased use of longer-maturity liabilities and variable rate loans should benefit a thrift institution's spread management and its liquidity management. The maturity of fixed return assets should coincide more closely with the maturity of fixed cost liabilities. Variable rate liabilities would be more closely matched by variable return assets. A more constant spread should lower the variability in earnings. Liquidity demands should be lessened because deposit flows can be maintained closer to the level of loan demands.

Linear Programming: A Technique for Wealth-Maximization

In this section we will indicate how linear programming can be employed to depict the more salient characteristics of one type of thrift institution, a savings and loan association. We will base the objective function on the wealth-maximization objective and, as in Chapter 5, we shall assume that wealth of the owners will be maximized by management's objective of maximizing the market value of the shareholders' equity. Therefore, the objective function of the model becomes

$$MAX \quad V_E = V_C X_C + V_G X_G + V_{SL} X_{SL} + V_B X_B + V_{CS} X_{CS} + V_M X_M + V_{OA} X_{OA}$$
$$+ V_{OA} X_{OA} - V_{UE} X_{UE} - V_{LR} X_{LR} - V_{OL} X_{OL}$$

where terms can be defined as follows: V_E = the market value of dollars expended for corresponding assets, or received in exchange for the respective liabilities; X_C = dollars in cash; X_G = dollars in government securities; X_H = dollars in mortgages in geographic area; X_O = dollars in mortgages outside of geographic area; X_L = dollars in other loans and long-term investments; X_M = dollars in municipal bonds; X_{SD} = dollars in savings deposits; X_{TD} = dollars in certificates of savings X_A = dollars in advances from the Federal Home Loan Board; and, X_B = dollars in other liabilities and reserves.

After establishing the objective function, we can now create linear constraints in an attempt to model the regulations and behaviors that typify the savings and loan association environment. There are basically two areas which concern us, asset management and liability management. Capital management will not be considered within this particular model because these decisions do not have the same importance attached to them as do the asset and liability management. Also, most savings and loan associations are mutual institutions, meaning there are no stockholders.

Under the heading of asset management, managers are concerned with liquidity and portfolio management. Liquidity constraints are placed on the associations by the Federal Home Loan Board which acts as a regulator and lender of last resort much like the Federal Reserve. The major difference is that while the Federal Reserve discourages borrowing except in emergencies, the FHLB does not. At the present time, savings and loan associations must keep 6 percent of their total savings in the form of liquid assets (that is, cash, government securities, and municipals of certain types and maturities). We will assume that the securities available in the model meet the requirements of the FHLB as liquid assets. Therefore, we can express the liquidity constraint as follows:

$$X_C + X_G + X_M \geq 0.06(X_{SD} + X_{TD}).$$

The next area of concern is portfolio management. Savings and loans were created to help funnel funds into the housing industry in their particular geographic area. Hence, savings and loans have generally restricted their loans to mortgage bonds in their area. In recent times, the associations have expanded their activity into mortgages outside the geographic area and other loans (e.g., consumer and mobile home loans). However, in our model, we will specify mortgages within the geographic area as the major component of the loan portfolio. The two constraints are modeled as follows:

1. The total amount of mortgages within the area must exceed three times the total of mortgages from outside the geographic area, or

$$X_H - 3H_O \geq 0.$$

2. The total amount of mortgages within the area must be ten times the total of other types of loans, or

$$X_H - 10H_L \geq 0.$$

Liability management is also very important to the management of the savings and loan association because most of its assets are long-term in nature (for example, mortgage bonds which turn over slowly). The sources of funds become important since interest rate fluctuations have a large effect on the spread between return on assets and cost of liabilities. The basic source of funds is savings that are divided into the more volatile savings deposits (which can practically be withdrawn on demand) and the more stable certificates of savings (which can be deemed as time deposits for they carry maturities of one to seven years). The more stable certificates have a higher cost associated with them. However, we will assume that management's concern with the volatility of savings requires that certificates be equal to or greater than total savings deposits. Therefore, the constraint becomes

$$X_{TD} - X_{SD} \geq 0.$$

Loans or advances from the FHLB are another profitable source of funds. Presently, savings and loan associations can borrow up to 25 percent of total savings from the FHLB. Hence, this constraint is

$$X_A \leq 0.25(X_{SD} + X_{TD}).$$

To complete the model, two final constraints must be added: non-negativity;

$$X_i \geq 0, \qquad \text{for all } i,$$

and the balance sheet identity constraint,

$$X_C + X_S + X_M + X_H + X_O + X_L - X_{SD} - X_{TD} - X_A - X_B = 0.$$

The above are by no means exhaustive of the possibilities of depicting savings and loan association behavior through linear constraints. These were expressed with the objective of presenting an example of how the savings and loan environment could be depicted within a linear programming model. One could assume that, due to uncertainties in the bond markets, management desires to limit its holdings of municipal bonds to less than 5 percent of total savings. The constraint would be

$$X_M \geq 0.05(X_{SD} + X_{TD}).$$

Other possibilities would be in maximizing the turnover of the bond portfolio, or constraining the composition of the portfolio.

Chapter 6

Review Questions

1. What are the two main categories of constraints on savings and loan associations? What are the limitations of each? In what ways are the Federal Reserve (banks) and Federal Home Loan Board (S&L's) the same? In what ways do they differ?

2. How are mutual savings banks more restricted than S & L's in capturing funds? In what ways do they have a more liberal choice in employing these funds?
3. What are the sources of funds to credit unions? How are they employed?
4. To what phenomena are thrift institutions especially susceptible? What asset-liability mix leaves the institution most vulnerable? Least vulnerable? With this knowledge, assume you are a manager of a thrift institution who is facing an upward sloping yield curve. What actions would you take concerning your asset-liability mix, and how would you take such actions?
5. What problems led to the slowed growth in deposits of thrift institutions in years like 1974? Why couldn't these institutions charge a sufficient rate to stop this? What are NOW accounts? Will NOW accounts help and which financial intermediary stands to suffer the most from their widespread utilization?
6. Describe the general trends in the asset mixes of the following institutions: savings and loan associations, mutual savings banks, and credit unions.
7. Liquidity and spread management are particularly difficult for thrift institutions. Why is this so? What two techniques were expounded to help alleviate some of these difficulties? Will the new GNMA mortgage futures market help?
8. Which of the three institutions discussed can compete more favorably with commercial banks? Why?

Selected References

Black, R. P. and Harless, D. E. *Nonbank Financial Institutions.* Richmond, Va.: Federal Reserve Bank of Richmond, 1969.

Croteau, John T. *The Economics of the Credit Union.* Detroit: Wayne State University Press, 1963.

Dougall, Herbert E. and Gaumnitz, Jack E. *Capital Markets and Institutions.* Englewood Cliffs, N.J.: Prentice-Hall, 1975.

Ehrbar, A. F. "Basic Problems of the S & L." *Fortune,* June 1975, p. 65.

Federal Home Loan Bank Board. *Study of the Savings and Loan Industry.* Washington, D.C.: Federal Home Loan Bank Board, 1969.

Goldfeld, S. M. "Savings and Loan Associations and the Market for Savings: Aspects of Allocational Efficiency." *Study of the Savings and Loan Industry.* Washington, D.C.: Federal Home Loan Bank Board, 1969.

Grebler, L. *The Future of Thrift Institutions.* Danville, Ill.: Joint Savings and Mutual Savings Banks Exchange Groups, 1969.

Kendall, L. T. *The Savings and Loan Business: Its Purposes, Functions, and Economic Justification.* Englewood Cliffs, N.J.: Prentice-Hall, 1962. A monograph prepared for the Commission on Money and Credit.

Krooss, Herman E. and Blyn, Martin R. *A History of Financial Intermediaries.* New York: Random House, 1971.

Morrissey, T. F. "The Demand for Mortgage Loans and the Concomitant Demand for Home Loan Bank Advances by Savings and Loan Associations." *Journal of Finance,* June 1971, pp. 687–698.

National Association of Mutual Savings Banks. *Mutual Savings Banks: Basic Characteristics and Role in the National Economy.* Englewood Cliffs, N.J.:

Prentice-Hall, 1969. A monograph prepared for the Commission on Money and Credit.

New York University Institute of Finance. "Cyclical and Growth Problems Facing the Savings and Loan Industry—Policy Implications and Suggested Reforms."*The Bulletin,* Nos. 46-47, March 1968.

Nicols, Alfred. *Management and Control in the Mutual Savings and Loan Association.* Lexington, Mass.: Heath, 1972.

Welfling, Weldon. *Mutual Savings Banks: The Evolution of a Financial Intermediary.* Cleveland: Case Western Reserve University press, 1968.

For current information see *The Federal Reserve Bulletins* (monthly), *The Savings and Loan Fact Book* (annually), and the *National Fact Book of Mutual Savings Banking* (annually).

Financial Management
of Insurance Companies

THE primary purpose of insurance is to provide individuals and organizations with a greater degree of certainty with respect to future plans and activities. Purchasers of insurance lower their risk of financial loss from specific hazards. This is accomplished by making periodic payments into a fund. If sufficient numbers of individuals or organizations contribute to this fund, the payments should be sufficient to support the loss claims that are presented against the fund. While insurance does not prevent the actual hazard, purchasers of insurance are able to decrease or avoid the uncertainties and consequences of specific types of large financial losses.

The primary functions of an insurance company are (1) to provide a means of reducing important financial uncertainties, (2) to provide added protection at the insurance company's risk, and (3) to provide other services while administering the collected funds. In order to provide protection and other services, insurance companies hold substantial amounts of assets. With these large asset holdings and cash inflows and outflows, insurance companies are capable of transferring funds from one sector of the economy to another.

The scope of the services provided by insurance companies is broad enough to encompass nearly every phase of our lives. Most people perceive of insurance as a policy created by a private company that protects both income and property. However, our vast structures of old-age and survivors insurance, employment security insurance, and other forms of insurance administered by the federal and state governments are also important parts of our nation's structure of insurance coverage. In this chapter, we limit our discussion to private insurance plans (public insurance plans are discussed briefly in Chapter 8). We consider two major categories of private insurance institutions: life insurance companies and property insurance companies. In recent years there has been a tendency toward multiple line profiles including both types of institutions' policies. Nevertheless, some of the functions of life and property companies are distinctive and the two institutions tend to appeal to different sources of funds and employ their funds differently. While our wealth-maximization model will be similar for both types, we will present the environmental and regulatory constraints, the historical pattern of performance, and specific financial management applications separately.

Financial Decisions of Insurance Companies

Life Insurance Companies

Life insurance companies must be licensed by the state in which they sell insurance and are regulated by state laws that are normally administered by insurance commissions or departments. The number of life insurance companies in the United States has grown rapidly since the end of World War II. At the end of 1945 there were 473 life insurance companies in operation. By the end of 1960 the number had grown to 1,441 and by mid-1974 there were 1,833 life insurance companies. Of the companies operating in mid-1974, there were 1,686 (or more than nine-tenths) owned by stockholders. The remaining 147 were mutual organizations. These mutual organizations, which are generally older and larger than the stockholder-owned companies, held about two-thirds of the assets of all United States life insurance companies and accounted for slightly more than one-half of all life insurance in force.[1]

Life insurance companies generally offer protection against three major categories of personal financial risk. First, there is the risk associated with premature death with the possible loss of family income. Second, there is the risk of insufficient income when the policyholder passes the prime earning age. Third, there is the risk of accident or sickness which disrupts the earning ability of the policyholder. When large numbers of individuals are involved (*e.g.*, group policies), the insurance company's actuary can accurately predict the number of policyholders which are likely to suffer these financial risks. The ability to accurately predict the needs of the entire group allows the individual members of the insured group to substitute certainty for uncertainty.

Life insurance companies sell a variety of forms of insurance to cover these categories of personal financial risk.[2] The principal types of contracts

---

[1]For greater detail on the number and organizational forms, see *Life Insurance Fact Book, 1975* (New York: Institute of Life Insurance, 1975).

[2]As mentioned earlier, public and private pension funds are also a source of insurance, particularly for the latter two categories of personal financial risk. Some property insurance companies also sell accident and health insurance.

are term life insurance, whole life insurance, endownment insurance, annuities, and accident and sickness insurance. These contracts can be sold separately to individuals or to groups of individuals who share some common bond. The principal types of contracts are briefly summarized in the following paragraphs.

Term line insurance is issued for a specified period of time — usually for one, five, ten, or twenty years — and provides for a fixed cash payment at the death of the policyholder. After the specified time period, no obligation remains on the part of the insurance company toward the insured. While many term policies do carry an option which allows renewal or conversion to another type of contract, the rate is typically higher since the risk of death has increased. Premiums (rates charged for insurance) are sufficiently high to cover the probability of death, which can be estimated reliably from mortality tables (Table 7-1); the operating expenses of the insurance company; and to provide for dividends or an addition to surplus for stockholders. Because no investment program is included with term insurance, the annual premiums are lower than for other types of contracts (Table 7-2). Term life insurance provides a much smaller capital accumulation for insurance companies than do other types of contracts since, with the absence of a savings or cash value component, the annual premium corresponds more closely to the basic cost of insurance protection.

Whole life insurance, on the other hand, stays in effect as long as the policyholder fulfills the contract agreements of the policy. The policy can require premiums for a fixed dollar per period for the life of the insured, as in *straight life insurance,* or for a specified number of years for limited payment life. The relatively large premiums during the early years of the policy are accumulated and invested in order to provide the necessary funds to meet loss settlements when the premium payments become inadequate. When one considers the effect of compound interest rates on the accumulated cash value, the total cost of whole life approximates the term insurance rate. However, under straight life insurance contracts, the policyholder has the option to receive the cash values accumulated, to borrow the entire amount from the insurer, or to convert the savings into retirement income rather than waiting for a death claim to be filed.

Endowment insurance is a contract which pays the entire amount of the policy at the maturity of the contract, or immediately if the insured should die before the maturity of the contract. This type of policy emphasizes the savings aspect of life insurance since the premiums collected and the investment income earned must be sufficient to allow for an immediate settlement or at the end of the contract period. Policyholders have the privilege of borrowing at any time against the cash value of the policy.

Annuities provide protection against the possibility of outliving one's financial resources. Annuity contracts generally provide for the disposition of an estate through its systematic liquidation. They can be specified to pay either current income or future income at regular intervals. While most annuities are intended to provide a predetermined amount of guaranteed retirement income for the life of the insured, there are many

TABLE 7-1   Mortality Tables—United States Total Population, 1969-1971

Age	Deaths per 1,000 Living	Expectation of Life (years)
20	1.40	53.00
21	1.47	52.07
22	1.52	51.15
23	1.53	50.22
24	1.51	49.30
25	1.47	48.37
26	1.43	47.44
27	1.42	46.51
28	1.44	45.58
29	1.49	44.64
30	1.55	43.71
31	1.63	42.77
32	1.72	41.84
33	1.83	40.92
34	1.95	39.99
35	2.09	39.07
36	2.25	38.15
37	2.44	37.23
38	2.66	36.32
39	2.90	35.42
40	3.14	34.52
41	3.41	33.63
42	3.70	32.74
43	4.04	31.86
44	4.43	30.99
45	4.84	30.12
46	5.28	29.27
47	5.74	28.42
48	6.24	27.58
49	6.78	26.75
50	7.38	25.93
51	8.04	25.12
52	8.76	24.32
53	9.57	23.53
54	10.43	22.75
55	11.36	21.99

Source: *Life Insurance Fact Book, 1975* (New York: Institute of Life Insurance, 1975), pp. 104-105.

different types of annuities. For example, under some versions payments are made only for a specified number of years. Under one form, the variable annuity, the payments may vary in amount. There are also choices as to the way the applicant pays for for the annuity—a lump sum or annual premium basis.

Accident and sickness insurance provides indemnity to the insured for loss of income due to accident or sickness and provides for the expenses incurred from hospital, surgical, and other medical requirements. Rising costs of medical services has meant that claims and premium payments have increased rapidly. This form of insurance does not provide much investment capital for insurance companies.

Most life insurance companies experience little or no demand for other

TABLE 7-2 Comparative Premiums for Different Insurance Contracts at Age 22

	Annual Rate per $1,000 of Insurance	Amount of Insurance Purchased by $100	Cash Value at Age 65 per $100 Premium
Term (5-year renewable and convertible)	$ 5.30	$19,000	$ 0
Straight life	12.22	8,000	4,660
Life-paid-up-at-65	13.46	7,200	4,986
20-year payment life	20.69	4,400	3,036
20-year endowment	42.60	2,100	(matured at age 42)
Retirement income at 65 (male)	$19.17	$4,000	$6,250

Source: Jerome B. Cohen, *Decade of Decision*, prepared by the Educational Division, Institute of Life Insurance, with the cooperation of the Health Insurance Institute, 1975. Material is adapted from tables on pages 14–22.

types of insurance contracts, such as industrial life insurance and credit life insurance. In addition, there are numerous variations and combinations of the basic types of contracts, such as family income protection and mortgage insurance.[3]

Group insurance is the other major form of contract to be discussed. Group insurance plans can include term life, whole life, accident, disability, and retirement policies sold under a single master policy to employees or members of an organization, generally without a medical examination. Coverage normally ceases when the individual leaves the organization, although term policies often permit conversion to permanent personal insurance and retirement plans vest with the employee or member after a specific period of time. In terms of numbers covered, group term life insurance dominates. The master contract of group term policies may require a flat premium for all members of the group, or the cost may be based on the amount of protection provided which is often determined by annual salaries. Group retirement plans represent a large source of investment capital for life insurance companies. Group annuities are the most common form. Other group retirement plans include terminally funded group plans, individual policy pension trusts, and tax-sheltered annuities.[4]

We wish to emphasize that an important consideration for life insurance contracts is that for most types of policies the timing and size of the insurance benefits can be predicted with considerable accuracy. Carrying large numbers of most types of contracts, a life insurance company can accurately predict its cash outflows for many years in the future. The fixed size of most insurance benefits also reduces the risk of unpredicted outflow patterns. Exceptions to this general pattern include the less predictable pattern of accident and sickness insurance, variable benefits under

---

[3]Other types of insurance constract and several combinations and variations are discussed in *Life Insurance Fact Book, 1975, op. cit.* pp. 20–42.

[4]The principal forms of group retirement insurance plans are discussed in *Life Insurance Fact Book, 1975, op. cit.* pp. 38–39.

variable annuities (the assets from which these benefits are paid are usually segregated), and the fact that policyholders usually have the right to borrow at any time against the cash value of their policy.

As we have indicated, the financial decisions of insurance companies are strongly influenced by the principal types of contracts used to insure against the primary forms of financial risk, and the insurance companies' abilities to predict their cash outlays for insurance benefits. In addition, their financial decisions are strongly affected by the contractual option of many insured persons to borrow the cash value of their insurance at a fixed rate, and by state regulations which specify the categories of investments that can be acquired, the standard of quality that investments in each permitted category must meet, and the required level of insurance reserves.

Most states set a maximum fixed interest rate for policy loans. Since most of these maximums are set at 5 or 6 percent, they have provided a strong incentive for policyholders to borrow during recent periods of high interest rates (for example, the prime bank lending rate reached 12 percent in 1974). Insurance companies are attempting to increase the maximum fixed rates or switch to variable rates on policy loans. Individual states determine the percentage of total assets which can be held in each category of investments and restrict the percentage of assets allocated to any single private borrower. Most states also place some geographic limitations on investments, and a few states require that a given percentage of reserves be invested in instruments originating in that state.

Many state laws dealing with investment media and investment quality are based on New York State regulations because of that state's early enactment of model legislation. In addition, the New York superintendent of insurance has the power to require insurance companies domiciled in other states, but licensed to sell insurance in New York, to comply with the investment laws established for New York-based firms. Corporate bonds must generally meet standards as to type and value of collateral or interest coverage or both; the latter requirement is usually stricter for unsecured obligations. Conventional mortgages must meet maximum loan-to-appraised-value ratios, and preferred stocks must meet specified tests of dividend coverage and payment. Common stocks, now permitted in at least limited amounts in most states, must ordinarily be listed and meet specified earnings and dividend tests. Income-producing real estate is restricted as to type and use of property. State laws also prescribe methods for valuation of securities and the preparation of financial statements. Finally, not only are companies regulated by the state of domicile, but companies domiciled in one state and doing business in others must also conform to the standards required of domestic insurers insofar as locally generated reserves are concerned.[5]

One additional environmental factor is that both mutual and

---

[5]These regulations are a summary of those contained in Herbert E. Dougall and Jack E. Gaumnitz, *Capital Markets and Institutions* (Englewood Cliffs, N.J.: Prentice-Hall, 1975). For a more detailed explanation of specific regulations by state, see *Life Insurance Companies as a Financial Institution* (Englewood Cliffs, N.J.: Prentice-Hall, 1962) — prepared for the Commission on Money and Credit by the Life Insurance Association of America.

stockholder-owned life insurance companies are able to reduce income taxes through additions to reserves and other means. The income tax rate paid by life insurance companies has been steadily increased in recent years, and we estimate that, on average, life insurance companies now pay an effective federal income tax rate of approximately 20 percent (up from 7–8 percent in 1960).

In summary, life insurance companies are chartered and regulated at the state level. They may be operated under either the corporate or mutual (policyholder) form of ownership. In most states insurance companies can offer most or all types of insurance contracts. They are able to influence the composition of their policies by pricing and selling efforts. Shifts among the types of contracts can have an influence over the size and form of life insurance assets. For example, a shift from whole life insurance to term insurance would tend to slow the institution's growth of assets. The three types of regulations most constraining to the financial management of insurance companies are (1) requirements to make policy loans at a relatively low fixed rate of interest; (2) restrictions on the categories of investments and the quality within these categories; and (3) required levels of reserves for the various types of insurance contracts. These regulations, with the exception of some quality standards which are often based on New York's legal list, vary widely from state to state. If the regulations are used as constraints, we believe life insurance companies can apply our basic wealth-maximization model for their financial management decisions.

Property Insurance Companies

Property insurance companies provide insurance to protect the insured against losses arising from physical damages to property or loss arising from damages to others for which the insured must be held liable. Property insurance companies are licensed and regulated by state laws administered by state departments or commissions (sometimes the same body that regulates life insurance companies). Most property insurance companies are organized under either the corporate or mutual (policyholder) form of ownership.[6] Corporate (stockholder-owned) companies comprised about two-thirds of the nearly 3,000 property insurance companies and accounted for roughly three-fourths of industry assets (approximately $86 billion) at the start of 1975. The environmental and regulatory conditions affecting financial decisions of property insurance are divided into three categories: (1) types of insurance contracts, (2) the nature of reserves, and (3) regulation of rates, reserves, and investments.

Property insurance is typically divided into four broad classifications: fire insurance, marine insurance, surety insurance, and casualty in-

---

[6]The other organizational forms of property insurance are reciprocal exchanges (cooperatives formed to provide coverage for members at cost) and American Lloyds (associations of unincorporated individuals that underwrite unusual risks) represent between 2 and 3 percent of the indusry in terms of assets held.

surance.[7] Basic *fire insurance* offers protection against the destruction of physical property as a result of fire. Most fire insurance policies can also protect against such perils to property as explosion, windstorm, and riot. In addition, contracts can be modified to include protection against losses incurred during the time the insured property is unable to be used. *Marine insurance* provides protection for transportation of merchandise, including both land and marine transportation. *Surety insurance* generally commits the insurance company to the insured as a result of failure on the part of a third party to perform as required by contract. Examples include insurance for the construction of a new plant as contracted, or fidelity bonds to insure against loss from the dishonest acts of employees. While *casualty insurance* basically seeks to protect the insured against liability for specified actions, it has been broadened to include all other forms of property insurance not covered by fire, marine, or surety. Examples of casualty insurance include automobile liability insurance that auto owners carry as protection against claims resulting from damage to other persons or property; insurance against theft; insurance against excessive bad debt loss; and insurance against claims resulting from occupational accidents. It is worth noting that the events insured under most property contracts are much less predictable than those insured under most life contracts.

The incidence of risk for property insurance is evenly distributed throughout the contract period. Premium income is generally allocated between two types of reserves for payment to policyholders—reserves for losses and reserves for unearned premiums. Reserves for losses represent a liability for claims that have been filed and that are anticipated (a 60 to 65 percent loss ratio is usually assumed). The reserves for unearned premiums equals the amount of collected premiums that would be returned to policyholders for unexpired terms if all policies were cancelled. This category of reserves causes net worth or policyholders' surplus to be understated since the acquisition costs have already been incurred and the risks could be reinsured for less than the prepaid premium.

The maximum premium rates charged for the various forms of property insurance are set by state commissions or regulatory departments in most states. This is particularly true for the better-known types of insurance covering the property of individuals, such as automobile liability insurance. Since applications for rate changes are based on past records, changes in rates tend to lag behind the actual incidence of claims. In some states the insurance commission or department sets lower as well as upper limits on premium rates in order to prevent cut-throat price competition.

State insurance departments or commissions or state law may also regulate the size and form of property insurance companies' reserves and

---

[7]One characteristic of the industry is the existence of multiple line companies offering various types of coverage through affiliated corporations. Some property companies offer life insurance through affiliated corporations. Some property companies offer life insurance through a subsidiary organization and some life insurance companies have property insurance subsidiaries.

the investment holdings of property insurance companies. For example, in New York State property insurance companies are required by law to hold fixed income obligations in an amount equal to their unearned premium reserve and loss reserve. This law, in effect, limits the common stock a New York company can legally hold to an amount equal to its capital and surplus.[8] While most states have some form of regulation on the investments of property insurance companies, these companies tend to have greater flexibility in their investment portfolio decisions than do life insurance companies.

A final environmental factor is the fact that property insurance companies (including most mutual companies) generally must pay taxes at regular corporate income tax rates. This implies that the marginal federal income tax rate for most property insurance companies is 48 percent.

In summary, while property insurance companies provide a medium for individuals and organizations to control types of financial risk similar to those covered by life insurance companies, the characteristics and constraints of the financial management of these two types of insurance companies are quite different. Property insurance companies tend to have less flexibility in setting rates (often set by a state regulatory body with a time lag) but have a greater flexibility to choose among investment alternatives than life insurance companies. The events insured by property companies are often less predictable, even with large numbers of contracts, than those insured by life companies.

Furthermore, the costs of the benefits paid by property insurance companies are less predictable and tend to rise with inflation. Even though property insurance companies are not required to make policy loans, they have greater liquidity needs than do life insurance companies. Property insurance companies tend to have a lower asset accumulation for investment than life companies because property contracts generally cover only one or a few years—there is little possibility of significant accumulation in the early years of a contract when probabilities of occurrence of the insured event may lower. Finally, property insurance companies typically pay more attention to the tax features of investments since they are subject to relatively high marginal income tax rates.

The Wealth-Maximization Model and Insurance Companies

While the environmental and regulatory characteristics of life and property insurance require that we adjust some of our variables slightly, we believe our basic conceptual model as developed in Chapter 2 can be applied to these insurance companies. To keep our example simple, we apply equation (4a)

$$W = \frac{R - (C + O + T)}{i + p}$$

---

[8]Murray E. Polakoff et al., *Financial Institutions and Markets* (Boston: Houghton Mifflin, 1970), p. 163.

which assumes constant average returns and costs for a hypothetical insurance company. We show what would happen to our hypothetical insurance company under two different premium benefit programs.

It is assumed that Sure Insurance Company has $100 million in assets to be distributed among A_1, short-term securities with low risks (both credit an interest rate risks) and low returns, A_2, longer-term securities with greater risks (particularly from interest rate fluctuations) and higher returns, and A_3, longer-term securities with even higher risks (both credit and interest rate risks) and higher returns. These assets are financed by $85 million in reserves which are obtained from either of two premium benefit programs. Under insurance program 1, the insurer based the premium charges on a promised return of 6 percent. Both the insurance benefits to be paid and the premium charges can be predicted with reasonable accuracy over the next few years. For program 2, the insurer based the premium charges on a promised return of 5.5 percent, and is much less certain about the net cash inflows which tend to fluctuate because of the less predictable nature of the benefit payments. Sure Insurance Company has $1 million of other expenses (overhead, $5 million of other liabilities, etc.) and has accumulated capital of $10 million. The returns and costs of these assets and reserves, the quantity of other expenses, the income tax rate, and the capitalization rate applied to various risk streams of benefits appear in Table 7-3. Given the alternatives available, we can make inferences about the optimal asset and deposit allocation decisions for the Sure Insurance Company.

Six possible situations are reviewed in Table 7-4. In the first three cases, it is assumed that Sure Insurance chose to obtain $85 million with insurance program 1. They then chose to invest $20 million in short-term securities, $60 million in high-quality, long-term securities, and $20 million in long-term, medium-quality securities. These insurance and asset decisions produced net benefits after expenses and taxes of $910,000. These benefits are capitalized at a 10 percent rate (which reflects the combined risk of the portfolios of assets, liabilities, and reserves) to produce a wealth position of $9.1 million for the company's owners. The same insurance program was employed in case 2; however, the company was considerably more aggressive in its asset management by employing $10 million less in short-term assets and $10 million more in medium-quality, long-term securities. Even if one assumes the capitalization rate rises to 12 percent because of the higher overall risk, the net benefits produce a higher wealth position of $10.5 million for the company's owners. In case 3, Sure Insurance Company reduces its liquidity position even further and reaches for higher returns by investing the $5 million decrease in short-term securities and $10 million reduction in high-quality, long-term securities in medium-quality, long-term securities. The additional income more than offsets the additional risk, and the value of the company's equity rises to $11.25 million. Given the capitalization and interest rate assumptions, the owners of Sure Insurance Company would be hurt by not taking the additional risk from reducing liquidity and adding higher-return, long-term assets (as in cases 2 and 3). Under the wealth-

TABLE 7-3   Assumptions About Sure Insurance Company

Balance Sheet Totals:

Assets	$100,000,000	Insurance reserves	$85,000,000
		Other liabilities	5,000,000
		Accumulated capital	10,000,000

Available Asset Returns:

A_1 (short-term securities) = 5%
A_2 (long-term, high-quality securities) = 8%
A_3 (long-term, medium-quality securities) = 10%

Cost of Acquiring Funds, Overhead, and Taxes:

I_1 (return for premium charges — stable benefits) = 6%
I_2 (return for premium charges — volatile benefits) = 5.5%
L (cost of other liabilities and reserves) = $400,000
O (overhead per period) = $1,000,000
t (income tax rate) = 30%
T = $0.5t(R - (C + O))$

Capitalization Rates:

			I_1	I_2
i	(riskless rate)	=	8%	8%
P_1	(low-risk premium)	=	2%	3%
P_2	(medium-risk premium)	=	4%	6%
P_3	(high-risk premium)	=	6%	9%

maximization objective, Sure Insurance's shareholders would prefer case 3 among the first three alternatives.[9]

We assumed that Sure Insurance Company obtained $85 million from insurance program 2 (lower average return and less certain benefit payments) when constructing cases 4, 5, and 6. The volatility of the net benefits resulted in the risk premiums for the capitalization rates to be higher. In case 4 Sure Insurance invested $20 million in short-term securities, $60 million in long-term, high-quality securities, and $20 million in long-term, medium-quality securities. This combination of insurance and asset-allocation decisions produced net benefits after expenses and taxes of $1,207,500, which resulted in an owners' wealth position of $10,997,000 when capitalized at the 11 percent rate. In case 5, net income after interest and taxes increased to $1,557,500 and the owners' wealth in-

---

[9]Two points merit attention. First, the higher effective return over longer periods of medium-quality securities as compared with higher-quality has been supported in several studies — cf. W. Braddock Hickman, *Corporate Bonds: Quality and Investment Performance*, (New York: National Bureau of Economic Research, 1957). Second, in spite of this research, state insurance commissions or departments may force insurance companies to be closer to case 2 than case 3. The primary reason for this difference is that insurance commissions or departments seem to believe it is their responsibility to see that insurance companies emphasize safety, even at the cost of lower insurance profits and higher insurance premiums.

TABLE 7-4 Alternative Decisions by Sure Insurance Company

	Case 1	Case 2	Case 3	Case 4	Case 5	Case 6
Balance Sheet						
A_1	$20,000,000	$10,000,000	$ 5,000,000	$20,000,000	$10,000,000	$ 5,000,000
A_2	60,000,000	60,000,000	50,000,000	20,000,000	60,000,000	50,000,000
A_3	20,000,000	30,000,000	45,000,000	20,000,000	30,000,000	45,000,000
I_1	85,000,000	85,000,000	85,000,000	85,000,000	0	0
I_2	0	0	0	0	85,000,000	85,000,000
L	5,000,000	5,000,000	5,000,000	5,000,000	5,000,000	5,000,000
E	10,000,000	10,000,000	10,000,000	10,000,000	10,000,000	10,000,000
Return and Costs						
R	7,800,000	8,300,000	8,750,000	7,800,000	8,300,000	8,750,000
C	5,500,000	5,500,000	5,500,000	5,075,000	5,075,000	5,075,000
O	1,000,000	1,000,000	1,000,000	1,000,000	1,000,000	1,000,000
T	390,000	540,000	675,000	517,500	667,500	802,500
B	910,000	1,260,000	1,575,000	1,207,500	1,557,500	1,872,500
Capitalization						
i	8%	8%	8%	8%	8%	8%
p	2%	4%	6%	3%	6%	9%
w	$910,000	$1,260,000	$1,575,000	$1,207,500	$1,557,500	$1,827,500
Rate and Wealth	0.10% or	0.12% or	0.14% or	0.11% or	0.14% or	0.17% or
	$ 9,100,000	$10,500,000	$11,250,000	$10,977,000	$11,125,000	$10,750,000
$W - E$	$ 900,000	$ 500,000	$ 1,250,000	$ 977,000	$ 1,125,000	$ 750,000

creased to $11,125,000 (based on a 14 percent capitalization rate) when the insurance company's portfolio of short-term securities was reduced $10 million and its longer-term, medium-quality securities were increased by the same amount. The shift to an even greater risk position exemplified in case 6 — reducing short-term securities $5 million and high-quality, longer-term securities $10 million and increasing medium-quality, longer-term securities by $15 million — resulted in higher net benefits but a lower owners' wealth position. The higher returns were more than offset by the greater risk which increased the capitalization rate to 17 percent. Among the cases considered under insurance program 2, case 5 would result in the largest wealth position for the company's shareholders.

Subdividing the Model for Management Decisions

While the criteria for every insurance company decision should be the effect of that decision on shareholders' net wealth, practical decision- making requires emphasis on selected variables. We believe that with minor adjustments the four interrelated categories identified in our general model in Chapter 2 are appropriate for insurance companies. The importance of the first category, control of overhead, is obvious and can be briefly summarized. Since there is less product differentiation in insurance than in most other financial products, price (premiums to the insured) can be a most important competitive force. Relative overhead cost would appear to be an important variable affecting the price of insurance because many of the other variables (*e.g.,* mortality tables) are similar for all companies.

Liquidity management is significantly different for life and property insurance to merit separate treatment. A life insurance company should be able to predict its net cash flows from insurance with a high degree of accuracy. Payments of benefits for most forms of insurance contracts can be accurately predicted from mortality tables which change very infrequently. With the exception of some accident and sickness policies and variable annuities, life insurance benefits are for a predetermined amount and are not affected by changes in the price level. Most premium payments are continuations of previous policies that are seldom cancelled. While the largest potential cause of change in net cash flows from insurance would appear to be premiums from new insurance contracts, it normally does not represent a large proportion of total life insurance premiums. Based on the fact that premiums should exceed benefits and overhead, one might conclude that the only financial decision of life insurance companies would be investment of new net cash flows and reinvestment of maturing securities. There is one potential confounding factor to this course of action. Most individual life insurance policies allow the insured to borrow, at a specified rate, an amount up to the cash value of the policy at any time. If other borrowing rates exceed the insurance borrowing rate, many insured persons would take advantage of the lower policy borrowing cost. Policy loans are, therefore, the major source of liquidity uncertainty faced by life insurance companies. While we will demonstrate later in this chapter that premium inflows have exceeded benefit payments, overhead cost, and net increases in policy loans even in periods of high interest rates, management of life insurance companies still must assess the effect of policy loans on all their company's policies.

Benefits from most property insurance contracts are considerably less predictable than those on life insurance contracts. It is more difficult to obtain reasonably large numbers of geographically diversified risks, even with the help of *coinsurance* which enables insurance companies to share the risk on a single policy. In addition, the insured risks are much less predictable over relatively short periods of time. Furthermore, the amount of benefits paid on property insurance tends to vary more and tends to increase with inflation. Premiums on property insurance are adjusted as benefits change, but the time lag may be considerable. As a result, the property insurance industry had little, if any, positive cash flow (from premium revenues, less benefits paid, and overhead) in recent years. Insurance cash flows for many individual property companies obviously fluctuate more than does the industry average. For many property companies, prudent liability management requires significant amounts of investment cash flows and asset holdings which can be converted into cash on short notice. The absence of policy loans and the fact that most policies are paid at the beginning of the insurance period are moderating factors.

Spread management for both types of insurance companies differs significantly from spread management for the financial institutions studied in the previous chapters. Conceptually, we have argued that commercial banks, savings and loan associations, and mutual savings banks should attempt to maintain an adequate spread by matching maturities of assets and liabilities, which are often short-term, and by charging variable rates. Life insurance companies are faced with significant fluctuations in promised returns to insured parties because most life insurance contracts are based on a fixed rate of return over long periods of time. In order to maintain their spread, management of life insurance companies generally seeks to obtain long-term assets promising fixed returns. Indeed, they tend to restrict investments in short-term assets, even if they provide a higher current spread, because of the possibility that interest movements may result in a deterioration in this spread at a later time. The relatively predictable and positive net cash inflows means that the assets of life insurance companies tend to grow each year. Management can, therefore, rationally accept securities without fixed maturities such as perpetual bonds, preferred stock, and common stock, if they believe the rates of return are sufficient. Regulatory restraints have tended to set maximum limits on how much life companies can invest in such assets.

Spread management is much different for property insurance companies. Because of the lower predictability of the outflows for the insured events, property companies require more liquid assets to protect against heavy insurance losses. On the other hand, since the cost of meeting benefits tends to rise with inflation, property insurance companies must purchase assets that serve as hedges against inflation. Such assets often require substantial credit and/or maturity risks as the institution attempts to obtain a sufficient spread.

The requirements for capital management depend on the form of organization and state regulation as well as the type of insurance contract. Mutual life and property insurance companies are generally expected to use residual cash inflows, after the required additions to reserves, for dividends to policyholders. Most states limit additions to the reserves of mutual companies. Life and property companies that are stockholder-owned charge considerably lower premiums, but generally do not pay policy dividends. As with other corporations, these insurance companies must determine whether residual inflows are to be paid as dividends to stockholders or be retained in the business. Such retained earnings are an important residual source of funds for corporate insurance companies. While incorporated insurance companies can also issue additional debt or equity capital, few have chosen to do so in recent years.

Historical Patterns of Performance by Insurance Companies

Having discussed environmental and regulatory constraints and a basic normative management model, we now review the past financial decisions of insurance companies. As aggregative data is presented, we are able to draw inferences for the financial decisions of individual insurance companies. Because of the substantial environmental and regulatory differences between life and property companies, their performances are considered separately.

Life Insurance Companies

Table 7-5 illustrates the stability and growth of total premium receipts of life insurance companies over the past 10 years. While growth rates differ considerably among individual companies, this stable pattern of premium inflows was also evident for a sample of companies examined separately. It seems that purchasers of life insurance generally treat premium payments as a contractual obligation. Further examination of Table 7-5 reveals that while ordinary (term, whole, and endowment) life insurance premiums remain the largest source of premium inflows, premiums for group annuities and group health insurance have experienced the most rapid growth in the last decade.

Table 7-6 presents evidence to support the predictability of benefit payments made by life insurance companies. The total benefits and the various categories of benefits display a smooth pattern of growth while total benefits have remained a stable percentage of total premiums. There is clearly a stable margin between premium inflows and benefit outlays for nearly all life insurance companies.

Table 7-7 summarizes the growth in policy reserves for the various types of life insurance contracts. The amount of reserves required for the various

TABLE 7-5 Premium Receipts of U.S. Life Insurance Companies (in $ millions)

Year	Ordinary Life Insurance Premiums	Group Life Insurance Premiums	Other Life Insurance Premiums[a]	Individual Annuity Considerations	Group Annuity Considerations	Individual Health Premiums	Group Health Premiums[b]	Total Premium Receipts
1965	$11,724	$2,928	$1,431	$ 548	$1,712	$1,974	$4,287	$24,604
1966	12,542	3,215	1,403	604	1,812	2,383	4,861	26,820
1967	13,247	3,452	1,395	681	1,990	2,495	5,392	28,652
1968	14,062	3,929	1,373	776	2,217	2,649	6,081	31,087
1969	14,833	4,289	1,369	855	2,907	2,812	6,931	33,996
1970	15,663	4,663	1,353	960	2,761	3,077	8,290	36,767
1971	16,567	5,039	1,329	1,207	3,703	3,471	9,426	40,742
1972	17,701	5,634	1,343	1,459	4,044	3,727	10,591	44,499
1973	18,758	5,052	2,563[a]	1,676	5,095	3,872	11,652[b]	48,668
1974	$19,823	$5,370	$2,557[a]	$1,924	$5,813	$4,310	$12,813[b]	$52,610

Source: Life Insurance Fact Books, 1966–1975 (New York: Institute of Life Insurance, 1966–1975).

[a] Primarily industrial life insurance; after 1972, also includes credit life insurance premiums which were previously included with ordinary or group life insurance premiums.

[b] After 1972 includes credit health insurance premiums which were previously included in both individual and group health insurance premiums.

TABLE 7-6   Benefits Paid by U.S. Life Insurance Companies (in $ millions)

Year	Death Payments	Matured Endowments	Disability Payments	Annuity Payments	Surrender Values	Payments from Supplementary Contracts	Health Insurance Benefit Payments	Total Insurance Benefit Payments
1965	$4,831	$ 931	$163	$1,039	$1,932	$2,030	$4,431	$15,357
1966	5,218	982	169	1,153	2,121	2,100	4,971	16,174
1967	5,665	1,017	175	1,261	2,243	2,130	5,352	17,843
1968	6,209	967	196	1,401	2,456	2,130	6,099	19,438
1969	6,758	953	205	1,559	2,722	2,150	6,874	21,221
1970	7,017	978	233	1,757	2,886	2,080	8,208	23,159
1971	7,423	990	257	1,944	2,882	2,090	9,064	24,650
1972	8,007	1,000	271	2,213	3,027	2,080	9,675	26,273
1973	8,572	1,026	317	2,598	3,418	2,260	10,300	28,491
1974	$8,885	$ 991	$374	$2,904	$3,642	$2,140	$12,100	$31,036

Source: Life Insurance Fact Books, 1966–1975 (New York: Institute of Life Insurance, 1966–1975).

types of contracts may be set by state regulation or company policy. The quantity of reserves varies greatly among the types of contracts. For example, in 1974 reserves were 11.8 percent of the $1,071,369 million of ordinary life insurance in force, 0.5 percent of the $896,505 million of group life insurance in force, and 30.8 percent of the $39,877 million of industrial life insurance in force. A life insurance company which stresses industrial and ordinary life insurance would, therefore, have substantially greater assets per dollar of insurance in force than one which emphasizes group life policies.

The finances of life insurance companies can perhaps be better understood when income flows are expressed in percentage terms. Table 7-8 reveals the major income and expenses of U.S. life insurance companies as a percentage of total income over the last decade. In this period, premium receipts have varied between 75.5 and 78.6 percent of total income. The majority of other income has been from the return on the companies' investments. Over the last decade operating expenses based on industry aggregates remained a stable 17 percent of income — roughly 7 percent for commissions to agents and 10 percent for expenses of home and field offices. Between 75 and 76 percent of industry income was required to meet current or future obligations including benefit payments, additions to policy reserve funds, and policy dividends. Residual income after operating expenses and current or future obligations averaged between 7 and 8 percent of industry income, and was used to pay taxes, pay dividends to stockholders (stock companies), and make additions to special reserve and surplus.

Some of the differences between stock and mutual life insurance companies are quite marked. For example, insurance premiums and annuity considerations were 73 percent of total income for mutual life insurance companies in 1974, while net investment and other income accounted for 27 percent. Premiums and payments for annuities accounted for 82.7 percent of total income of stock companies, while the balance, chiefly investment earnings, contributed 17.3 percent. One reason for this difference is that a larger proportion of the stock companies' business consists of group life and group insurance which carry smaller reserves than ordinary life insurance and thus smaller levels of investment earnings relative to the level of premium income. The other primary reason is that the premium rates for participating policies of mutual companies (policyholders are returned a portion of their premiums in the form of policy dividends) are considerably higher than the rates on the nonparticipating policies of stock companies.[10]

Another area of difference is in the use of after-tax earnings. Mutual companies should not have any after-tax earnings after operating expenses, benefits, and addition to policy reserves and special reserves are returned to policyholders. On an aggregate company basis, dividends to

---

[10]*LIfe Insurance Fact Book, 1975* (New York: Institute of Life Insurance, 1975), pp. 57–59.

TABLE 7-7 Policy Reserves by Type for U.S. Life Insurance Companies (in $ millions)

End of Year	Life Insurance			Annuities		Supplementary Contracts with Life Contingencies	Supplementary Contracts without Life Contingencies	Health Insurance	Total	Yearly Net Addition to Total Reserves
	Ordinary	Group	Industrial	Individual	Group					
1965	$ 76,865	$2,011	$11,919	$ 5,028	$22,187	$3,281	$4,897	$1,432	$127,620	$ 6,922
1966	81,018	2,166	12,132	5,340	24,029	3,381	4,809	1,836	134,711	7,091
1967	85,810	2,362	11,931	5,746	26,193	3,483	4,749	2,144	142,418	7,707
1968	90,284	2,594	12,032	6,264	28,434	3,610	4,618	2,472	150,308	7,890
1969	95,082	2,836	12,173	6,348	31,213	3,665	4,404	2,879	158,550	8,242
1970	100,076	3,093	12,273	6,911	33,826	3,726	4,177	3,474	167,556	9,006
1971	105,782	3,429	12,374	7,606	38,126	3,905	4,136	3,892	179,250	11,694
1972	111,931	3,957	12,369	8,502	42,948	3,937	4,155	4,347	192,146	12,996
1973	118,933	3,985	12,374	9,418	45,818	4,066	4,164	4,910	203,668	11,522
1974	$125,536	$4,453	$12,284	$10,438	$48,874	$4,176	$4,079	$5,607	$215,447	$11,779

Source: Life Insurance Fact Books, 1966–1975 (New York: Institute of Life Insurance, 1966–1975).

178

TABLE 7-8 Major Sources and Uses of Income for U.S. Life Insurance Companies (percentage distribution)

Year	Premium Receipts[a]	Net Investment and Other Income[b]	Commissions to Agents	Home & Field Office Expense	Benefit Payments & Policy Dividends	Additions to Policy Reserve Funds	Taxes[b]	Dividends to Stockholders	Addition to Surplus & Special Reserves
1965	78.2%	21.8%	7.3%	9.6%	53.0%	22.6%	4.0%	0.8%	2.7%
1966	78.1	21.9	7.2	9.6	53.9	21.4	4.2	0.8	2.9
1967	77.9	22.1	7.2	9.8	53.7	21.8	4.2	0.7	2.6
1968	78.1	21.9	7.2	9.8	54.4	21.2	4.5	1.0	1.9
1969	78.2	21.8	7.2	10.0	54.9	20.8	4.4	1.0	1.7
1970	78.4	21.6	7.1	10.2	55.8	20.1	4.4	1.0	1.4
1971	78.6	21.4	7.0	10.0	53.9	22.2	4.3	1.0	1.6
1972	78.3	21.7	7.2	9.8	52.7	22.4	4.5	1.1	2.3
1973	77.7	22.3	7.0	9.9	52.5	22.7	4.7	1.0	2.2
1974	77.5%	22.5%	6.9%	10.1%	52.5%	23.1%	4.6%	1.1%	1.7%

Source: Life Insurance Fact Books, 1966–1975 (New York: Institute of Life Insurance, 1966–1975).

[a]Certain offsetting items (such as considerations for supplemental contracts) are excluded.

[b]Direct investment taxes (such as real estate) are excluded from taxes and are deducted, with other investment expenses, from investment income. Federal income taxes, however, are included in taxes.

shareholders amounted to 1.1 percent of total income. For stock life insurance companies, dividends to shareholders amounted to 2.3 percent of the total income, whereas no dividends were paid for mutual life insurance companies.[11]

Table 7-9 presents an estimated source and use of funds statement for all U.S. life insurance companies from 1970 to 1974. While the flow of funds could be depicted in several ways, the form we use provides several interesting insights into the financial management of life insurance companies. Premiums less commissions to agents are treated as the primary source of funds from insurance. Total benefit payments, operating expenses, taxes (excluding those relating directly to investment), and dividends to policyholders (for mutuals) and to shareholders (for stock companies) were subtracted from these net premium receipts to obtain estimated fund inflows from insurance operations. Net inflows from income on investments and other income and inflows from maturing long-term (original maturity over 1 year) debt and mortgages are added to net insurance inflows for estimated total fund inflows. Uses of these inflows are separated into policy loans, long-term government securities, long-term corporate debt, mortgages, and all other assets. The other assets category includes changes in position, all purchases and sales of securities with original maturities of less than a year, purchases and sales of corporate stocks and changes in the market value of stocks held, and changes in any other assets not included in the mentioned categories. We have been unable to isolate changes in market value of common stock from purchases and sales of common stock.

A brief analysis of the sources and uses of funds for the last five years reveals that insurance companies generally have positive net cash inflows from their total insurance operations. The average annual net inflow from such operations was slightly over $1 billion during the last five years, with only one year having a negative inflow. When net investment and other income (rising steadily from $10 to $15 million over the last five years) and maturing long-term debt and mortgages (ranging from $11 to $16 billion in that period) are added to new insurance inflows, the amounts available for investment are quite large—increasing from $20 billion to nearly $32 billion over the last five years.

Changes in investment holdings of life insurance companies are easier to assess if we examine Table 7-10 in conjunction with Table 7-9. We find that the net increase in policy loans ranged between slightly under $1 billion to nearly $2.7 billion. For the entire five-year period this net increase averaged 6.5 percent of the total funds available for investment. The $6–$7 billion of acquisitions of short-term government securities and $74–$75 billion of short-term corporate debt purchased in 1973 and 1974 were almost entirely reinvestment of maturing similar securities, and resulted in total net additions to both categories of only $1 billion in these two years. Acquisitions of long-term government securities averaged

---

[11]*Ibid.*

TABLE 7-9   Estimated Sources and Uses of Funds for U.S. Life Insurance Companies (in $ billions)

	1970	1971	1972	1973	1974
Sources					
Premium receipts	$36,767	$40,742	$44,499	$48,668	$52,610
Less estimated commissions to agents	− 3,318	− 3,608	− 4,045	− 4,331	− 4,635
Net premium receipts	$33,449	$37,134	$40,454	$44,337	$47,975
Less benefit payments	− 23,159	− 24,650	− 26,273	− 28,491	− 31,036
Home and field office expense	− 4,767	− 5,155	− 5,510	− 6,125	− 6,780
Policy dividends	− 3,577	− 3,681	− 4,055	− 4,383	− 4,655
Taxes	− 2,055	− 2,216	− 2,530	− 2,908	− 3,090
Shareholder dividends	− 467	− 515	− 610	− 620	− 740
Net inflows from insurance	$− 576	$ 917	$ 1,476	$ 1,810	$ 1,674
Net investment and other income	10,095	11,030	12,200	13,798	15,110
Operating funds available	$ 9,519	$11,942	$13,676	$15,608	$16,784
Maturing long-term debt and mortgages	10,809	14,296	16,180	15,446	14,892
Total available for investment	$20,328	$26,243	$29,856	$31,054	$31,676
Uses					
Net increase in policy loans	$ 2,239	$ 1,001	$ 938	$ 2,196	$ 2,663
Acquisition of long-term government securities	796	1,635	1,604	1,385	1,456
Acquisition of long-term corporate debt	6,808	11,727	14,257	12,741	11,266
Mortgage loans made	7,181	7,573	8,696	11,463	11,339
Net change in cash, short-term securities, corporate stock, and other assets	3,304	4,307	4,361	3,269	4,952
Total uses of funds	$20,328	$26,243	$29,856	$31,054	$31,676

Source: Life Insurance Fact Books, 1966-1975 (New York: Institute of Life Insurance, 1966-1975).

roughly $1.3 billion over the last five years, and the amount of such securities held has grown little. The rapid growth in life insurance investments has been in long-term corporate debt and in mortgages.[12] In the last five years, nearly three-fourths of the total funds available for investments have been allocated between these two major categories. Net increases in total holdings in these two categories have averaged nearly $10 billion for the last two years. Table 7-10 indicates that holdings of preferred stock have increased in the last two years. While over $6 billion in 1973 and nearly $4 billion in 1974 were used to acquire common stocks, sales and sharp declines in the market values of most common stocks led to a decline of nearly $7 billion in the market value of that account from the beginning of 1973 through 1974.

---

[12]Later we show nearly three-fourths of these mortgages are for multifamily writs and commercial (nonfarm, nonresidential) structures.

TABLE 7-10   Detailed Acquisitions and Changes in Holdings of Investments,
U.S. Life Insurance Companies (in $ billions)

	1973			1974		
			Change in			Change in
	Acquired	Held at	Holdings	Acquired	Held at	Holdings
Type of Investment	in Year	Year-End	in Year	in Year	Year-End	in Year
Government Securities						
Short-term; (1 year or less):						
U.S. Treasury	$ 5,317	$ 262	$ - 76	$ 4,287	$ 284	$ + 22
U.S. federal agency	1,536	36	+ 16	1,817	63	+ 27
Foreign government and international agency	52	5	+ 2	49	4	- 1
	6,905	303	- 58	6,153	351	+ 48
Other (over 1 year):						
U.S. Treasury	229	3,182	- 307	242	3,088	- 94
U.S. federal agency	239	848	+ 133	282	1,002	+ 154
U.S. state and local	501	3,412	+ 45	552	3,667	+ 255
Foreign government and international agency	416	3,658	+ 218	380	3,857	+ 199
	1,385	11,100	+ 89	1,456	11,614	+ 514
Total government securities	$8,290	$11,403	$ + 31	$7,609	$11,965	$ + 562
Corporate securities (bonds, debentures, and notes):						
Short-term: 1 year or less	74,318	3,004	+ 23	75,390	4,070	+ 1,066
Other: over 1 year						
U.S.	12,298	83,974	+ 5,496	10,790	85,575	+ 3,601
Foreign	443	4,818	+ 137	476	5,007	+ 189
	87,059	91,796	+ 5,656	86,656	96,652	+ 4,856
Stocks:						
Common (market value)	6,492	19,606	- 2,187	3,930	14,946	- 4,660
Preferred	1,706	6,313	+ 1,261	902	6,974	+ 661
	8,198	25,919	- 926	4,832	21,920	- 3,999
Total corporate securities	$95,257	$117,715	$ + 4,730	$91,488	$118,572	$ + 857
Mortgages:						
Farm	1,006	5,996	+ 318	1,007	6,327	+ 331
Nonfarm:						
F.H.A.	281	9,209	- 754	170	8,544	- 664
N.H.A.	21	532	- 18	63	571	+ 39
V.A.	237	4,402	- 258	185	4,178	- 224
Conventional	9,918	61,231	+ 5,133	9,914	66,614	+ 5,383
Total mortgages	$11,463	$81,369	$ + 4,421	$11,339	$86,234	$ + 4,865
Policy loans	$4,602	$20,199	$ + 2,196	$5,332	$22,862	$ + 2,662

Source: Life Insurance Fact Books, 1966-1975 (New York: Institute of Life Insurance, 1966-1975).

Table 7-11 presents summary balance sheets for all U.S. life insurance companies for selected years from 1950 to 1974. The mixture of the primary sources of life insurance funds has changed little over this 25-year period; however, several trends in the employment of funds are discernible. Government securities declined from 25 percent of insurance assets in 1950 to less than 5 percent of these assets by 1974. Three categories of assets—policy loans, mortgages, and common stock—were emphasized as replacements for government securities. Policy loans grew from less than 4 percent in 1950 to nearly 9 percent of total assets in 1974. Most of this relative growth occurred during the latter 1960s and early 1970 when interest rates were at historically high levels. Mortgages, as a proportion of total insurance assets, grew during the period from the 1950s to the early 1960s and then declined slightly. Holdings of common stock grew from under 2 percent of insurance assets in 1950 to 6 percent in 1974. Corporate debt remained between 35 and 40 percent of assets throughout the 25-year period.

Property Insurance Companies

Table 7-12 summarizes the net sources and uses of funds for all property insurance companies. The net sources do not include maturing long-term securities, but we are able to isolate net acquisitions of common stocks from changes in their market values. The less stable pattern of cash inflows relative to life insurance companies is evident in the wide yearly swings in policyholder surplus. The primary causes of this less stable pattern of insurance inflows are less predictable insurance benefits and a regulatory lag in setting some premium rates. The uses of funds of property companies depends on whether the major source of funds is unearned premium or loss reserves or surplus. Table 7-12 shows that common stock has been a more popular use of funds in years when surplus increased rapidly (*i.e.*, profits from the insurance portion of the business were high), while U.S. government and other more marketable securities grew faster in years when growth in reserves dominated as a source of funds. The major use of funds in the last decade, however, was net increases in tax-free state and local securities.

Table 7-13 illustrates the dollar and percentage distribution of assets and liabilities of all property insurance companies for selected years from 1960 to 1974. Two characteristics are particularly noticeable. First, the decline in relative holdings of federal government and agency securities has been absorbed primarily by increases in holdings of state and local securities and, to a lesser extent, by corporate bonds and stocks. Second, loss reserves have replaced policyholder surplus as the largest source of liabilities and reserves. It is also interesting to note that the total assets of stock companies are over three times the total assets of mutual property insurance companies. Since mutual companies lack stockholders to serve as a cushion against losses in asset values (surplus belongs to policyholders), they tend to be more conservative than stock companies in their use of funds.[13]

---

[13]Herbert E. Dougall and Jack E. Gaumitz, *Capital Markets and Institutions* (Englewood Cliffs: Prentice-Hall, 1975), pp. 92–95.

TABLE 7-11 Assets and Liabilities of U.S. Life Insurance Companies (in $ billions)

	1950 $	1950 %	1960 $	1960 %	1965 $	1965 %	1970 $	1970 %	1974 $	1974 %
Assets										
Government securities	$16.1	25.2%	$11.8	9.9%	$11.9	7.5%	$11.1	5.4%	$12.0	4.6%
Mortgages	16.1	25.1	41.8	34.9	60.0	37.8	74.4	35.9	86.2	32.7
Corporate bonds	23.2	36.3	46.7	39.1	58.3	36.7	73.1	35.3	96.7	36.7
Preferred stock	1.0	1.5	1.8	1.5	2.9	1.9	3.5	1.7	6.1	2.3
Common stock (market values)	1.1	1.6	3.2	2.7	6.2	3.8	11.9	5.7	15.8	6.0
Real estate	1.4	2.2	3.8	3.2	4.7	3.0	6.3	3.0	8.3	3.2
Policy loans	2.4	3.8	5.2	4.3	7.7	4.5	16.1	7.8	22.9	8.7
Miscellaneous assets (incl. cash)	2.6	4.1	5.3	4.4	7.2	4.5	10.8	5.2	15.4	5.8
Total	$63.9	100.0%	$119.6	100.0%	$158.9	100.0%	$207.3	100.0%	$263.3	100.0%
Liabilities and Net Worth										
Policy reserves	$54.3	85.0%	$98.5	82.4%	$127.6	80.3%	$167.6	80.8%	$215.4	81.8%
Policy dividend accumulation	1.5	2.3	3.4	2.8	4.3	2.7	6.1	2.9	8.1	3.1
Funds for dividends	.8	1.3	1.8	1.5	2.6	1.6	3.5	1.7	4.6	1.7
Other obligations	2.9	4.5	6.3	5.3	10.5	6.6	12.8	6.2	16.6	6.3
Capital and surplus	4.4	6.9	9.6	8.0	13.9	8.7	17.4	8.4	18.6	7.1
Total	$63.9	100.0%	$119.6	100.0%	$158.9	100.0%	$207.3	100.0%	$263.3	100.0%

Source: *Life Insurance Fact Books, 1966–1975* (New York: Institute of Life Insurance, 1966–1975).

185

TABLE 7-12 Estimated Net Sources and Uses of Funds for U.S. Property Insurance Companies (in $ billions)

	1965	1966	1967	1968	1969	1970	1971	1972	1973	1974
Additions to major liability and surplus accounts:										
Unearned premium reserves	$0.6	$0.7	$0.7	$0.7	$1.1	$1.7	$1.1	$1.3	$1.2	$1.1
Loss reserves	1.0	1.2	1.4	1.8	2.1	2.2	2.7	3.7	3.8	4.0
Surplus[a]	0.3	1.0	0.6	0.6	0.3	1.3	2.4	2.5	2.0	1.3
Total available for investment	$2.0	$2.9	$2.7	$3.0	3.6	$5.1	$6.2	$7.6	$7.0	$6.4
Uses of funds:										
U.S. government securities	$0.0	$0.2	$ -0.8	$ -0.1	$ -0.3	$0.0	$0.0	$ -0.5	$ -0.1	$ -0.4
Agency securities	0.2	0.1	0.0	0.1	0.0	0.1	-0.2	-0.1	0.0	0.2
State and local securities	0.5	1.0	1.5	0.8	1.1	1.3	3.5	3.5	3.3	2.5
Corporate bonds	0.6	0.7	0.6	1.2	0.8	1.5	0.3	0.8	-0.2	1.5
Corporate stocks[a]	-0.1	0.2	0.9	0.6	0.7	1.1	2.5	2.5	2.8	-0.5
Cash and other assets	0.8	0.7	0.5	0.5	1.3	1.1	0.0	1.4	1.2	3.1
Total net uses	$2.0	$2.9	$ 2.7	$ 3.0	$ 3.6	$5.1	$6.2	$ 7.6	$ 7.0	$ 6.4

Source: Best's Aggregates and Averages, Property-Liability, 1965–1975 (New York: Alfred M. Best Co., Inc., 1965–1975).
[a]Net of changes in market value.

TABLE 7–13 Assets and Liabilities of Property–Liability Insurance Companies (in $ billions)

	1950[b]		1960		1965		1970		1974	
	$	%	$	%	$	%	$	%	$	%
Assets										
Cash			$ 1.4	4.6%	$ 1.3	3.1%	$ 1.4	2.4%	$ 1.6	2.0%
Federal government and agencies			6.0	20.0	6.5	15.6	5.4	9.1	6.2	7.6
State and local securities			8.2	27.3	11.2	26.8	16.8	29.0	30.2	37.1
Corporate bonds			1.7	5.6	2.6	6.2	8.1	14.0	8.3	10.2
Preferred stock			.8	2.7	1.1	2.6	1.6	2.8	2.8	3.4
Common stock[a]			8.6	28.6	14.1	33.7	16.0	27.6	17.5	21.5
Premium balances			2.0	6.6	2.6	6.2	4.3	7.5	6.9	8.5
Other assets			1.4	4.6	2.4	6.2	4.4	7.6	7.8	9.6
Total	$13.5	100.0%	$30.1	100.0%	$41.8	100.0%	$58.0	100.0%	$81.3	100.0%
Liabilities and Reserves										
Liabilities and other			$ 2.8	9.3%	$ 2.3	5.5%	$ 4.9	8.4%	$ 6.4	7.9%
Loss reserves			7.5	24.9	12.1	28.9	20.6	35.5	31.7	39.0
Unearned premiums			8.2	27.2	10.6	25.4	14.5	25.0	18.8	23.1
Policyholders surplus			11.6	38.5	16.8	40.2	18.0	31.0	24.4	30.0
Total	$13.5	100.0%	$30.1	100.0%	$41.8	100.0%	$58.0	100.0%	$81.3	100.0%

Source: Best's Aggregates and Averages, Property–Liability, 1950–1975 (New York: Alfred N. Best Co., Inc., 1965–1975).

[a]Market value.

[b]Detailed asset breakdown not available for 1950.

Financial Strategies for Insurance Companies

Having adapted our conceptual model of insurance companies and observed that most actions of insurance companies are consistent with this model, we now turn to some suggested financial strategies that insurance companies may employ beneficially. While we emphasize the appropriate use of funds after they have been obtained (investment strategies), a brief statement on attracting funds is made at the outset.

Both life and property insurance companies face strong competitive pressures. Limits on product differentiation constrain company control over the types of insurance contracts it chooses to emphasize and result in an emphasis on marketing efforts and pricing (for policies on which flexibility is permitted). Given these constraints, insurance companies should carefully decide which types of insurance they will write and which forms they will emphasize in their marketing and pricing efforts.[14] Two factors deserve particular attention. First, identifying the types of contracts which are appealing to potential purchasers; for example, endowment life insurance contracts may not attract many customers, while variable annuities might appeal to a large, relatively untapped market. For property insurance, potential insurees are often given the price of numerous insurance possibilities and then choose the ones essential to their interests. Second, the type of contracts emphasized often have a substantial effect on asset accumulation and investment decisions. While the total annual premium volumes of all property insurance companies and all life insurance companies are comparable, the property insurance industry is only about one-fourth the size of the life insurance industry as measured by total assets. A life insurance company emphasizing term individual policies or group policies will have considerably fewer assets than one that emphasizes whole life policies.

Differences in investment policies depend on factors such as the sources of funds, stability of underwriting flows, and potential liquidity demands. Because of substantial differences in these factors, investment strategies for life and property companies are discussed separately.

Most life insurance contracts are essentially long-term. While some contracts mature every day, the pattern of cash outlay can be forecast with considerable accuracy as can cash inflows from net new premiums, the maturing of bonds and mortgages, and investment income. These cash flow patterns enable life insurance companies to place investments in any maturity asset—from short-term securities which would continually be reinvested at maturity to infinite maturity preferred and common stocks. The logical preference should be debt obligations with longer-term maturities that roughly coincide with expected settlement claims. Longer-term maturities are preferable to shorter-term securities for two reasons.

---

[14]Stock life and property companies set premiums when the insurance is offered; mutual companies have higher premiums but pay a dividend to policyholders. The size of this dividend depends on the company's expenses and benefit program.

First, for most past periods of at least several years in duration, the average return on long-term securities has exceeded the average return on short-term securities. Second, longer-term maturities enable the life company to more accurately predict a fixed earnings rate to be used in computing premiums on insurance contracts. Fluctuations in short-term rates would cause companies to use low earnings rates.

Since insurance settlements can usually be financed out of current net premium inflows, one might wonder why debt with maturities in excess of expected settlement dates or securities with infinite maturities are not emphasized. While regulatory constraints are in part an answer, we believe there are reasons to discourage placing investment emphasis on very long- or infinite-maturity securities. The main reason is that life companies' abilities to compete with each other depend on current returns on long-term debt securities. A company with settlements averaging 20 years is afraid to tie down a 9 percent interest rate for 50 years because, if rates rise substantially, it will be unable to charge premium rates sufficiently low (because of lower investment returns) to compete effectively. Of course, the company would be better off locking in this fixed return if they can correctly forecast that rates will fall (but this is a risk few life insurance companies want to take). Fixed income securities tend to be preferred over equities for this reason and because the promised insurance return is generally fixed for the life of the policy. An exception is variable rate annuities and other insurance contracts which promise returns that vary with changes in the prices of equities in which most of the funds are invested.

One may also ask what quality and marketability of long-term debt is acceptable for investment emphasis by life insurance companies. Our opinion is that life insurance companies should emphasize less marketable, medium-quality securities. The primary constraints on marketability and quality should generally be regulatory rather than imposed by managers of the company. Statements that management should emphasize government bonds, real estate mortgages that are guaranteed or insured by government agencies, and marketable, high-grade bonds seem improper to us. There is virtually no cash flow pressure to sell long-term securities which, in fact, are nearly always held to maturity. The higher yield available from less marketable issues produces a reward with virtually no additional risk to the insurance company. The higher-realized returns from diversified holdings of a medium-quality versus high-grade security if both are held to maturity has been well-documented in numerous studies.[15] In our opinion, life insurance companies should take advantage of their atypical pattern of highly predictable cash flows and emphasize such investments as directly placed corporate debt issues and mortgages on income-producing or multiple-dwelling property.

Finally, the rapidly rising tax rate on investment income of life in-

---

[15]For example, see W. Braddock Hickman, *Corporate Bonds: Quality and Investment Performance* (New York: National Bureau of Economic Resource Occasional Paper No. 59, 1957).

surance companies must be carefully monitored for opportunities in state and local securities whose interest is not subject to income taxes. Most insurance companies remain in an under-30-percent marginal tax rate, and have bought few high-yielding revenue bonds. However, we seem to be rapidly approaching the day when directly placed, medium-quality municipal bonds are very attractive to life insurance companies.

Life insurance management must also consider any potential sources of liquidity even though underwriting inflows are generally positive (and when investment income and maturities are added cash flows are strongly positive). Cash is required to meet normal receipts and disbursement transactions and to provide for less predictable events, such as unforeseen benefit payments (unusual), heavy cash value refunds resulting from policy surrenders, and policyholder loans. The least predictable and largest liquidity concern is loans to policyholders which typically rise in times when returns on alternative investments are very high. Our cash flow data (Table 7-8), however, indicates that these loans have constituted less than one-sixth of net investable cash inflows in the recent years of very high interest rates. Insurance companies are concerned that these might grow even more if there is a serious depression (policyholder loans reached a record high of 18.3 percent of assets in 1932); however, policyholder loans might not be highly desirable in such a period because other interest rates would tend to be very low. Finally, some short-term liquid assets might be maintained to exploit favorable interest rate opportunities. In general, we believe it is better for life insurance companies to invest funds longer-term as they become available, rather than gamble on changes in the bond market.

Property insurance companies must also comply with state regulations on their investments. After meeting these requirements, property insurance companies should strive to balance the conflicting needs for liquidity and high investment income. The liquidity needs of property companies are much greater than those of life companies because of the uncertain pattern of claims and the dangers of calamitous loss. Furthermore, length of property policies are generally 1-3 years. If a property company were to cease writing new business, it would pay out on existing claims approximately the loss reserve plus that portion of the unearned premium credited to loss reserves as the policies neared expiration. This payment coverage would require extreme liquidity. Actually, in most years, many property insurance companies can meet both expenses and losses from net premium income. This income relieves much of the pressure for liquidity, but it does not remove the price risk on the portfolio. The possible need to sell securities in large amounts to meet catastrophic losses requires limited vulnerability to fluctuations in the market value of a significant part of portfolio assets. Sizable investments in short-term, high-quality marketable government or corporate securities seem essential. Directly placed corporate bonds or long-term mortgages seem nearly as undesirable for property insurance companies as they are desirable for life companies.

A concern for high investment income to help offset the rising cost of many property risks coupled with the high marginal income tax rate of most property companies encourages emphasis on state and local debt and corporate stocks in the portfolio, remaining after liquidity needs have been covered. Longer-term, high-yielding state and local debt produces relatively high after-tax returns. Since only 15 percent of total dividends on domestic preferred or common stock are included in taxable income, these investments also tend to produce comparatively high after-tax returns. Possible growth in price and the lower tax rate on capital gains encourages the use of common stock as an investment vehicle.

Adapting Linear Programming to Insurance Companies

In this section we will attempt to model the major characteristics of the insurance company environment. As before, this will be accomplished within our wealth-maximization objective, by maximizing the value of shareholder equity. We will also compare the environments of life and property insurance companies by presenting constraints depicting both environments.

As far as building constraints, we are primarily concerned with asset management. Liability management is not of much concern since the vast majority of liabilities is composed of reserves arising from the underwriting function. Further, the constraints in the insurance environment primarily affect the composition of the company's portfolio.

As before, the objective function can be written as follows:

$$MAX \; V_E = V_C X_C + V_G X_G + V_{SL} X_{SL} + V_B X_B + V_{CS} X_{CS} + V_M X_M + V_{OA} X_{OA}$$
$$- V_{OA} X_{OA} - V_{UE} X_{UE} - V_{LR} X_{LR} - V_{OL} X_{OL}$$

where V_i = the value of the dollars invested in the ith asset or obtained from the ith liability; X_i = dollars in the ith asset or liability with i equal to any of the following: C, cash; G, short-term government securities; SL, state and local government securities; B, bonds; CS, common stock; M, mortgages; OA, other assets; UE, unearned premium reserve; LR, loss reserve; and OL, other liabilities.

The constraints for both life and property insurance companies are fairly simple. Both sets will be presented so as to fit the above objective function.

One of the constraints for life insurance companies is a mild liquidity constraint. The constraint is based on the ability of policyholders to borrow on the cash value of their insurance policies. Little or no liquidity is necessary for benefit payments, for the cash flows from the insurance underwriting has been shown by actuarial science to be fairly stable. Hence, the life insurance company is constrained to keep the liquidity for policy loans and it is assumed that management requires a percentage of reserves in liquid assets:

$$X_C + X_G \geq 0.075(X_{UE} + X_{LR}).$$

States often control the composition by requiring insurance companies to maintain a percentage of reserves in securities of state and local governments. We assume that the state requires life insurance companies to keep at least 5 percent of their reserves in state and local securities. Therefore, the constraint is

$$X_{SL} \geq 0.05(X_{UE} + X_{LR}).$$

Finally, we have indicated that the profit spread for life insurance companies will be more stable when management matches the asset maturities with that of its liabilities. Therefore, life insurance companies should invest in medium or longer-term securities since their liabilities are primarily long-term and their liquidity needs are small (due to the relative certainty of insurance cash flows). Hence, to model this behavior, we propose the following constraint:

$$A = X_C + X_G + X_{SL} + X_B + X_{CS} + X_M + X_{OA}$$

$$0.06A \leq X_B + X_{CS} + X_M.$$

A property insurance company has greater liquidity needs than its life insurer counterpart since, in addition to the borrowings on cash value, the cash flows of the insurance function is more uncertain. To reflect this increased uncertainty, the liquidity constraint is

$$X_C + X_G \geq 0.15(X_{UE} + X_{LR}).$$

Also, the uncertain nature of the property insurance business demands that management actively seek the high-yielding securities. This requires that a greater portion of its assets be in state and local securities and common stock. Hence, this constraint can be depicted by

$$0.6A \leq X_{SL} + X_{CS}.$$

Finally, to complete the model, the nonnegativity and balance sheet identity constraints are needed:

$$X_i \geq 0 \qquad \text{for all } i,$$

$$X_C + X_G + X_{SL} + X_{CS} + X_M + X_{OA} - X_{UE} - X_{LR} - X_{OL} = NW.$$

Chapter 7

Review Questions

1. Briefly describe the following types of life insurance policies: term life, whole life, endowment, and group.

2. Life insurance companies are able to predict their cash flow many years into the future. Why is this so?

3. The financial decisions of life insurance companies are obviously heavily influenced by the types of policies and obligations of the company. Describe how this concept would affect the asset mix of a life insurance company. What other factors affect financial decisions?

4. Discuss the environmental factors affecting the financial structure of the property insurance company, and indicate the nature of these effects.

5. Explain why property insurance companies have problems with their cash flow, and how these problems lead to lower profitability of assets relative to life insurance companies.

6. Indicate how spread management is different between life and property insurance companies.

7. What factors affect the investment policies of insurance companies? If you were making investment policy for a life insurance company, what types of securities would you emphasize? If you were doing the same thing for a property insurance company, what would your policy directives be?

Selected References

American Mutual Insurance Alliance et al. *Property and Casualty Insurance Companies: Their Role as Financial Intermediaries.* Englewood Cliffs, N.J.: Prentice-Hall, 1962. A monograph prepared for the Commission on Money and Credit.

Brimmer, A. F. *Life Insurance Companies in the Capital Market.* East Lansing, Mich.: Bureau of Business and Economic Research, Graduate School of Business Administration, Michigan State University, 1962.

Dougall, Herbert D. and Gaumnitz, Jack E. *Capital Markets and Institutions.* Englewood Cliffs, N.J.: Prentice-Hall, 1975.

Jones, L. D. *Investment Policies of Life Insurance Companies.* Boston: Division of Research, Graduate School of Business, Harvard University, 1968.

Life Insurance Association of America. *Life Insurance Companies as Financial Institutions.* Englewood Cliffs, N.J.: Prentice-Hall, 1962. A monograph prepared for the Commission on Money and Credit.

McDiarmid, Fergus J. *Investing for a Financial Institution.* New York: Life Office Management Association, 1967.

Magee, John H. and Serbein, Oscar N. *Property and Liability Insurance.* 4th ed. Homewood, Ill.: Irwin, 1967.

Schott, F. H. "Disintermediation through Policy Loans at Life Insurance Companies." *Journal of Finance,* June 1971, pp. 719-729.

Financial Management
of Other Financial Institutions

THERE are several other major types of financial institutions in addition to commercial banks, thrift institutions, and insurance companies. In this chapter we study the financial management of the three remaining major categories of financial institutions: investment companies, pension funds, and finance companies. As in previous chapters, we (1) consider the environmental characteristics that affect each type of financial institution; (2) examine the historical pattern of their performance; and (3) discuss some specific financial management decisions for wealth-maximization in each type of institution. We leave to the reader the adaptation of our wealth-maximization model developed in Chapter 2 and the development of specific linear programming or similar models (these tasks were done in detail for the institutions examined in Chapters 5, 6, and 7 and seem to be repetitive).

We do not discuss some organizations which are often categorized as financial institutions, such as investment banks, mortgage banks, and some governmental agencies. These institutions tend to be smaller in asset size and more specialized in their functions. We, nevertheless, believe that our basic model is appropriate to most of the financial management decisions of such institutions.

Financial Management of Investment Companies

Investment companies obtain funds through the sale of their own securities and invest these pooled funds in a portfolio of securities. This portfolio is presumably managed so as to obtain benefits such as professional selection of securities, skillful timing of purchases and sales, and diversification that an individual investor may be unable to achieve on his own. Two characteristics are common to all forms of investment companies: (1) their primary function is investment, not investment to meet their financial obligations (as insurance companies or banks) or to acquire securities for purposes of control (as holding companies); (2) income from investments is usually exempt from corporate income taxes (48 percent) if the investment company meets certain qualifications and if it distributes at least 90 percent of its income to its shareholders.

The four types of financial institutions that meet these criteria are: fixed trust investment companies, closed-end investment companies, open-end investment companies, and real estate investment trusts. The first three emphasize the purchase of stocks and bonds with the pool of funds obtained from investors; the fourth, as its name implies, emphasizes real estate investments in its portfolios. After briefly describing fixed trust investment companies, closed-end investment companies, and real estate investment trusts, we will present a more detailed analysis of the financial management of open-end investment companies.

Fixed trust investment companies operate with a fixed fund that involves an initial selection of a group of securities that are deposited in trust for a fixed number of years. Shares that remain outstanding for the duration of the trust are issued for the securities purchased. This type of investment company was popular during the 1920s. The inflexibility of this form (*i.e.,* inability to grow, inability to switch assets, the fixed maturity, and the poor record of these companies in the early 1930s) caused this form of investment company to decline in popularity. Aggregate figures for the financial assets or liabilities of these companies are not available because the amounts are currently relatively small.

Closed-end investment companies operate as ordinary business corporations. That is, from time to time they offer their own securities at a predetermined price. The securities offered are usually common stock, but the closed-end investment company can also seek financial leverage by issuing preferred stock or debentures. The issued securities are sold on an exchange or in the over-the-counter market in a similar way to the securities of typical nonfinancial corporations. Closed-end investment companies use the funds they have raised to acquire a diversified list of securities, usually emphasizing common stocks. In contrast to the fixed trust, the closed-end company places great emphasis on portfolio management. Large blocks of common stock are bought and sold in accord with management's interpretation of future performance. As with fixed trusts, closed-end investment companies enjoyed their greatest popularity during the 1920s; however, approximately 40 new closed-end companies (generally emphasizing income as a primary objective) were started in the first half of the 1970s. New common shares have seldom been offered in the last decade by existing closed-end companies because most of these shares have market values that are substantially lower than their book values. As of the beginning of 1976, there were nearly 200 closed-end investment companies registered with the Securities and Exchange Commission with total assets of approximately $9 billion.[1]

Real estate investment trusts (REITs) are similar to closed-end investment companies in that to raise funds securities are offered to investors that hold shares of the REITs. Shares are traded on an exchange or in the over-the-counter market. Consequently, as with closed-end companies, REIT shares may sell above or below their net asset values, and REITs tend to leverage themselves with short- and long-term borrowing. The major difference is that REITs are confined primarily to real estate investments, mortgages, and construction loans. REITs that emphasize the purchase of real estate are generally referred to as "equity" REITs, while those that typically invest in mortgages or construction loans are called "Mortgage" REITs. REITs have been in existence in one form or another for many years; however, they have grown from less than $1 billion in assets to nearly $20 billion in assets from the late 1960s to early 1974. Poor management and security selection in conjunction with a declining market for real estate in 1974 and 1975 led to declines in the REITs' asset values in the mid-1970s.

Open-end investment companies, or mutual funds as they are popularly called, have three characteristics which differentiate them from the previously discussed types of investment companies. First, they can only issue one type of liability — ownership shares. They cannot issue preferred stock or borrow. Second, they continuously offer their own shares at current asset value per share plus a selling charge, if any. The selling charge usually runs 8–9 percent for sales of up to about $10,000 (it is gradually reduced for larger sales); however, some mutual funds have no selling commission because they rely on advertising or word of mouth publicity. Third, mutual funds agree to redeem their shares at any time at their current asset value. The per share asset value for selling or redeeming shares is calculated at regular intervals, usually twice daily, and is determined by dividing the market value of all securities (plus any cash or other assets less any liabilities) by the number of shares outstanding.

The other characteristics of most mutual funds are similar to other investment companies. Nearly all mutual funds are qualified as regulated investment companies. So long as all net investment income and capital gains are credited to shareholders (who are taxed on such returns), the fund itself is not taxed. The mutual fund makes no commitment to shareholders apart from a willingness to redeem shares at their asset value and to supervise management of the assets in accordance with the objectives stated in the fund prospectus. Some of the more common investment objectives include: (1) primarily current income, (2) emphasis on capital appreciation, and (3) moderate income and appreciation. While manage-

---

[1] *Annual Report of the Securities and Exchange Commission,* Washington, D.C.: Government Printing Office, 1976.

ment can be accomplished by the fund itself, most mutual funds have management contracts with organizations that provide all of the necessary administrative services as well as portfolio management.

The growth of mutual fund assets from 1950 to 1974, the composition of these assets in selected years during that period, and the distribution of mutual funds by size and type are reported in Tables 8-1, 8-2, and 8-3. The data in Table 8-1 indicate that mutual funds grew rapidly, albeit irregularly, from the early 1950s through the late 1960s. In 1970 gross sales turned downward with large increases in redemptions in 1972 and 1973, leading to negative net sales in those two years. These cash outflows accompanied by large declines in market values in 1973 and 1974 led to a decline in net asset value from $55.8 billion in 1972 to $45.8 million in 1975. The distributions of mutual fund assets in Table 8-2 indicate that although common stock remains by far the most widely held asset, the proportion of corporate bonds has risen markedly in recent years. Reasons include the higher returns on these fixed income securities in recent years and the sharply falling stock prices in the 1973–1974 period.

The data in Table 8-3 indicate that on December 31, 1974, 452 of the 586 open-end investment companies had total assets of less than $50 billion; however, these smaller companies constituted only 15 percent of the combined assets of the industry. Open-end companies which emphasized common stocks dominated among those funds which had capital gains and growth as their objective.

In keeping with our statement at the beginning of this chapter, we will examine only selected topics in the financial management of open-end investment companies. The two topics examined are the instability of net cash inflows and the correlation between management fees and management performance.

The instability of net inflows to mutual funds (net sales) is illustrated in Table 8-1. It is a particularly worrisome financial management problem for mutual funds because of the instability in this time pattern. The data in Table 8-1 demonstrate that net sales tended to rise when market values had risen appreciably, while net sales tended to decline after market values had fallen. This relationship over time between net sales inflows and market values forces mutual funds to purchase more securities when market values, on average, are high and to sell more securities when market values, on average, are low. Thus, while decisions as to the purchase of sale of individual securities are at management's discretion, managers of mutual funds are generally forced to increase and decrease (or increase at a slower rate) their total portfolio at inopportune times. Existing shareholders are hurt because management is restricted in its ability to buy securities at depressed prices. Furthermore, mutual funds tend to suffer bad publicity from those shareholders who incurred losses and from suggesting that they contribute to the instability of some securities (those with high proportions of institutional ownership) and of capital markets in general.

TABLE 8-1   Growth of Mutual Funds* (in $ billions)

Year	Total Net Assets	Gross Sales	Redemptions	Net Sales	Change in Market Value of Assets	Redemption Rate (%)	Number of Shareholder Accounts	Number of Funds
1950	$ 2.5	$0.5	$0.3	$0.2	$ 0.3	12.5%	938,651	98
1951	3.1	0.7	0.3	0.4	0.2	11.4	1,110,432	103
1952	3.9	0.8	0.2	0.6	0.2	5.6	1,359,000	110
1953	4.1	0.7	0.2	0.4	−0.2	5.9	1,537,250	110
1954	6.1	0.9	0.4	0.5	1.5	7.8	1,703,846	115
1955	7.8	1.2	0.4	0.8	1.0	6.4	2,085,325	125
1956	9.0	1.3	0.4	0.9	0.3	5.1	2,518,049	135
1957	8.7	1.4	0.4	1.0	−1.3	4.6	3,110,392	143
1958	13.2	1.6	0.5	1.1	3.4	4.7	3,630,096	151
1959	15.8	2.3	0.8	1.5	1.0	5.4	4,276,077	155
1960	17.0	2.1	0.8	1.3	−0.5	5.1	4,897,600	161
1961	22.8	3.0	1.2	1.8	4.0	5.8	5,319,201	170
1962	21.3	2.7	1.1	1.6	−3.1	5.1	5,910,455	169
1963	25.2	2.5	1.5	1.0	3.0	6.5	6,151,935	165
1964	29.1	3.4	1.9	1.5	2.4	6.9	6,301,908	159
1965	35.2	4.4	2.0	2.4	3.7	6.1	6,709,343	170
1966	34.8	4.7	2.0	2.7	−3.1	5.7	7,701,656	182
1967	44.7	4.7	2.7	1.9	7.9	6.9	7,904,132	204
1968	52.7	6.8	3.7	3.0	5.0	7.9	9,080,168	240
1969	48.3	6.7	3.8	3.1	−7.4	7.3	10,391,534	269
1970	47.6	4.6	3.0	1.6	−2.3	6.2	10,690,312	356
1971	55.0	5.1	4.8	0.4	7.0	9.3	10,900,952	392
1972	59.8	4.9	6.6	1.7**	6.5	11.4	10,635,287	410
1973	46.5	4.4	5.7	1.3**	−12.0	10.6	10,330,862	421
1974	$35.8	$5.3	$3.9	$1.4	$−12.1	9.6%	10,247,162	431

Source: Arthur Wiesenberger Service, Inc., *Investment Companies* (New York: Arthur Wiesenberger Service, Inc., 1975), p. 19.

*Data pertain to member companies of the Investment Company Institute Total net assets at the 1974 year-end are 94 percent of the combined assets of all mutual funds listed in this table, including 569 regular funds and 14 tax-free exchange funds. Institute Gross Sales figures include the proceeds of initial fund underwritings prior to 1970.

**Net redemptions.

TABLE 8–2 Assets and Liabilities of Open-end Investment Companies* (in $ billions)

	1950 $	1950 %	1960 $	1960 %	1965 $	1965 %	1970 $	1970 %	1975 $	1975 %
Assets										
Cash (net)	$ .1	3.0	$ .4	2.4	$ 1.0	2.8	$ 2.7	5.7	$ 1.2	2.6%
U.S. government securities	.1	3.0	.6	3.5	.8	2.3	.9	2.0	2.0	4.4
Corporate notes and bonds	.2	6.1	1.2	7.1	2.5	7.3	4.3	9.0	8.8	19.2
Preferred Stock	.1	3.0	.7	4.1	.6	1.7	1.1	2.4	1.2	2.6
Common stock[a]	2.8	84.9	14.1	82.9	30.3	85.9	38.5	80.9	32.6	71.2
Total	$3.3	100.0%	$17.0	100.0%	$35.2	100.0%	$47.6	100.0%	$45.8	100.0%
Liabilities										
Shares	$3.3	100.0%	$17.0	100.0%	$35.2	100.0%	$47.6	100.0%	$45.8	100.0%

Source: Investment Company Institute, *1976 Mutual Fund Fact Book* (Washington, D.C.: Investment Company Institute, 1976).

*Data pertain to member companies of Investment Company Institute. Total net assets for 431 member companies at the end of 1975 were approximately 95 percent of $.5 billion of assets for all 586 open-end investment companies.

[a]Market values.

TABLE 8-3   Classification of Mutual Funds by Size and Type, December 31, 1974

Size of Fund	Number of Funds	Combined Assets (000 omitted)	Percent of Total
Over one billion	5	$ 6,835,400	17.7%
$500 million — $1 billion	13	8,309,900	21.5
$300 million — $500 million	10	3,858,900	10.0
$100 million — $300 million	66	10,947,500	28.3
$ 50 million — $100 million	40	2,897,300	7.5
$ 10 million — $ 50 million	201	4,895,600	12.7
$ 1 million — $ 10 million	192	862,400	2.2
Under one million	59	28,599	0.1
Total	586	$38,545,599	100.0%

Type of Fund	Number of Funds	Combined Assets (000 omitted)	Percent of Total
Common Stock:			
Maximum Capital Gain	139	$ 3,680,000	9.5%
Growth	170	10,754,100	28.0
Growth and Income	103	11,845,400	30.7
Specialized	26	530,600	1.4
Balanced	23	4,014,400	10.4
Income	65	3,576,400	9.3
Bond and/or Preferred Stock	27	1,212,800	3.1
Money Market	19	2,384,600	6.2
Tax-Free Exchange	14	547,200	1.4
Total	586	$38,545,599	100.0%

Source: Arthur Wiesenberger Service, Inc., *Investment Companies* (New York: Arthur Wiesenberger Service, Inc. 1975). p. 50.

It is impossible for mutual funds to completely overcome this instability; however, two suggestions may prove useful. First, many mutual funds could allow their cash (short-term securities) position to vary more widely — increasing as the market and net cash inflows increase and declining as the market and rate of increase in net cash inflows decreases. Second, mutual funds could emphasize securities with lower Betas (security variability related to market variability) as the market and net cash inflows increased.

The relationship between management fees and mutual fund performance is interesting. Several studies, which have compared the performance of mutual funds paying (1) high management fees (typically in excess of 1.3 percent of the fund's assets), (2) low management fees (typically less than 0.7 percent of the fund's assets), and (3) management fees on the basis of the fund's performance, produced similar results for the period from the late 1950s to the early 1970s. The level of management fees does not affect either the rates of return or the variability of returns in a statistically significant way. Whether the funds pay fixed or incentive management fees did, however, have a statistically significant effect on fund performance. Funds which had fees tied to the rate of return on the fund earned a considerably higher return and had considerably greater variability in these returns than did funds that paid fixed fees (whether high or low).

Financial Management of Pension Funds

For the purposes of our discussion, we divide pension funds into three major categories: federal government retirement funds, state and local government employees retirement funds, and private pension funds. Each category is discussed with primary attention given to state and local government employee retirement funds and private pension funds.

Federal Retirement Funds

There are four major federal government retirement funds: (1) social security (Old Age Survivors' Insurance), (2) the Civil Service Retirement and Disability Fund, (3) the Disability and Insurance Trust Fund, and (4) the Railroad Retirement Fund. Table 8-4 indicates the relative size and growth in the assets for these federal government retirement funds. Their assets have not grown as rapidly as state and local employee retirement funds or private pension funds primarily because they cover only a small proportion of promised future benefits (operating on close to a pay-as-you-go basis). Federal government retirement benefits have increased sharply because of inflation, political popularity, and comparison with the other types of pension funds. Contributions have not increased at a commensurate rate, however, and there is some concern about the ability to meet promised future benefits, in particular those under social security.

TABLE 8-4   Total Assets of Federal Government Retirement Funds (in $ billions)

	1950	1960	1965	1970	1974
Old Age Survivors Insurance	$12.9	$20.8	$19.9	$32.6	$37.9
Civil Service Retirement and Disability	5.0	10.4	15.9	23.1	34.5
Disability and Insurance Trust	.0	2.5	2.0	5.6	8.3
Railroad Retirement	3.2	3.7	3.9	4.4	3.9
Total	$21.1	$37.4	$41.7	$65.7	$84.6

Sources: Social Security Bulletins (Washington, D.C.: Social Security Administration, selected issues through 1975); *Treasury Bulletin* (Washington, D.C.: Securities and Exchange Commission, selected issues 1961–1976).

Most of the assets of these federal government retirement funds are invested in special Treasury issues. These nonmarketable securities can be bought at the maturity selected by the particular retirement fund and at rates of return similar to those on the same maturity of marketable Treasury issues. The primary economic effect of purchasing this form of debt is to reduce the supply of marketable Treasury securities below the level it might otherwise reach. The remaining assets of federal government retirement funds are marketable Treasury securities. Therefore, the only two decisions the managers of these retirement funds have is to choose between marketable and nonmarketable Treasury issues and to choose the appropriate maturity of these issues. On the average, management appears to have been on the conservative side, emphasizing short-term nonmarketable special issues. The possibility of greater returns by selecting more longer-term Treasury issues should be considered. The risk of lower liquidity from following this strategy could be reduced by buying more marketable rather than nonmarketable Treasury issues. Proposals that federal government retirement funds have the discretion to buy securities other than Treasury issues appear to have merit from an economic viewpoint, but seem unlikely to be enacted in the near future.

State and Local Retirement Funds

According to the Governments Division of the Bureau of the Census, there are slightly over 2,000 separate state and local government employee retirement funds. The asset funding of future benefits of these funds varies widely—from approximately pay-as-you-go to fully funded—as do the investment policies and restrictions. In general, these funds tended in recent years to have lower funding of future benefits, fewer investment restrictions, and more aggressive investment policies. The investment policies and practices of most state and local government employee retirement funds have tended to move toward those of private pension funds and away from those of the federal retirement funds in recent years. In the following paragraphs we will briefly discuss the nature of cash flows for state and local employee retirement funds, present evidence on how their investment policies have changed and why, and discuss some public policy questions regarding the low funding of some state and local government retirement funds.

Table 8-5 presents the total and net receipts for all state and local government employee retirement funds reporting to the Governments Division of the Bureau of the Census for the last decade. Probably the most important characteristic for nearly all of the flows in this exhibit is their remarkable consistency over time. Among the inflows, government contributions have consistently constituted nearly 45 percent, employee contributions have declined from roughly 30 to 25 percent, and earnings on investments have increased slightly from approximately 25 to 30 percent of total receipts over the last decade. We have been unable to obtain figures on either the amount of maturing securities or securities sold. The consistency of benefit payments (averaging one-third of total receipts) has meant that net cash receipts have grown at a very consistent rate. These consistencies, if true for individual funds, have the implication that there is little need for liquidity. Investment policies and practices should reflect this condition. As a warning, some individual funds do mature and those responsible for managing the funds must be careful that their liquidity and investment practices reflect this specific need and not the needs of funds in general.

Table 8-6 discloses the major categories of asset holdings of state and local retirement funds. As late as the early 1950s most of these funds were limited to investment in debt securities of state or local governments and of the U.S. government or its agencies. Table 8-6 indicates that over 80 percent of state and local retirement funds were invested in such securities in 1950. Reasons for such severe investment limitations included (1) the desire on the part of state and local officials to strengthen the market for their securities, (2) the small size of many retirement funds, and (3) the lack of investment expertise or experience among many officials appointed as trustees or managers of such funds.

By the early 1960s, however, these limitations were liberalized for many state and local retirement funds. For example, Table 8-6 indicates that the securities of state, local, and federal government and its agencies were only approximately 8 percent of total assets at the end of 1975 and that the absolute amount of state and local securities held is lower in 1975 than in 1960. Corporate bonds, nearly all acquired in the open market (versus direct placement that was prevalent in many insurance companies), were the primary investment media of state and local retirement funds in the 1960s. Such securities rose to over half of all asset holdings by 1970. Mortgages also grew increasingly popular as an investment media in the 1960s; however, their popularity appeared to decline in the early 1970s. As late as 1965 common stock composed less than 5 percent of the assets of state and local retirement funds. Recent liberalization of restrictions for many funds has meant that common stock has grown to slightly above 20 percent of all fund asset holdings.

TABLE 8-5 Total and Net Receipts of State and Local Government Employee Retirement Funds, 1964–1975 (in $ billions)

	1964	1965	1966	1967	1968	1969	1970	1971	1972	1973	1974	1975
Employee contributions	$1.5	$1.6	$1.8	$2.0	$2.2	$2.5	$2.8	$3.2	$3.4	$4.2	$4.2	$4.5
Government contributions	2.3	2.4	2.6	3.1	3.6	4.0	4.6	5.2	5.8	6.7	7.8	9.1
Earnings on investments	1.1	1.2	1.4	1.6	1.8	2.1	2.5	2.9	3.5	4.1	4.5	5.3
Total receipts	$4.8	5.3	$5.8	$6.6	$7.6	$8.6	$9.9	$11.3	$12.7	$14.9	$16.5	$18.9
Benefit payments	1.5	1.7	1.9	2.1	2.3	2.6	3.0	3.5	4.1	5.0	5.7	6.5
Withdrawals	0.3	0.3	0.4	0.5	0.5	0.6	0.6	0.6	0.7	0.9	1.0	1.0
Net receipts	$3.0	$3.3	$3.6	$4.0	$4.8	$5.4	$6.3	$7.2	$8.0	$9.1	$9.8	$11.4

Source: U.S. Bureau of the Census, *Governmental Finance* (Washington, D.C.: U.S. Government Printing Office, annual issues 1964–1976).

Note: Total and net receipts may differ slightly from direct addition and subtraction of components because of rounding differences.

203

TABLE 8-6 Assets and Liabilities of State and Local Government Employee Retirement Funds (in $ billions)

	1950 $	1950 %	1960 $	1960 %	1965 $	1965 %	1970 $	1970 %	1975 $	1975 %
Assets										
Cash	$0.1	2.0%	$0.2	1.0%	$0.2	0.9%	$0.6	1.0%	$0.6	0.6%
Federal government and agency securities	2.5	50.0	5.9	30.1	7.6	22.9	6.9	11.9	6.9	6.5
State and local securities	1.6	32.0	4.4	22.4	2.6	7.8	2.0	3.4	1.9	1.8
Corporate bonds	0.6	12.0	6.7	34.2	16.6	50.0	31.8	54.8	59.1	55.5
Preferred stock	*	-	*	-	0.2	0.6	0.4	0.7	0.9	0.8
Common stock	*	-	0.4	2.0	1.4	4.2	7.6	13.1	23.8	22.3
Mortgages	0.1	2.0	1.5	7.7	3.7	11.1	6.8	11.7	7.2	6.7
Other assets	0.1	2.0	0.5	2.6	0.8	2.4	1.9	3.3	6.1	5.7
Total	$5.0	100.0%	$19.6	100.0%	$33.2	100.0%	$58.0	100.0%	$106.5	100.0%
Liabilities										
Contributions and reserves	$5.0		$19.6		$33.2		$58.0		$106.5	

Source: Federal Reserve Bulletins (Washington, D.C.: Board of Governors of the Federal Reserve System, selected issues 1951–1976).
*Under $0.05 billion.

In our opinion, the liberalization of investment restrictions on state and local retirement funds and the resultant portfolio changes seems reasonable. The fact that such retirement funds are not taxed precludes the holding of tax-exempt state or local securities. Because most state and local retirement funds have little need for liquidity, they can reasonably purchase more long-term and less marketable securities. Further, as retirement benefits become increasingly tied to increases in wages, the cost of living, and productivity, state and local retirement funds will probably be forced to continue to take higher risks (e.g., buying corporate bonds instead of Treasury bonds) in order to achieve the required returns. Future years may see heavier commitments in privately placed corporate bonds, mortgages on income property, and common stock.

While investment practices appear to be improving, there are potential problems in both the funding and other financial practices associated with some individual state and local employee retirement funds. For example, in *The Unions and the Cities,* Wellington and Winter remark:

> Where state and local pensions are concerned, major concessions may be politically tempting since there is no immediate impact on the taxpayer or city budget. Whereas actuarial soundness would be insisted on by a profit-seeking entity like a firm, it may be a secondary concern to politicians whose conduct is determined by relatively short-run considerations. The impact of failing to adhere to actuarial principles will frequently fall upon a different mayor and a different city council. In those circumstances, concessions that condemn a city to future impoverishment may not seem intolerable.[2]

The potential problem areas which are beginning to surface include:

1. Relationships with social security benefits
   a. many state and local employees are not covered
   b. where coverage has been started, no recognition in state or local pension scheme
2. Vesting (portability)—employees hurt and job mobility reduced because of severe restrictions on vesting of state or local government contributions
3. Funding
   a. often actuarial tables are inadequate to evaluate funding
   b. some locally administered systems have very little funding
   c. horror stories, such as in Hamtramck, Michigan, where local official paid current operating bills from pension funds until they ran out
4. Impact of increased unionization and collective bargaining
   a. special benefits
   b. lower, if any, employee contribution
   c. younger normal retirement and early retirement plans
   d. short-term interest of many state and local political officials
5. Questionable fiduciary rules and investment decisions

---

[2]Harry H. Wellington and Ralph K. Winter, Jr., *The Unions and the Cities* (Washington, D.C.: The Brookings Institution, 1971).

The impact of these and similar problems associated with state and local requirement funds is felt in different ways by different groups. The impact on state and local employees is direct and consequential—strict vesting requirements reduce their mobility, inadequate funding raises questions about promised benefits, early retirement causes worries, and so on.

The impact of pension costs on the financial position of the pension-sponsoring state or local governmental unit is another area of serious concern. For example, New York State organizations representing state workers have been bargaining for retirement at half pay after 20 years of service, and for full pay after 35 years of service, based on the highest one year's salary. Before this proposed benefit, the total public pension cost in New York State was $1.4 billion in 1970 (roughly 11 percent of tax receipts) and was expected to reach approximately $3 billion by 1976. The financial problems of many locally administered systems seem even more severe. Philadelphia's $1 billion of unfunded pension costs is greater than the city's general obligation indebtedness. Philadelphia experienced an increase from $47 million in 1972 to $88 million in 1973 in the costs to meet the current normal funding of its retirement systems. In 1973, Detroit's police and fire pension appropriations represented slightly over half of its total police and fire payrolls. In 1974, Hamtramck, Michigan, had unfunded pension liabilities of $30 million, compared with $1 million of general obligations and a general fund budget of approximately $5 million. Clearly, as Representative Martha W. Griffith pointed out:

> At some point, a sensible set of rules setting forth how much the public can finance in retirement benefits will simply have to be arrived at, and methods of estimating future burdens from present grants and benefits will have to be developed and made general for federal, state, and local systems alike. . . . People must awaken to the tax burden that is being placed on the average taxpayer by these retirement systems.[3]

The Employee Retirement Income Security Act of 1974, which mandated sweeping private pension reform, required that a Congressional study of public employee retirement systems be completed by December 31, 1976. There is a distinct possibility that in response to the findings of such a study, Congress will require substantial changes in the funding, vesting, benefits, investment limitations, and fiduciary provisions of public employee retirement systems.

Private Pension Funds

In early 1975 there were roughly 170,000 private pension funds with assets totaling over $190 billion covering approximately 30 million employees (nearly half of all wage and salary workers). In this section we will discuss

---

[3]Statement by Representative Martha W. Griffith in *Tax Review* (January), 1972.

the financial management of uninsured private pension funds. (Insured pension funds, which had nearly $60 billion in assets in early 1975, are administered by life insurance companies, generally as a special part of their annuity program. The financial management of these insured pension funds was discussed in Chapter 7.) Our discussion will emphasize the development of a foundation for financial management from fund inflows and outflows, an analysis of pension portfolio policy, and changes in the pension fund environment as a result of passage of the Employee Retirement Income Security Act of 1974.

We begin by assuming the existence of an uninsured pension fund associated with a typical pension plan that promises benefits to retired persons based on the level of their wages and their years of service. For an employee who enters the plan at age 30 and plans to retire at 65, the liability of the fund will be to make the appropriate payments after 35 years. Over the 35 years the employee is with the company, contributions to the fund together with their earnings must cumulate to the discounted value of future benefit payments. Since earnings and demographic characteristics are not precisely foreseeable, required contributions must be estimated actuarially.

There are two particularly interesting implications for the management decisions of this (the most common) form of pension plan. First, higher earnings from aggressive financial management reduces the required contributions. A lower level of required contributions generally pleases the sponsoring company since employers contribute an average of 90 percent of total pension contributions (Table 8-7). Second, the net growth (contributions exceeding benefits) of the fund as a whole is likely to continue for at least the first generation of employees and often longer. For example, an expanding number of covered employees or liberalization of promised benefit payments (leading to higher current contributions) can delay the time when net growth ceases.

The characteristics of the two other popular forms of pension plans, *fixed contribution-variable benefit schemes* and *profit-sharing plans,* are somewhat different. The inflow of contributions to the former type vary directly with the number of covered employees and not on the basis of actuarial estimates. Employees, rather than the employer, benefit from better portfolio management. Net growth will occur so long as contributions on behalf of active employees exceed disbursements; therefore, an increasing number of covered employees (but not benefits that are dependent on contributions) can cause net growth to continue. Net growth of deferred-benefit, profit-sharing plans will be the net results of employer profits and fund earnings.

Aggregative data on total and net receipts for the last 15 years are summarized in Table 8-7. The increased importance of employer contributions for private pension funds compared with state and local retirement funds is immediately evident. There is also some evidence of a slowing in the rate of net growth and maturity. As recently as the early 1960s investment and other income exceeded benefit payments. By the mid-1970s,

TABLE 8-7 Total and Net Receipts of Uninsured Private Pension Funds (in $ billions)

	1960	1961	1962	1963	1964	1965	1966	1967	1968	1969	1970	1971	1972	1973	1974
Employee contributions	$0.5	$0.5	$0.6	$0.6	$0.6	$0.7	$0.7	$0.8	$0.9	$1.0	$1.1	$1.1	$1.2	$1.3	$1.5
Employer contributions	3.5	3.7	4.0	4.2	4.9	5.6	6.4	7.0	7.7	8.5	9.7	11.3	12.7	14.4	17.0
Investment and other income	1.3	1.5	1.6	1.8	2.1	2.5	2.7	3.0	3.3	3.7	4.0	4.2	4.4	5.0	6.1
Gain (loss) on sale of securities	0.1	0.3	0.1	0.2	0.4	0.6	0.5	1.0	1.3	1.0	(1.6)	0.9	1.7	(0.9)	(3.5)
Total receipts	$5.4	$5.9	$6.3	$6.8	$7.9	$9.3	$10.3	$11.8	$13.2	$14.2	$13.2	$17.5	$20.0	$19.7	$21.0
Benefit payments	1.3	1.5	1.8	2.0	2.4	2.8	3.4	3.9	4.5	5.3	6.0	7.1	8.3	9.3	10.7
Other disbursements	0.1	0.1	0.1	0.1	0.1	0.1	0.1	0.1	0.1	0.1	0.2	0.2	0.2	0.2	0.3
Net receipts	$4.0	$4.3	$4.4	$4.7	$5.5	$6.4	$6.8	$7.8	$8.5	$8.7	$7.0	$10.3	$11.6	$10.1	$10.0

Source: Securities and Exchange Statistical Bulletins (Washington, D.C.: Securities and Exchange Commission, selected issues 1960–1975).

Note: Total and net receipts may differ slightly from direct addition and subtraction because of rounding differences.

such income had fallen to slightly above half of benefit payments; nevertheless, total contributions and benefits were more than twice the size of benefit payments. Growth in the number of covered employees and amount of benefits meant that the liquidity demands for most private pension funds were minimal.

Several other factors also affect the financial management of private uninsured pension funds. First, nearly all of the cash outflows from these funds are for benefit payments, which are fairly predictable. Beneficiaries can demand payments only when preestablished events (generally retirement, disability, or death) occur and the size of benefit payment for most pensions is established when the employee retires. The timing of employee retirement and employee turnover and mortality can be predicted within reasonable limits. The predictability of benefit payments is decreased if benefits vary after retirement (for example, if they are tied to some price index) and if employment in a firm is unstable. Second, as in the case of federal and state and local retirement funds, investment income is exempt from income taxes. Third, most private pension funds carry their assets at book values rather than market values. Fourth, managers of private uninsured pension funds are not subject to many limitations or restrictions on their reasonable activities. For example, the prudent man rule and reasonable disclosure are required for investment activities, but few funds are prohibited from buying entire categories of securities, as is still the case for many public retirement funds.

There is intense competition for the business of managing pension funds. Most private uninsured pension funds are managed by trust departments of commercial banks. By the early 1970s such pension funds constituted over 35 percent of the assets of the trust departments of banks.[4] A few investment banking firms and investment management firms also manage pension funds; however, self-administered pension funds are the second most common form of management. This arrangement probably reflects the incentive of some corporate executives to employ their company's pension plan assets aggressively in hopes of lowering retirement costs. These managers of self-administered funds must be careful that they fulfill their fiduciary responsibility. Finally, a few private pension funds are managed by union officials.

The net investment results of the minimal liquidity demands and other factors affecting pension funds are shown in Table 8-8. Most private uninsured pension funds chose to emphasize taxable, long-term debt issues and common stocks throughout the 1960s and early 1970s. Their strategy was that, without the hazard of forced liquidiation, they could wait until debts mature and wait out wide changes in market prices. The tax advantages of preferred stock and municipal bonds do not appeal to these tax-exempt funds. Types of investments that may have an increased appeal in the future (particularly if their returns exceed those on corporate bonds and common stock) include mortgages, mortgage-backed federal agency securities, and bonds of foreign governments and countries.

---

[4]Edna E. Ehrlich, "The Functions and Investment Policies of Personal Trust Departments." Federal Reserve Bank of New York, *Monthly Review,* October 1972, pp. 255-270

TABLE 8-8 Assets and Liabilities of Uninsured Private Pension Funds (in $ billions)

	1950 $	1950 %	1960 $	1960 %	1965 $	1965 %	1970 $	1970 %	1974 $	1974 %
Assets										
Cash	$0.3	4.5%	$ 0.9	2.4%	$ 0.9	1.2%	$ 1.8	1.9%	$ 4.3	3.2%
Governmental securities	2.0	29.9	3.1	8.3	3.6	4.9	3.0	3.1	5.5	4.1
Corporate bonds	2.8	41.8	14.1	37.9	21.2	29.1	29.7	30.6	35.0	26.2
Preferred stock	0.4	6.0	0.7	1.9	0.8	1.1	1.7	1.8	1.1	0.8
Common stock[a]	0.7	10.4	15.7	42.2	40.0	54.8	51.7	53.3	79.3	59.3
Mortgages	0.1	1.5	1.3	3.5	3.4	4.7	4.2	4.3	2.4	1.8
Other assets	0.4	6.0	1.4	3.8	3.0	4.1	4.7	4.9	6.1	4.6
Total	$6.7	100.0%	$37.1	100.0%	$72.9	100.0%	$97.0	100.0%	$133.7	100.0%
Liabilities										
Contributions and reserves	$6.7	100.0%	$37.1	100.0%	$72.9	100.0%	$97.0	100.0%	$133.7	100.0%

Source: SEC *Statistical Bulletins* (Washington, D.C.: Securities and Exchange Commission, selected issues 1950–1975).

[a]Book value.

The demand to improve pension fund performance will tend to accelerate in future years because several provisions in the Employment Retirement Income Security Act of 1974 will increase the cost of pensions to employers. In summary, the provisions affecting financial management of pension funds include the following:

1. Funding—each plan must fund normal costs (accruing liabilities based on actuarial measurement) currently. Unfunded past service liabilities are to be amortized over a 40-year period. The Secretary of Labor may, however, waive these requirements if this presents an undue hardship.
2. Fiduciary responsibilities—each system is to be established and maintained pursuant to written instruments naming one or more fiduciaries who will manage the system. The fiduciary is required to operate in a manner consistent with those of a prudent man. Assets are to be held in trust and governed by a trustee or named fiduciary.
3. Benefit accrual—for defined benefit plans based on years of service, benefits must not be less than 3 percent of the maximum possible benefits (ie., considering maximum length of service) times the years of service up through 33⅓ years. For defined benefit plans based on average earnings, this average amount must be based on highest average earnings for any 10 consecutive years of service. These benefit provisions are not retroactively applicable.
4. Vesting—normal retirement benefits become nonforfeitable upon the attainment of normal retirement age. The Act provides that employee benefits derived from own contributions are nonforfeitable. In addition a plan must satisfy one of the following vesting schemes:
   a. after 10 years service an employee is entitled to 100 percent of the accrued benefits with no rights until then, or
   b. at least 25 percent vesting after 5 years of service and an additional 5 percent for each year through 10 years of service and an additional 10 percent for each succeeding year through 15 years of service, or
   c. at least 50 percent when an employee's years of service and age total 45 plus 10 percent additional vesting for every succeeding year. (An employee with 10 years of service must be at least 50 percent vested, however.)
5. Reporting and disclosure—each system must provide (1) a summary plan description for members, (2) a comprehensive plan description in a format prescribed by the Secretary of Labor, (3) a detailed annual report which is to include a financial statement and opinion provided by an independent, certified accountant and an actuarial statement and opinion provided by an approved actuary, and (4) detailed reports when aspects of the plan are changed. In addition, each system is required to provide a requesting member with information as to accrued benefits.
6. Participation—the Act basically requires that an employee be allowed to participate in a plan if he or she is at least 25 years old or after one year of service.
7. Plan termination insurance—Title IV of the Act creates the Pension Benefit Guaranty Corporation within the Department of Labor. It is to collect premiums from the benefit system and will provide payments to the members of defaulting systems.[5]

---

[5]Excerpts from *Information Bulletin No. 74-11*, Washington, D.C.: General Post Office, December 1974, Prepared by the Advisory Commission on Intergovernmental Relations.

Financial Management of Finance Companies

Finance companies have traditionally been classified into three categories: consumer finance companies, sales finance companies, and commercial finance companies. The distinction between these categories has been disappearing in recent years as most finance companies have been forced to diversify their lending activities. Nevertheless, we will begin this section by briefly describing the characteristics of each category of finance company so as to introduce the primary function of finance companies. We examine recent trends in the finance industry, discuss the primary assets and liabilities and major sources and uses of funds for all finance companies, and then turn to the pressing financial management problems facing these companies.

Consumer finance companies are primarily engaged in making cash loans for a variety of purposes. Most frequently, these loans are of a remedial or service nature such as payment of medical bills, educational expenditures, travel, or perhaps for the consolidation of small personal bills. Many companies also handle moderate amounts of the low-dollar, unit-sized, installment sales business generated by appliance dealers, furniture stores, camera shops, and other retail stores. In acquiring this type of paper (negotiable notes) the advance is based largely on the credit of the individual purchaser rather than on the value of the collateral involved.

Sales finance companies emphasize direct and indirect installment financing of consumer durables, and can be further subdivided according to their form of ownership. Independent sales finance companies previously emphasized installment financing for new and used automobiles. When commercial banks entered the installment finance field in force, competition increased, rates fell, and the quality of receivables declined. Faced with a declining share of the automobile finance business and lower profit margins, the sales finance companies gradually turned to other sources of financing to bolster earnings. Today, the paper generated from the financing of automobiles accounts for less than 50 percent of many portfolios and it would be difficult to find a single company in this group that has not diversified to some extent. The balance consists of receivables arising from other types of financing activities, including direct personal loans, major appliance financing, home improvement loans, financing of mobile homes and shell homes, boat financing, leasing, and in some cases, various types of commercial financing.

Captive sales finance companies are owned by companies not identified with the finance business. Captives are ostensibly organized for the purpose of providing supplementary financing facilities as a selling aid to distributors, dealers, and end-users of the parent company's products. Because company philosophies differ, even those captive companies operating in similar product fields are often quite dissimilar in their operations. In addition, there is wide product variation between companies, which produces even greater differences among them.

The third category of companies in the finance industry are the *commercial finance companies,* so called because their activities deal largely with the financing of commercial and industrial business. Our modern day commercial finance company is perhaps best described as a supplier of additional working funds for a variety of beneficial purposes to all types of businesses in amounts that would not normally be available on an unsecured basis from other sources because of the disproportionate ratio of need to net worth or working capital. While the purposes for which funds might be needed are virtually limitless in number, some indication of their range is suggested by a brochure of one company that lists as eligible for financing such activities as mergers and acquisitions, research, design and tooling, inventory accumulation of seasonal products, and installment or lease contracts. Advances are usually fully secured by varying types of collateral, often in the form of an assignment of accounts receivable, a pledge of inventories, a mortgage on owned machinery or other chattels, or combinations thereof.

Several trends pertaining to finance companies have important management implications. First, as previously mentioned, by the mid-1970s many of the distinctions between consumer finance companies, sales finance companies (with the exception of captive sales finance companies), and commercial finance companies had disappeared and the trend was clearly toward finance with diversified activities. Second, the number of finance companies has decreased significantly, largely as a result of mergers, but the average size of finance companies has increased significantly over the last decade or so. There were only half as many finance companies in 1970 (slightly under 3,500) as there were in 1960 (slightly over 7,000)[6], while Table 8-9 indicates that the assets of all finance companies more than doubled over the same decade. Third, while some small proprietorships or partnerships with individual offices still remain, the corporate form with extensive branching operations has become increasingly important. Advantages of these larger organizations include access to the money and capital markets (rather than being restricted to owner's investment and retained earnings), geographic diversification, and mobility of financial resources. Finally, finance companies are subject to more intensive competition from commercial banks, who increasingly seek profitable loans to consumers and smaller businesses, and larger nonfinancial businesses, who seek profits from financing their own sales. This intense competition has narrowed the margin of net income to total revenues from 15 percent in the mid-1960s to under 10 percent in the mid-1970s, and has probably led to lower quality loan portfolios, more mergers, and more failures among finance companies.[7]

The primary assets and liabilities of all finance companies for selected years from 1950 to 1974 are summarized in Table 8-9. This information

---

[6]*1975 Finance Facts Yearbook* (Washington: National Consumer Finance Association, 1975), pp. 54–73.
[7]Ibid.

TABLE 8-9 Assets and Liabilities of Finance Companies (in $ billions)

	1950 $	1950 %	1960 $	1960 %	1965 $	1965 %	1970 $	1970 %	1974 $	1974 %
Assets										
Cash and deposits	$ 1.0	8.8%	$ 1.5	6.0%	$ 1.5	4.1%	$ 2.0	3.3%	$ 3.6	3.9%
Loans to consumers	6.3	55.8	14.0	56.0	20.4	56.2	29.8	49.2	45.2	48.4
Loans to business	2.5	22.1	7.6	30.4	11.8	32.5	21.1	34.8	32.2	34.5
Other assets	1.5	13.3	1.9	7.6	2.6	7.2	7.7	12.7	12.4	13.3
	$11.3	100.0%	$25.0	100.0%	$36.3	100.0%	$60.6	100.0%	$93.4	100.0%
Liabilities										
Short-term liabilities	$ 5.2	46.0%	$11.6	46.4%	$17.7	48.8%	$33.8	55.8%	$49.8	53.3%
Long-term liabilities	2.7	23.9	9.3	37.2	13.2	36.3	16.9	27.9	32.4	34.7
Capital and surplus	3.4	30.1	4.1	16.4	5.4	14.9	9.9	16.3	11.2	12.0
	$11.3	100.0%	$25.0	100.0%	$36.3	100.0%	$60.6	100.0%	$93.4	100.0%

Source: *Federal Reserve Bulletins* (Washington, D.C.; Board of Governors of the Federal Reserve System, selected issues 1951–1975), and *Finance Fact Yearbook* (Washington, D.C.: National Consumer Finance Association, selected issues 1951–1975).

indicates that even though the proportion has declined slightly in the last decade, loans to consumers are roughly half of all finance company assets. In recent years, between 35 and 40 percent of these consumer loans have been cash loans with nearly all of the remainder being sales installment loans.[8] Loans to business have grown to slightly over one-third of all finance company assets in recent years. Other assets, which consist primarily of other loans and investments, have grown to roughly one-eighth of all finance company assets in recent years.

Table 8-9 also indicates there have been some modest changes in the major sources of financing available to finance companies. Short-term liabilities, generally one-quarter to one-third of which were loans from banks and two-thirds to three-quarters commercial paper (mostly directly placed), constituted over one-half of finance companies' sources of funds. While long-term debt has fluctuated considerably, on the average it has constituted about one-third of finance company liabilities over the last decade or so. Common stock (proceeds from stock issues and retained earnings) has declined from slightly above 16 percent of total liabilities in 1960 to approximately 12 percent in 1974.

The relative importance of the three main forms of borrowing— borrowing from banks, commercial paper, and long-term debt—varies according to the differentials in interest rates at which they can be secured; but it also differs among the three categories of finance companies as a result of their different sizes and needs. The larger size of many sales finance companies (including many captive companies) and many commercial finance companies means they usually have access to lower interest costs in the commercial paper market. Most consumer finance companies and smaller sales and commercial finance companies rely on direct bank borrowing for their short-term financing. Consumer and sales finance companies have, on average, tended to use more long-term debt than commercial finance companies.[9]

While financing via short- and long-term borrowing and equity is an important source of funds, we should not ignore the cash flows from repayments or outstanding loans. For example, $35, $38, and $40 billion of repayment were received and $38, $43, and $41 billion of new loans were extended in 1972, 1973, and 1974, respectively, for the consumer and sales finance companies surveyed by the National Consumer Finance Association.[10] While we were unable to find industrywide data, most of the new loans extended were clearly financed with repayments of existing loans as opposed to retained earnings or new external financing.

Many of the problems faced by finance companies—high fixed cost of smaller loans, high interest costs, weaker quality loans, competition from commercial banks and nonfinancial businesses—are likely to continue for

---

[8]Ibid.

[9]Raymond W. Goldsmith, *Financial Institutions* (New York: Random House, 1968), pp. 94–98.

[10]*1975 Finance Facts Yearbook*, p. 57.

the next several years. We strongly believe that finance companies can continue to remain viable financial institutions if they maintain prudent management policies and procedures. One area of continuing effort should be the drive for legislative reform on restrictions such as maximum limits on the size of consumer loans, maximum interest rates under usury laws, and increasing regulation of consumer loans.

On a more positive note, several of the points in our general model for the management of a financial institution seem to deserve emphasis by finance companies. The concept of maintaining an adequate spread seems particularly important. In spite of increased competition, finance companies should charge high enough interest rates to earn an adequate rate of return. Finance companies should be careful that these rates are not obtained at the cost of drastically lowering the quality of assets. Instead, finance companies should continue to look for innovative areas in consumer and business financing that offer adequate rates for taking reasonable levels of risks. In our opinion, finance companies must become increasingly marketing conscious to attain such a goal.

Finance companies also must be able to obtain financing in as efficient a manner as possible. If the finance company is strong enough to use commercial paper, it should carefully compare the cost of commercial paper with the cost of bank borrowing. Commercial paper costs include the cost of any required backup lines of credit and the risk that the impersonal commercial paper market will not accommodate their needs. In the case of bank loans, the cost of compensating balances required at the bank less the benefits of any services the bank provides should be added to the interest cost. Some banks have begun charging a higher interest fee and not demanding any compensating balance.

The task of comparing long-term borrowing with either or both forms of primary short-term borrowing leads to another important financial management concern for finance companies. The rates which finance companies charge for their loans to individuals or businesses are often fixed for the term of the loan (generally two to five years). The fact that over half of these loans were financed with interest sensitive short-term loans in many finance companies did not appear to harm finance companies appreciably until the late 1960s. The sharp swings to very high interest rates in 1969-1970 and again in 1973-1974, however, demonstrated that most finance companies could no longer afford the luxury of intermediate-term portfolios financed in large part with interest-sensitive short-term funds. Finance companies must move toward a greater matching of the maturities of their assets and liabilities in a manner similar to that suggested for commercial banks and thrift institutions.

Chapter 8

Review Questions

1. How does a mutual fund differ from a closed-end investment company? How is the current asset value of the mutual fund's shares calculated?

2. Investment companies are unusual in that their profits can escape corporate income taxes. What must the company do to enjoy this right?
3. What is the biggest problem for investment companies? How does it adversely affect a fund's portfolio activity? What are two ways of alleviating this problem?
4. What have been the past trends in the asset mix of state and local government pension funds? What are some of the problems of these plans?
5. What are two ways in which net growth for pension funds will continue? In what ways are private pension funds similar to life insurance companies? Why would pension fund managers be interested in the index fund controversy?
6. In many ways the problems of finance companies are not unlike those of other institutions. List some of the problems facing finance companies. Unstable monetary periods such as 1973–1974 made finance companies more aware of a basic problem in their financial structure. What was this problem, and what must they do to alleviate it?

Selected References

Bartel, H. R., Jr. and Simpson, E. T. *Pension Funds of Multiemployer Industrial Groups, Unions, and Nonprofit Organizations.* New York: National Bureau of Economic Research, 1968.

Dougall, Herbert E. and Gaumnitz, Jack E. *Capital Markets and Financial Institutions.* Englewood Cliffs, N.J.: Prentice-Hall, 1975.

Ehrlich, Edna E. "The Functions and Investment Policies of Personal Trust Departments." Federal Reserve Bank of New York, *Monthly Review,* October 1972, pp. 255–270.

"Finance Companies: An Era of Change." *Banker's Monthly,* July 1975, pp. 24–28.

Friend, I., Blume, M., and Crockett, J. *Mutual Funds and Other Insitutional Investors: A New Perspective.* New York: McGraw-Hill, 1970.

Goldsmith, Raymond W. *Financial Institutions.* New York: Random House, 1968.

Never, N. "Open-end v. Mutual Fund Companies." *Inland Printer/American Lithographer,* July 1975, pp. 50–51.

Phelps, Clyde William. *The Role of Factoring in Modern Business Finance.* Baltimore: Educational Division, Commercial Credit Company, Studies in Commercial Financing, No. 1, 1956.

A Study of Mutual Funds. Report of the Committee on Interstate and Foreign Commerce, 87th Congress, 2d Session, Washington, D.C.: Government Printing Office, 1962. Prepared for the Securities and Exchange Commission by the Wharton School of Finance and Commerce, August, 1962.

Wrightman, D. "Pension Funds and Economic Concentration." *Quarterly Review of Economics and Business,* Winter 1967, pp. 29–36.

For current information see *Federal Reserve Bulletins* (monthly), *Mutual Fund Fact Books* (annually), *Annual Reports of the Securities and Exchange Commission* (annually), *Social Security Bulletins* (monthly), *Treasury Bulletins* (monthly), and *Finance Facts Yearbooks* (annually).

Financial Management
of Financial Institutions
in Future Years

THE primary theme of this book has been that most financial institutions can be effectively managed by employing the wealth-maximization model we presented in Chapter 2. In Chapters 5 through 8 we demonstrated how this general wealth-maximization model could be adapted to the current environment (determined by regulatory and legal constraints, past management practices, money and capital market conditions, etc.) in which each particular form of financial institution operates.) In this chapter we indicate that the environment in which financial institutions must operate is not static but dynamic. Indeed, both academicians and practitioners alike would agree that the rate of change in the environment of financial institutions seems to be increasing at a faster and faster pace. We then present evidence on how this environment may change in the next few years. While we conclude that financial institutions in tomorrow's environment will be considerably different from todays' financial institutions, we strongly believe our general wealth-maximization model will remain the appropriate criteria for financial management decisions.

The Dynamic Nature of Financial Institutions and Their Environment

A brief review of the changes since the early 1960s in the financial institutions themselves and the environment in which they must operate illustrates the dynamic nature of these institutions. Furthermore, the current pressures for further change lead us to conclude that the pace of change may quicken rather than decrease.

In the early 1960s commercial banks were, on the average, rather lethargic, slow-growing institutions. There were few bank holding companies or bank failures, and liability management was not considered a part of a bank manager's activities. Savings and loan associations were the fastest-growing financial institutions — investing the funds obtained from passbook savings in long-term mortgages. Life insurance companies were also growing rapidly and utilizing the proceeds from policies which promised fixed returns to buy good quality, fixed return assets. Open-end investment companies and private pension funds were becoming more popular because of their emphasis on investments in common stocks. Some of today's financial institutions, such as money market funds and real estate investment trusts, were small and relatively unknown.

The position of financial institutions is definitely a function of the economic environment. In the 1960s the economy seemed to be capable of generating adequate savings to finance the investment needed to sustain economic growth. While the economy had experienced cyclical swings in the 1960s they were moderate and unemployment was relatively low, inflation was at a reasonable rate, and interest rates were increasing at a very moderate pace. Financial institutions were basically regulated by the statutes written in the 1930s.

When reviewing the differences in financial institutions in the mid-1970s, we see that marked changes have occurred. Commercial banks have become more aggressive institutions emphasizing both profitability and growth. These trends began in the early 1960s as some banks began to aggressively seek funds by such techniques as aggressive marketing, competitive rates to savers, and new financial liabilities, such as the certificate of deposit (used to attract short-term corporate funds). These trends were supported in the mid- and later 1960s by the holding company movement, the philosophy that a bank could buy money at a price whenever it required funds, and the heightened interest in international banking. Both the regulatory and economic environments explicitly or implicitly supported these trends. Aggressive competiton for savings was encouraged and some bank holding companies remained virtually unregulated for a period of time. Demands for credit, intensified by inflation, were generally so high that even very expensive purchased money could be profitably lent to deficit units.

The environment from the mid-1960s through the mid-1970s also led to substantial changes in other financial institutions. When interest rates rose rapidly, the long-maturity asset and short-maturity liability positions of savings and loan associations and mutual savings banks caused them to suffer from low spreads and a weakened competitive ability to obtain funds. The rapid growth of savings and loan associations in the postwar period tended to slow and become much more erratic. Attempts to counteract these trends by issuing intermediate-term savings deposits and by making variable rate mortgages have been modestly successful. The growth of life insurance companies also slowed, probably because their fixed return contracts became less attractive in an inflationary environment. The insurance companies' attempts to overcome this problem with variable return policies and by acquiring mutual funds were not very successful. The slower growth in savings and loan associations, mutual savings banks, and life insurance companies led to problems in financing housing. Private financing of housing was so low in the credit crunch years of 1966, 1969–1970, and 1973–1974 that government guarantees or direct lending by government agencies was necessary for roughly half of the financial requirements in the residential housing sector in those years.

Open-end investment companies continued to grow until the early 1970s when the industry experienced net outflows for three years as public confidence appeared to be disturbed by stock market declines. Real estate investment trusts climbed from less than $1 billion in assets in the late 1960s to over $20 billion in 1973, but have declined precipitously in the last few years. Finance companies have reacted to intensified competitive pressures from commercial banks by shifting their portfolios to make cash loans to individuals and intermediate-term loans to businesses with higher credit risks. State and local retirement funds have reacted to fewer restrictions on their investments in most states by following much more aggressive investment policies. The problem of federal retirement funds has changed from concern over accumulating too high a level of assets to concern about difficulties in meeting future benefits.

Changes in the financial management of private pension funds is a recent and final example of how a changing environment changes the financial decisions of a financial institution. The Employment Retirement Income Security Act of 1974 (reviewed in detail in Chapter 8) is already causing changes in the financial management of private pension. Because of the more stringent vesting, funding, and reporting requirements, a sizeable number of smaller companies have dropped their pension plans.[1] Companies continuing their pension plans are increasing their contributions to the pension plans and are demanding improved fund performance because the new act has sharply increased the cost of pensions to corporations. Managers of pension funds seem to be turning to medium-quality, long-term debt securities and common stocks; however, they are becoming more concerned about their fiduciary responsibility.

While the changes over the last decade or so have been numerous and often significant, current demands for further changes and an uncertain economic environment lead us to believe that financial institutions may have to change even more in the coming decade. (A few examples of these demands are summarized in the following paragraphs.) Recent banking failures have led to charges that the current regulatory system is antiquated and must be completely restructured. Banking regulations have generally evolved to deal with banks operating within a limited geographical area and offering only standard (traditional) banking ser-

---

[1]Pension Benefit Guaranty Corporation (see Chapter 8 for description) received notices of intent to terminate 5,035 pension plans in 1975, about four times the number anticipated when the Employment Retirement Income Security Act was passed in 1974. *Cf. Wall Street Journal,* January 7, 1976, p. 3.

vices. The development of banks that are actually worldwide financial conglomerates has rendered some aspects of regulation obsolete. The pressures for regulatory change are coming from many sources. Congress has recommended that bank regulation be centralized no later than 1980. Further, they have discussed the advisability of regulating bank activities in areas such as foreign exchange speculation.

The steady deterioration of banks' capital positions has also been of concern to both banks and their regulators. Many regulators have expressed the opinion that capital ratios have declined as far as they reasonably can. A major contributor to this shortage has been the relative inaccessibility of money and capital markets in recent years, to the point where few banks are able to raise additional capital at reasonable terms. Some have claimed that regulators' actions are responsible for the reluctance of investors to purchase bank equity and capital notes.

The increased cyclical instability of funds available for residential housing has led to several proposals that would significantly affect commercial banks, life insurance companies, savings and loan associations, and mutual savings banks. One proposal is that commercial banks and life insurance companies should be forced to allocate a certain percentage of their loans and securities to mortgages financing residential housing. Another proposal is that savings and loan associations and mutual savings banks should be given broader powers to attract funds so that these institutions would consistently have more funds available for residential mortgages.

The Employment Retirement Income Security Act only dealt with private pension funds. Pressures are mounting for similar reforms for public pension funds. Some examples of questionable practices in state and local retirement funds were reviewed in Chapter 8, and the 1974 Act called for a two-year study of state and local retirement systems. There is widespread concern that contributions to federal retirement systems will be inadequate to finance increasing benefits.

The very existence of many financial institutions in the real estate investment trust, open-end investment trust, and sales finance company industries currently seems subject to serious concern. Furthermore, many of the securities markets in which financial institutions are active are subject to continued impetus for change. It is too soon to be certain what will be the impact of new securities or securities experiencing greatly increased activity, such as the variable rate mortgage, options, or mortgage and Treasury bill futures. The market for state and local securities may never fully recover from the impact of New York's financial problems in 1975, and the markets for common stocks have been changing rapidly in recent years.

The Hunt Commission Report

The best example of the demands for change and possibly the most important influence on the future operation of financial institutions is the recommendations of the Hunt Commission which were first presented in

1972. The Commission was created in 1970 as a result of the disruption of financial markets in the second half of the 1960s. The purpose of the Commission was to make recommendations that would bring about a greater degree of stability in the financial markets in the United States. The Commission was charged specifically with formulating policy actions that would insure a more even flow of credit to the home-building industry. Most of the Hunt Commission's recommendations related to the loan, investment, and deposit powers of commercial banks (including bank trust departments), mutual savings banks, savings and loan associations, and credit unions. However, selected activities of life insurance companies and pension funds are also covered. The recommendations summarized below seemed to be the major ones:

1. *Regulation Q-type ceilings* covering rates paid on time and savings deposits would be removed. Standby ceiling authorities which would be invoked in case of need, were suggested for consumer-type deposits.
2. *Third party payment accommodations* (e.g., automatic bill-paying and transfer systems, checking accounts, or credit cards) would be offered by any deposit-type institution (commercial bank, savings bank, S & L s, or credit union). Institutions offering such services would, in most cases, be subject to the same reserve requirement, tax treatment, and supervision.
3. *Reserve requirements* on time and savings deposits would be eliminated, and requirements for demand deposits would be the same for all, with no distinction as to size of institution or city location.
4. *Loan and investment powers:* Savings banks and S & Ls would experience the greatest increase in latitude, having hitherto faced relatively greater restrictions. They would be permitted to make mortgage loans on all kinds of properties; invest directly in real estate; make consumer loans in amounts totaling not more than 10 percent of total assets; invest in a full range of investment-grade debt instruments; provide construction credit in the same manner as commercial banks; and lend on mobile homes. For commercial banks, restrictions covering real estate loans and the amount of acceptances that could be created would be removed.
5. *The mortgage market* would also be affected by other recommendations. Interest rate ceilings (statutory and administrative) on residential mortgages would be abolished. It was suggested that Congress consider programs to insure lenders against interest rate risks arising from holding long-term, fixed-rate residential mortgages during periods of rising interest rates. Direct subsidization was advocated in the event that the mortgage credit generated under regular means is insufficient to meet national housing goals.
6. *Regulation and supervision,* mainly affecting commercial banks, would be shifted and consolidated, and some deposit insurance functions would be amalgamated. The independence of the Federal Reserve System was reaffirmed, and it would continue to supervise bank holding companies and Edge Act corporations, as well as administer regulations affecting banks' international activities.
7. *Branching and chartering* would be altered. State-wide branching authority for deposit-type institutions was suggested, but proposals for interstate branching or metropolitan-area branching that crosses state lines were rejected Federal charters would be made more widely available for thrift institutions.

8. *Powers and responsibilities of pensions, trusts, and fiduciaries* would be more clearly defined, and in some cases broadened, under the recommendations. A federal prudent-man investment rule was advocated. Regular reviews would be made of the distribution of brokerage commissions, situations in which there might be conflicts of interest, and the ways in which voting responsibility is conducted in the cases of equity ownership. Reporting would be more comprehensive, including annual independent audits and actuarial reports for pension operations. Savings banks and S & Ls would be permitted to offer certain fiduciary and insurance services to individual and nonbusiness entities, and these institutions, along with commercial banks, would be permitted to manage and sell mutual funds (including commingled agency accounts).[2]

As might be expected, the reaction to the Hunt Commission recommendations has varied considerably. This was to be expected given the sweeping nature of their suggested changes in the financial structure. Without arguing the pros and cons of the specific recommendations, many have criticized the Commission's lack of analytical or empirical support for their findings. This deficiency seems surprising since in many cases significant research findings were available. For example, the Commission's recommendations that the prohibition of interest on demand deposits be continued is an example of a decision that is contrary to the existing evidence. Nevertheless, it is the general feeling that the Hunt Commission's recommendations would serve to increase the stability of financial markets.

While it is too early to determine the final effects of the Hunt Commission's report on the future environment in which financial institutions must operate, it is certain to have a significant influence. Already some recommendations have been partially adopted. For example, in several states third-party transfers are already a reality for savings and loans and savings banks. Rate maximums under Regulation Q have been removed from deposits of over $100,000 and rates are now equal for all smaller-denomination, similar-maturity time deposits of commerical banks, savings and loans, and savings banks. Several rulings regarding loans and investments by savings and loan associations have been liberalized, and effective income tax rates for savings and loans and savings banks have been increased. Perhaps more important, President Ford proposed a comprehensive Financial Institution Act in 1975 which encompassed many of the Hunt Commission's recommendations. A revised version of this Act passed in the Senate by a wide margin in 1976; however, the House of Representatives was unable to achieve agreement on several controversial parts of the Act. It seems very likely a version of this legislation will be reconsidered by both Houses of Congress in 1977 or 1978.

The Effect of Future Changes on Financial Institutions

While we do not pretend to be soothsayers, current trends make the probability of some future changes fairly high at the present time. Drastic

---

[2]Adapted from *Business in Brief,* The Chase Manhattan Bank, February, 1972.

changes in the external environment could, of course, alter these predic-
tions. Nevertheless, is seems helpful to briefly explore several of the future
changes that seem likely to occur and to surmise some of their effects on
the financial management of financial institutions. The four areas of
change examined are (1) the trend toward open and freer competition
among deposit-type financial institutions, (2) the revision of the regulatory
structure, (3) the reform of state and local retirement funds, and (4) the
continuing evolution of financial securities and their markets.

The trend toward open and freer competition among deposit-type
financial institutions for savings, deposits, loans, and investments seems
practically irreversible. It seems likely that thrift institutions will obtain
demand-type accounts and that an interest return will be paid for at least
some demand-type accounts at commercial banks and thrift institutions. It
also seems highly probable that thrift institutions will obtain much broader
lending powers, for example, getting into previously untapped areas such
as consumer installment loans and commercial loans. These broad liability
and asset powers are only the beginning. Geographic competitive boundaries will continue to erode at an increasing rate. The use of shared electronic systems will increase. Commercial banks and thrift institutions will
place even more emphasis on attracting funds from consumers. And if the
increased competition among the deposit-type financial institutions is not
sufficient, it seems likely that nonfinancial businesses will continue to increase their involvement in many areas of finance.

One effect of these changes will be to make the efficient financial
management of these institutions even more essential. Reductions in
geographic, asset, and liability restrictions will narrow spreads for
deposit-type institutions. Efficiency and cost control efforts should be at a
premium. These institutions should be able to lower liquidity and price
fluctuation risks because they will generally be more able to match
maturities of assets and liabilities. On the other hand, there may well be
increased pressures for taking greater credit risks because of lower spreads,
lower liquidity, and price fluctuation risks. The fact that such a competitive environment still may not provide adequate financing for residential housing makes some economists concerned about increased government involvement in this area.

Substantial changes in the regulation and supervision of several financial institutions also seems very likely. The top candidate for change is
commercial banking, which is regulated by 3 federal and 50 state
regulatory agencies. Mix in three failures of large banks in the last two or
three years and serious problems in several other large banks, add a Congress that seems anxious for reform, and the result is tremendous pressure
for reform of bank regulation and supervision. Substantial regulatory
change for savings and loan associations, mutual savings banks, and credit
unions seems likely to occur as part of the restructuring of commercial
bank supervision. The regulation of private pension funds was altered
substantially in 1974 and there appears to be considerable pressure for

changes in the supervision and regulation of other financial institutions, such as state and local retirement funds and open-end investment trusts.

The House Banking Committee's proposal for regulatory reform provides an example of what may be coming. This proposal calls for the creation of a federal depository institution's commission to supplant the U.S. Comptroller's office, the regulatory and supervisory functions of the Federal Reserve System, the Federal Deposit Insurance Corporation, the Federal Home Loan Bank Board, and the National Credit Union Administration. The new commission would be responsible for chartering, conversion, mergers, examination, supervision, and regulation of federally chartered depository institutions, their holding companies, and foreign bank operations in the United States. A single separate insurance corporation is proposed to insure the deposits in all depository financial institutions. While the Senate will probably propose a different structure and existing regulatory authorities will fight to retain their powers, the pressures for some form of centralization of supervisory and regulatory functions seem great indeed. At the very least, managers of financial institutions can expect a far tougher regulatory climate in coming years, with more reports required and closer scrutiny by the supervisors.

We believe it is only a matter of time before state and local retirement funds will be under statutes and supervision similar to that which private pension funds have had to operate under since the 1974 Employment Retirement Income Security Act. Rapid vesting, full funding, and strong disclosure requirements will cause major changes in the management of many state and local retirement funds. The rate of growth in benefits is likely to slow sharply for some retirement funds as taxpayers become aware of the full cost of rapidly increasing benefits. Full funding will call for sharply increased amounts to be invested and the demand for aggressive investment performance will be much greater. Common stocks and medium-grade, fixed-income securities will probably become a more prominent proportion of many portfolios.

Finally, financial institutions will have to react to rapid changes in the securities markets and in the available menu of financial assets and liabilities. Examples are given for two rapidly developing securities, variable rate mortgages and mortgage futures, after which we make a couple of educated guesses about the types of securities and markets that may appear in coming years.

The increased acceptance of the variable rate mortgage and the recent development of a mortgage futures market have expanded the investment opportunities of those financial institutions that deal in the mortgage market. Both innovations allow the manager of such a financial institution to decrease the sensitivity of profit spreads to interest rate movements. As we mentioned in Chapter 2, the profit spread of financial institutions that issue demand (or short-term) liabilities while purchasing long-term fixed income assets (bonds, mortgages) is very sensitive to changes in the general level of interest rates. During a period of rising rates, costs of liabilities must increase in order to prevent severe deposit withdrawals. On the other hand, the nature of the asset position is such that average returns change very slowly as new mortgages are made at the higher rates. The deleterious effects on savings and loans of rising rates during the late 1960s and early 1970s are well documented.

The variable rate mortgage represents a possible solution to the problems introduced by fluctuating interest rates. Very simply, such mortgages would allow the financial institution to more closely match the maturity structure of its asset and liability poisitions. In this way, when interest rates rise, the return on its mortgage portfolio will increase along with the cost of liabilities, thereby "locking in" the spread.

The mortgage futures market began in October 1975 at the Chicago Board of Trade. Basically, this market offers opportunities similar to those provided by commodity and foreign exchange futures markets.[3] The basic unit to be traded is $100,000 with an 8 percent interest rate. Maximum daily price changes are limited to 0.75 percent of par value.

The usefulness of this mortgage futures market to some financial institutions can be demonstrated with a simple example. Suppose an institutional investor such as a savings and loan wishes to take advantage of the current high level of mortgage interest rates but will not have funds to invest until some future date. The savings and loan can lock in the current favorable rate by purchasing a futures contract. When the funds become available, it can purchase mortgages in the cash (spot) market and simultaneously sell the futures contract. Regardless of the movement in rates, the investor has accomplished its goal of locking in a favorable rate of return. As an example, if rates actually decreased, the profit on the futures contract would allow for a greater dollar investment into the lower yielding mortgages purchased in the cash market.

One new security that may appear in the next few years is a fully taxable and possibly federally guaranteed state and local government bond. Opposition by municipal officials to such a financial instrument has declined markedly in the last year or so. Such a security might be appealing to life insurance companies and retirement funds that are not heavily taxed and which have reasonably predictable cash outflows. Among the markets for securities, we see the greatest changes occurring in the markets for common stocks of corporations and in the market for state and local debt. Security brokers and dealers selling common stocks will experience continued change as competition forces lower margins amid greater demands for services. Most services to other financial institutions will be financed by fees covering the services provided. Fixed commissions are a thing of the past. Nondealer or broker financial institutions and foreign-controlled brokerage firms will be members of stock exchanges and there probably will be a national securities market. In the market for state and local securities, dealers and participants will find that demands for full

---

[3]See Appendix 2 for an explanation of the forward foreign exchange market.

disclosure will increase markedly and the market may be unsettled for several years as a result of New York's financial problems.

Chapter 9

Review Questions

1. Contrast the activities of financial institutions in the 1960s with their activities in the 1970s.
2. What reasons were given as an indication that commercial banks will be changing more in the future?
3. What was the Hunt Commission? What was its specific purpose? What were the Commission's recommendations affecting interest rate ceilings? Loan and investment power? Reserve requirements? Bank regulation and supervision?
4. Discuss the trends leading to a more open, freer, more competitive financial system. How are financial institutions going to react if these trends continue?
5. What types of institutions will be aided by variable rate mortgages and the mortgage futures market? Why will these changes help these institutions?

Selected References

Baker, D. I. "Maybe It's Time to Make Changes in the System." *Bankers Magazine,* August 1974, pp. 67-71.

Commission on Financial Structure and Regulation. *Report of the Commission.* Washington, D.C.: Government Printing Office, 1971.

"The Drive for Sweeping Financial Reform." *Business Week,* May 26, 1975, pp. 83-86.

Grebler, L. *The Future of Thrift Institutions.* Danville, Ill.: Joint Savings and Mutual Savings Banks Exchange Groups, 1969.

Haywood, Charles F. and McGee, L. Randolph. *The Expansion of Bank Funds in the 1970s.* New York: Association of Reserve City Bankers, 1970.

Monroe, John S. "Can Your Bank Compete in Tomorrow's Market?" *The Magazine of Bank Administration,* June 1974.

Prochnow, Herbert V. and Prochnow, Herbert V., Jr. *The Changing World of Banking.* New York: Harper & Row, 1974.

"Restructuring of Financial Institutions, Regulators Slated for Hearings in House." *Wall Street Journal,* December 15, 1975, p. 3.

Robinson, R. I. "The Hunt Commission Report: A Search for Politically Feasible Solutions to the Problems of Financial Structure." *Journal of Finance,* September 1972, pp. 765-778.

Appendix A
Linear Programming:
Basic Concepts and
Summary of Techniques

Foreword

LINEAR programming is a powerful mathematical tool that can be employed in order to determine the optimal allocation of scarce resources. Specific restrictions and constraints can be modeled to determine the optimal allocation to competing objectives. Thus, linear programming has two integral parts:

1. an objective function—this depicts the particular objective of the decision-maker (i.e., maximize profit or minimize cost)
2. a set of linear constraints—these constraints specify certain regulatory and behavioral aspects of the decision-maker's environment so as to make the solution of the objective function more realistic

Our wealth-maximization hypothesis allows for the implementation of linear programming. Here, we have a financial institution with limited financial resources desiring to construct an asset mix and capital structure which will maximize the wealth of its shareholders. Each dollar of particular assets adds a certain amount to the wealth of stockholders, while each dollar of liabilities decreases stockholder wealth by a certain amount. The institution cannot expand assets without bound, for the regulatory and behavioral environment will limit the purchase of assets. Linear programming is used in this case to determine the quantity of each asset to purchase so as to maximize shareholder wealth.

Geometric Approach to Linear Programming

One might ask how linear programming performs its optimization task. We will illustrate the geometric approach to linear programming which, although limited to two dimensions, is very helpful in describing the conceptual underpinnings of linear programming. A very simple two-variable problem will be used in the development of these concepts.

Example

The Ninth National Bank of North Waukegan has $15,000 in excess funds which it can invest in two assets, short-term government obligations and mortgages. Each dollar of the short-term investment adds 20 cents to profit, and each dollar of mortgages adds 40 cents to profit. Thus, the objective function becomes

$$\text{MAX } P = 0.20X_1 + 0.40X_2$$

where X_1 = dollars in the short-term investment and X_2 = dollars in the long-term investment.

The management wants no more than $10,000 in short-term securities and a maximum of $5,000 in mortgages. Further, for every dollar in short-term securities, management would like $1.50 in mortgages. The three constraints are

$$X_1 \leq \$10,000,$$
$$X_2 \leq \$\ 5,000,$$
$$X_1 + 1.5X_2 \leq \$15,000.$$

To these constraints we now add the nonnegativity constraints necessary to the use of linear programming. So the situation for the Ninth National Bank is as follows:

$$\text{MAX } P = 0.20X_1 + 0.40X_2$$

subject to

$$X_1 \leq \$10,000$$
$$X_2 \leq \$\ 5,000$$
$$X_1 + 1.5X_2 \geq \$15,000$$
$$X_i \leq 0, \qquad \text{for all } i.$$

Now the constraints must be graphed. The inequalities are changed to equalities, graphed, and a solution set will be obtained by the boundaries of the constraint. This is done below:

$$X_1 + 1.5X_2 = \$15,000$$

if $X_2 = 0$, $X_1 = \$15,000$

if $X_1 = 0$, $X_2 = \$10,000$

$$X_1 = \$10,000$$
$$X_2 = \$5,000$$
$$X_1, X_2 \neq 0.$$

Graphing these equations gives the area of feasibility for answers, as denoted by the shaded area in Figure 1.

Our answer as to what portion of funds will go into mortgages and what goes into short-term obligations will be some point in the area of feasible solutions. Any combination falling outside the area of feasible solutions will not satisfy the problem since one or more of the constraints will be violated.

How do we find the optimal point that leads to wealth-maximization? We can do this geometrically by plotting the line of the objective function, starting at zero and making parallel shifts upward and to the right since these shifts would result in higher profits. In other words, we are plotting isoprofit lines until we get a line which is tangent to the area of feasible solutions. This point of tangency would be the optimum allocation point (Figure 2).

Figure 1.

(In Thousands of Dollars)

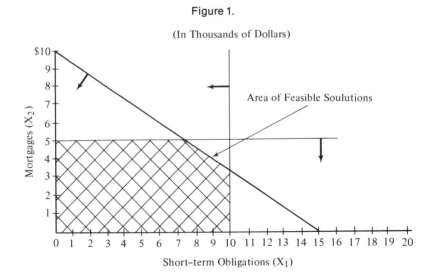

Mortgages (X_2)

Area of Feasible Soulutions

Short–term Obligations (X_1)

Figure 2.

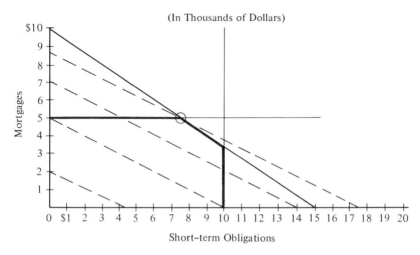

(In Thousands of Dollars)

$P_{MAX} = \$3,500$ Point of Tangency: $(X_1, X_2) = \$7,500, \$5,000)$

Hence, the point of tangency is $X_1 = \$5,000$, $X_2 = \$4,500$, and the profit is maximized at $P = \$2,900$.

Several important points are evidenced from this solution:

1. The optimal decision will always be a solution set within the area of feasible solutions.
2. It will always lie on the boundary of the area of feasible solutions.
3. If a unique solution exists, it will be found at one of the "corners" of the area of feasible solutions (i.e., it will be found at the intersection of the lines formed by the constraints).

This two-variable case can also be solved algebraically. The equations of the constraints are solved simultaneously to obtain a set of possible solutions. Each member of the solution set is then substituted into the objective function, and the member that satisfies the objective function (whether it be a maximizing or minimizing problem) is the point of optimal allocation of available resources.

Let us now extend the linear programming approach to the multivariable case.

Linear Programming on the Multivariable Level—The Simplex Method

In the multivariable case, we move out of the two-dimension geometric space into the n-dimension space (where n = number of variables). For example, in extending the geometric approach to three variables, we are dealing in three-dimensional space, and looking at extreme points determined by the intersection of three planes. The optimal solution will be at one of these extreme points.

If we extend the concept of linear programming to four or more variables, we cannot portray the configuration geometrically. However, the optimal solution will still occur at an extreme point, with these points generated by the intersection of hyperplanes. The extreme points might be examined by the algebraic method, but as n increases, the number of simultaneous equations to be solved increases dramatically, and makes this approach nearly impossible once the number of variables reaches a moderate number. What is needed is another way of systematically examining extreme points for optimality in light of a given objective function.

We do have such a systematic search method at our disposal. This method is called the *simplex method* for linear programming. It is an algorithm which begins at the origin and searches for other feasible solutions that improve the objective function. Each step is taken on the basis of the results of the last step since each iteration will only be taken if the objective function can be improved. Thus, the simplex method converges on an optimal solution.

As in the geometric approach, when the simplex algorithm is employed, we must convert the inequality constraints into equations. Under the simplex rule, this will require us to convert the inequalities by using slack, surplus, and artificial variables in the following way:

$\geq$ "greater than" — add a surplus variable and subtract an artificial

$\leq$ "less than" — add a slack variable

$=$ "equal to" — subtract an artificial variable.

The slack, surplus, or artificial variables are treated as real variables in the simplex algorithm, but they are given zero values in the objective function since they represent nonexisting resources. These variables may or may not appear in the final solution, and when they do, they make no contribution to the optimization of the objective function.

An example will help illustrate the points involved with the simplex algorithm.[1] A firm uses two types of labor, manufacturing and assembly labor, to make three different products. There are 120 hours of manufacturing labor and 260 hours of assembly labor available. One unit of product 1 (X_1) requires 0.10 hours of manufacturing labor and 0.20 hours of assembly labor. One unit of product 2 (X_2) requires 0.25 hours of manufacturing labor and 0.30 hours of assembly labor. One unit of product 3 (X_3) requires no manufacturing labor, but needs 0.40 hours of assembly labor. The profit contribution of products 1, 2, and 3 is $3, $4, and $5, respectively.

---

[1]This example was taken from a text example in Robert L. Childress, *Mathematics for Managerial Decisions,* p. 204.

The problem is

$$\text{MAX } P = 3X_1 + 4X_2 + 5X_3$$

subject to:

$$0.1X_1 + 0.25X_2 + 0X_3 \leq 120$$
$$0.2X_1 + 0.3X_3 + 0.4X_3 \leq 260$$
$$X_i \geq 0 \qquad \text{for all } i.$$

This problem must be restated to simplex form by using slack variables due to the "less than or equal to" constraints. The problem restated is

$$\text{MAX } P = 3X_1 + 5X_3 + 0X_4 + 0X_5$$

subject to:

$$0.1X_1 + 0.25X_2 = 0X_3 + X_4 + 0X_5 = 120$$
$$0.2X_1 + 0.3X_2 + 0.4X_3 + 0X_4 + X_5 = 260$$
$$X_i \geq 0 \text{ for all } i.$$

The fact that in all cases when slack, surplus, or artificial variables are added there are more variables than equations provides the basis for the simplex algorithm. The algorithm converges on the optimal solution by employing a technique similar to the Gaussian elimination method for solving simultaneous equations. To see how the iterations work, we must put the problem in tableau form:

X_1	X_2	X_3	X_4	X_5	Solution
0.1	0.25	0	1	0	$120 = X_4$
0.2	0.3	0.4	0	1	$260 = X_5$
3	4	5	0	0	$0 = P$

This is known as the basic feasible solution. As you can see, profit is equal to zero, and X_4 and X_5 are in the basis.

What we will do now is perform iterations that will move variables in and out of the basis until we have an optimal solution. We perform the iterations by the following pivot technique:

1. Look at the bottom row in the tableau. Since this is a maximization problem we want to pick the column with the largest positive number, so as to add the most to profit.
2. We then divided the number in the Solution column by the number in the row picked in technique 1—the row with the smallest non-negative quotient with a

positive denominator. This is the row we will pivot on with the column picked in technique 1.

3. We then perform row operations so as to give us a 1 at the pivot point, and zeros in the rest of the column. This helps form the identity matrix needed in the Gaussian elimination technique for solving simultaneous equations.

4. Techniques 1–3 are performed until we have all zeros or negative numbers in the bottom row.

We will now employ techniques 1–4 in our example. Restating the original tableau:

X_1	X_2	X_3	X_4	X_5	Solution
0.1	0.25	0	1	0	$120 = X_4$
0.2	0.3	(0.4)	0	1	$260 = X_5$
3	4	5	0	0	$0 = P$

We pick the X_3 column since every unit of X_3 that we bring into the basis will add \$5 to profit. We pivot on the 2-5 element since it gave us the minimum quotient. The next tableau after performing the necessary row operations is:

X_1	X_2	X_3	X_4	X_5	Solution
(0.1)	0.25	0	1	0	$120 = X_4$
0.5	0.75	1	0	2.5	$650 = X_3$
0.50	0.25	0	0	-12.50	$3,250 = P$

So, by moving X_3 into the basis, we have increased profit to \$3,250. The next pivot is on 1-1 element for the reasons outlined in techniques 1 and 2 above. Row operations are performed as needed, and the final tableau is:

X_1	X_2	X_3	X_4	X_5	Solution
1	2.50	0	10	0	$1,200 = X_1$
0	-0.50	1	-5	2.50	$50 = X_3$
0	-1	0	-5	-12.50	$3,850 = P$

Profit is maximized at \$3,850 since there are all zeros or negative numbers in the bottom row. The numbers in the bottom row are called the marginal value of the resources. For example, the \$$-12.50$ says that an additional hour of assembly labor can add \$12.50 to profit. Thus, if the cost of that hour is less than \$12.50, it should be acquired.

This appendix is intended only to familiarize the reader with the basic concepts and important techniques of linear programming. Several other benefits can be obtained from linear programming (*e.g.*, duality and sensitivity analysis). To obtain knowledge of the omitted topics in linear programming, the student is encouraged to refer to any of a number of mathematics texts.

Appendix B
Understanding the
Foreign Exchange Market
and Foreign Investments

THE continuing trend toward greater worldwide financial integration makes it necessary for managers of financial institutions to possess at least a minimum competency in the area of international finance. The purpose of this appendix is twofold: (1) to explain the functions and the structure of the foreign exchange market, and (2) to demonstrate how the manager of a financial institution might obtain higher returns on the asset portfolio by expanding the menu of available investment opportunities to include financial liabilities of foreign governments and businesses.

What Is the Foreign Exchange Market?

Very simply, the foreign exchange market allows one to convert purchasing power held in one country's currency into any of several traded currencies. Since both the total volume of transactions and the size of each individual transaction are extremely large, transaction costs tend to be minimal.[1] For most widely traded currencies there is a spot market and several forward markets. In the *spot market,* one can obtain an immediate balance in one currency by selling one's position in another currency. As an example, suppose you desire to convert £200 (£ denotes British pound sterling) into U.S. dollars. If the current spot rate is $2.40/£, the sale of 200 would bring $480. When making the transaction, you would be required to surrender the £ balance before receipt of the $ deposit.

---

[1] Transaction costs are proportionately larger for some transactions since one must employ a correspondent relationship with a commercial bank or a foreign exchange trader.

Transactions in the *forward market* are contracted at a specific date in the future. As an example, suppose the 90-day forward rate is $2.38/£. Since the $ is relatively more expensive in the forward market, it is said to be trading at a "premium" against the £. For most of the major international currencies there exist fairly broad forward markets up to one year. In rare cases the $ has been traded in the forward market up to five years in the future.

While the same currencies are being traded in many financial centers throughout the world (New York, London, Paris, Zurich, etc.), there is rarely a significant difference in the quoted exchange rates. Individuals undertaking exchange rate arbitrage insure this near-equality of rates. Very simply, this activity involves the simultaneous sale and purchase of the same currency in different financial centers. Suppose the spot rate in New York is $2.40/£ while the rate in London is $2.39/£. With these rates one could gain a profit by purchasing $s in New York (where the $ is relatively inexpensive) and selling $s in London. This activity would tend to bring the exchange rates into equality, since the added $ demand in New York would increase the $ price while the $ sales in London would reduce its price. Exchange rate arbitrage also occurs in the forward currency markets.

Functions of the Foreign Exchange Market

Basically, the functions of the foreign exchange market can be divided into those facilitating the transfer of goods and services and those facilitating the transfer of financial capital.

Exchange of Goods and Services

When a British exporter receives payment for his product the contract might specify payment in either £ s or the currency of the importer. In either case, the exporter will ultimately require £ in order to pay for the labor and materials employed. The foreign exchange market allows the exporter to easily convert most foreign currencies into £ s.

An individual engaging in international trade might also have use for the forward markets in order to *hedge* on the risk of a change in exchange rates. Suppose the British exporter is to receive a specified number of $s in 90 days. If he waits for payment and converts into £s in the spot market in 90 days, he runs the risk that a lower $ price might wipe out the profits from the export sale. In order to avoid the risk from holding a "long" position in $s, he could sell $s in the 90-day forward market for a guaranteed number of £s. Since no funds change hands until the 90-day contract comes due, the exporter can use the incoming $s to satisfy his commitment on the forward contract. Regardless of the movement in the spot or forward rates, the exporter is assured of a specific inflow of £s in 90 days since the long position in $s which resulted from the export transaction has been cancelled by an equal (balancing) short position in the forward market.

Transfer of Financial Capital

When an investor desires to purchase a foreign financial asset, he uses the foreign exchange market to transfer the funds. As an example, if an Englishman purchases General Motors stock he must first obtain $s for £s in the foreign exchange market.

The phenomenon of *interest rate arbitrage* is responsible for much of the volume in the foreign exchange market. An example of such a transaction is as follows:

Suppose an investor in the United States faces the following interest rates and exchange rates:

90-day bill rate in London:	8%
90-day bill rate in New York:	6%
Spot rate:	$2.40/£
90-day forward rate:	$2.40/£

Let us assume the investor desires the higher bill rate in London, but is unwilling to take the risk that a change in the spot rate 90 days in the future will adversely affect the return. This risk can be avoided by simultaneously purchasing £s in the spot market and selling £s in the 90-day forward market. The £s obtained from the spot purchase are used to obtain an 8 percent bill in London. When the bill matures, these £s will be used to satisfy the forward £ commitment. Thus, the investor has guaranteed himself the higher return since he isn't required to enter the foreign exchange market at any time in the future. One would expect that the additional demand for £s in the spot market would increase the spot £ price while the additional supply of £s forward would reduce the forward price.

The forward foreign exchange market also allows one to take a speculative position in hopes of obtaining a profit from a change in rates. If one expects a decrease in the price of the $ (devaluation), he would obtain a profit by selling $s forward at the current rate and then buying the required $s in the spot market 90 days hence. If the $ is devalued, these $s can be obtained more cheaply in 90 days. The speculator hopes to obtain a profit by purposefully taking a short position in the currency he expects to decrease in price.

Foreign Investment Opportunities

In an earlier example, we demonstrated how the foreign exchange market can allow an investor to obtain a higher return by purchasing a foreign currency-denominated financial asset. While the computation of alternative rates of return is trivial when spot and forward rates are equal, this situation rarely exists in the currency markets. In most cases the effect on actual return from *hedging* in the forward market will be quite substantial. In order to obtain the hedged, or covered, return to a U.S. investor from a foreign currency-denominated financial asset, one must deduct the cost of forward cover (positive or negative) from the asset's stated rate of return.

Computation of forward cover on an annualized basis is quite simple. As an example, on February 28, 1975, the following interest rates and foreign exchange rates were available:

	United States	England
Three-month Treasury bill rate	5.36%	10.02%
Spot rate = $2.4305/£		
Three-month forward rate = $2.3920/£		

The annual cost of forward cover (CFC) for a U.S. investor is computed by:

$$CFC = \left[\frac{2.4305 - 2.3920}{2.4305} \right] 4 = 6.34\%$$

Since the 90-day interest rates are quoted on an annual basis, we must multiply the bracketed term by four in order to annualize the 90-day cost of cover.

Since the £ is selling at a discount in the forward market, the CFC is a positive cost which will decrease the covered rate of return below the stated rate. In the preceding example, the covered equivalent of the 90-day investment in English bills is only 3.68% = 10.02% − 6.34%. Thus, the U.S. Treasury bill actually offers the better return since the cost of forward cover more than compensates for the favorable differential in stated rates.

In the following table we compare the rates of return available on February 28, 1975, for three different maturity bank time deposits in the United States, Canada, and England. The net rates on the foreign deposits assume a covered foreign exchange position. The positive effect on return from forward cover in the Canadian dollar indicates that the Canadian dollar is selling at a premium in the forward markets. Casual inspection of the net rates indicates that the U.S. investor could obtain a significantly higher return on Canadian dollar-denominated time deposits than on U.S. bank time deposits. A similar table can be constructed to allow the investor to compare rates on other foreign currency-denominated financial assets (Treasury bills, commercial paper, etc.) in any country whose currency is broadly traded in the foreign exchange market.

Bank Time Deposits in Local Currency		30 days	90 Days	180 Days
United States	Net	6.25	6.38	6.38
Canada		6.50	6.75	6.75
Forward cover		+ 0.24	+ 0.32	+ 0.36
	Net	6.74	7.07	7.11
United Kingdom		11.63	11.13	11.13
Forward cover		− 6.91	− 6.34	− 5.68
	Net	4.72	4.79	5.45

Appendix C
The Application of
Portfolio Analysis
to the Bond Market

I_N this appendix we present a fairly rigorous demonstration of how techniques of portfolio analysis can be applied to investment decisions for fixed income financial assets. It is our hope that the materials contained in this appendix will serve two different though related purposes. First, we explain the effect of maturity on a bond's riskiness using both a mathematical and a statistical demonstration. Such information should prove helpful in assessing the impact on bond prices and yields from specific phenomena that influence the bond market, such as a new Treasury issue in the three- to five-year maturity range. Secondly, we present a workable method for obtaining optimal bond portfolios from a given term structure of interest rates. The usefulness of such a technique certainly needs no explanation.

While the majority of our presentation is concerned with the selection of portfolios of default-free government bonds, we conclude with a brief discussion of the selection of other fixed income financial assets — municipal and corporate bonds.

The Influence of Maturity on a Bond's Risk

One phenomenon is most important in order to understand the investment opportunities available from different maturity government bonds — the nonlinearity of the risk–maturity relationship. Table 1 lists actual standard deviation in price data for each maturity government bond. These figures were obtained from monthly yield observations during the

**TABLE 1   Risk and Return Data for Government Bonds,
June 1953 to November 1972**

Maturity	σ Return	Mean Return	Mean Coupon
1 month	0	0.278	0.278
3 months	0.146	0.295	0.296
1 year	0.308	0.313	0.324
2 years	0.569	0.317	0.340
3 years	0.777	0.315	0.350
4 years	0.942	0.310	0.358
5 years	1.076	0.304	0.362
10 years	1.414	0.260	0.367
20 years	1.758	0.230	0.363
30 years	1.935	0.215	0.365
S & P 500	3.090	0.991	

period from June 1953 to November 1972. In computing the price data we assumed the bonds to be selling at par value—where coupon is identical to yield. Graphing standard deviation in price against maturity in Figure 1, one is aware of the direct though decreasing effect of maturity on price volatility.

The effect of maturity on a bond's risk (price change) can be attributed to two phenomena: (1) the natural mathematics of the price change–maturity relationship, and (2) the stable relationship between a bond's maturity and the relative size of its yield changes.

One can compute the price of a par bond n-years from maturity by summing the present values of the stream of coupon payments and the payment to be received at maturity.

$$P_n = \sum_{t=1}^{n} \frac{C_t}{(1+R_n)^t} + \frac{A}{(1+R_n)^n} \tag{1}$$

where C = dollar value of coupon payment; A = dollar value of payment at maturity; t = period in which payment is made; R_n = yield to maturity; and n = maturity period.

Yield to maturity is computed by

$$R_n = [(1+R_1)(1+{}_1r_1)(1+{}_2r_1)\ldots(1+{}_{n-1}r_1)]^{1/n} - 1 \tag{2}$$

Where R_1 = current one-year yield, and ${}^iR_1$ = expected (forward) one-year yield i years from the present.

The mathematics of the risk-maturity can be easily demonstrated. First, we substitute $A = {}^{C_t}/_{R_n}$ since we assume the bond is selling at par. Taking differential of equation (1) we obtain

$$dP_n = \left\{ -\left[1 - \frac{1}{(1+R_n)^n} \right] \frac{C_t}{R_n^2} \right\} dr_n. \tag{3}$$

Figure 1. Risk Versus Maturity*

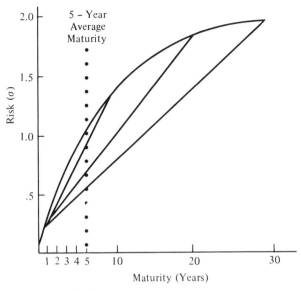

*Data from Table 1.

The direct effect of maturity on price change, for a given change in all yields (*i.e.,* $dR_n = dR$ for all n), can be shown by differentiating $|dP_n|$ with respect to n (assume $C_t = 1$ for simplicity).

$$\frac{d|dP_n|}{dn} = \frac{[\log_e(1 + R_n)]}{(1 + R_n)^n R_n^2}|dR| > 0 \qquad (4)$$

Differentiating a second time with respect to n, we have an explicit measure of the decreasing effect of maturity on price change.

$$\frac{d^2|dP_n|}{dn^2} = \frac{[\log_e(1 + R_n)^2]}{(1 + R_n)^n R_n^2}|dR| < 0 \qquad (5)$$

One could then infer from equations (4) and (5) that, even if all yields were to change by equal amounts, the graph of price change versus maturity would be curvilinear. We have referred to this phenomenon as the natural mathematics of the maturity-price volatility relationship. This phenomenon is demonstrated in the following example: Consider the case where we have two bonds, both selling at par and with a 5 percent yield to maturity. Bond A matures in 5 years and bond B in 10 years. Let us assume that a so-called parallel shift in the yield curve causes all rates to increase by 25 basis points (0.25 percent). While bond B will experience a greater deterioration in price (1.93 percent) than will bond A (1.09 percent), its price change will be less than twice that of A. But, as evidenced by the data in Table 2, yield volatility was found to decrease monotonically with maturity over the period of our study.[1] This greater volatility of short rates further amplifies the nonlinearity of the price change–maturity relationship.

Obtaining Optimal Portfolios from a Given Yield Curve

We demonstrated in Chapter 3 that the risk-pooling benefits from combining assets in a portfolio will be larger, the less-positively correlated are the asset's rates of return. As evidenced in Table 2 (Chapter 3), it is not uncommon for the risk of a two-asset portfolio to be less than the risk of either of the individual assets taken separately.

The risk-pooling benefits from applying portfolio analysis to the government bond market are severly limited by the near-perfect positive correlation between price changes on different maturity bonds (i.e., note the lack of risk-pooling benefits in Table 2 (Chapter 3) for large positive ρs). Nevertheless, the absence of diversification benefits in no way precludes the successful application of portfolio analysis to the government bond market, since we find that the combinations obtained on the efficient frontier offer significantly higher returns than many of the alternative equal risk portfolios.

The near-perfect positive correlation between price changes on different maturity bonds allows for a significant simplification in the selection process. Namely, all possible risk–return combinations from combining two different maturity bonds will plot on a straight line connecting the risk and return of each individual bond. The validity of this statement can be demonstrated quite simply. From equation (6) (Chapter 3), the risk of a two-asset portfolio is given by

$$\sigma p = \sqrt{X_a^2 \sigma_a^2 + X_b^2 \sigma_b^2 + 2X_a X_b \sigma_a \sigma_b \rho_{ab}}.$$

TABLE 2   Yield Volatility Versus Maturity*

Years to Maturity	Mean Absolute Change in Yield
1	0.212179%
2	0.209786
3	0.192564
4	0.180641
5	0.169914
10	0.127692
20	0.101026
30	0.089231%

Source: for yield data, Salomon Brothers, *An Analytical Record of Yields and Yield Spreads,* New York, 1973.

*The mean change in yield is the average of the absolute values of the monthly yield changes over the period May 1973 to November 1972.

---

[1]This relationship is consistent with the generally accepted hypothesis of a less than unitary elasticity of expectations between changes in the current short-term rate and changes in expected (forward) future short rates.

Figure 2. Risk–Return Possibilities from Combining a Single Maturity
Bond with the Riskless Security

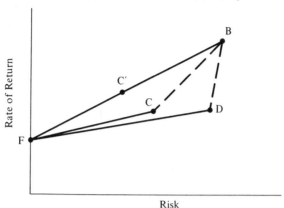

For $\rho_{ab} = 1$,

$$\sigma p = \sqrt{(X_a\sigma_a + X_b\sigma_b)^2} = X_a\sigma_a + X_b\sigma_b. \tag{6}$$

In this form, σ_p is simply a weighted average of the risk of the individual assets.

At this point, it might be instructive to consider portfolios that can be constructed from a given maturity bond and the riskless asset (zero maturity bond). In Figure 2 we plot the risk and return combinations offered by three different maturity bonds (denoted **A, B,** and **C**) and the riskless asset (denoted by **F**). From equation (6) above, we are able to obtain portfolios having risk–return combinations on the line segments $\overline{FA}$, $\overline{FB}$, and $\overline{FC}$ when one of the three maturity bonds is combined in varying proportion with the riskless asset. Linear combinations on $\overline{AB}$, $\overline{AC}$, and $\overline{BC}$ could also be obtained from two-maturity portfolios. Security **B** is said to dominate **A** and **C** since there exists some combination of **B** with the riskless asset which is preferable to **A** or **C**. As an example, the combination of **B** and **F** at **C'** has both a higher expected return and less risk than security **C**.[2] This type of comparison for attainable risk–return combinations from a given yield curve serves as a basis for generating the efficient frontier of government securities.

A commonly used summary measure of an asset's risk–return tradeoff is "return to variability." In the Sharpe model, return to variability is expressed as the ratio

$$V_i = \frac{E_i - E_f}{COV_{im}} \tag{7}$$

---

[2] If the return on **A** or **C** exceeded that of **B,** one would need the additional assumption that investors can borrow at the riskless rate in order to demonstrate the superiority of **B.**

where E_i is the expected return on asset i, E_f is the riskless return: and COV_{im} measures the contribution of asset i to the total nondiversifiable risks in the capital markets. Because of the high correlation between price changes on different maturity bonds, we can replace COV_{im} with σ_i and not alter the *relative* measure of return to variability within the bond market. In this form,

$$Vi' = \frac{E_i - E_f}{\sigma_i} \tag{8}$$

A bond's return to variability is simply the slope of the line segment connecting the risk–return combination (Figure 2) with the riskless asset. Using this means of comparison, asset **B** in Figure 2 is clearly superior.

Transforming the Yield Curve to a Risk–Return Axis

Since risk and maturity are not *linearly* related for government securities, generating an efficient frontier on the conventional return-maturity axis would be unduly complicated. Therefore, the first step in our analysis must be to transform the yield curve to a risk-return axis. The major problem is obtaining satisfactory measures for each bond's expected return and risk. Diagramatically, Figure 3 portrays the transformation that requires one to substitute expected return (E) and risk (σ) measures for each security's yield (R) and maturity (N).

Figure 3. Transformation of a Yield Curve to a Risk–Return Axis

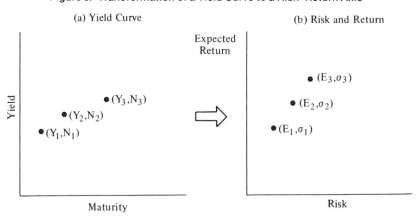

(a) Yield Curve   (b) Risk and Return

The Risk Index

The measure of a bond's risk is taken to be the standard deviation in its monthly price. We feel that this variable best represents the risk in return over the holding period since the other component of return, the cash flow,

TABLE 3   Relative Risk Indices for Each Maturity Government Bond

	3 months	1 year	2 years	3 years	4 years	5 years	10 years	20 years	30 years
1959	0.0552	0.1384	0.2518	0.3597	0.4503	0.5235	0.7925	0.9476	1
1960	0.0562	0.1503	0.2740	0.3590	0.4419	0.5111	0.6427	0.8752	1
1961	0.0500	0.1489	0.2781	0.3609	0.4500	0.5310	0.6759	0.9132	1
1962	0.0543	0.1573	0.2964	0.3719	0.4651	0.5521	0.6823	0.8979	1
1963	0.0556	0.1574	0.2984	0.3692	0.4646	0.5553	0.6866	0.8701	1
1964	0.0560	0.1545	0.3068	0.3779	0.4691	0.5682	0.6638	0.8865	1
1965	0.0471	0.1322	0.3087	0.3632	0.4427	0.5296	0.6266	0.8383	1
1966	0.0669	0.1260	0.2756	0.3373	0.4029	0.4606	0.5997	0.7900	1
1967	0.0592	0.1463	0.3187	0.4515	0.5539	0.6248	0.8384	0.8968	1
1968	0.0409	0.1347	0.2769	0.3965	0.4865	0.5557	0.7546	0.8829	1
1969	0.0371	0.1255	0.2538	0.3663	0.4471	0.5098	0.7047	0.8674	1
1970	0.0401	0.1217	0.2589	0.3778	0.4617	0.5333	0.7242	0.9088	1
1971	0.0413	0.1293	0.2642	0.3827	0.4624	0.5304	0.7177	0.9167	1
1972	0.0459	0.1427	0.2850	0.4115	0.4925	0.5591	0.7589	0.9229	1

is known with certainty. We are able to obtain a series on bond prices by employing historical yield data in conjunction with convential bond tables. Sixty observations (5 years) are used to compute the standard deviation in price for each maturity bond. The risk figures were revised annually by deleting the oldest 12 observations and adding the most recent 12 months of data. Our choice of yearly intervals between revisions in the risk measure is based on the practical limitations of a strategy requiring reestimation on a monthly basis and the relative insensitivity of the risk measures to the replacement of a single observation in the data base.

Table 3 contains the risk indices of each maturity bond for each of 14 consecutive years, 1959–1973. The risk index is obtained by dividing a given maturity's σ in price by the σ in price of the riskiest security — the 30-year par bond; it is a measure of the risk of each bond relative to the maximum attainable risk in the government bond market. Since our goal in this section is to obtain an efficient frontier from the available menu of governmental securities, we can employ the risk index in our analysis.

Even in the event that the absolute riskiness of the bond market were to change, we assume that there would be no change in the relative comparisons between different maturity bonds. That is, if one maturity dominates another in terms of its ratio of "excess return" to its risk index, it will dominate when the risk index is replaced by the absolute risk measure (*i.e.*, standard deviation).

The Expected Return

It is assumed that all bonds are available at par with yield to maturity equal to coupon.[3] The most obvious candidate for a bond's expected return is simply its yield. The shortcoming of using yield for expected return is that it precludes the quantification of nonzero expected price changes when generating the efficient frontier. For this reason, we suggest a method whereby such expectations can be captured in the estimate of each bond's expected return.

The Efficient Frontier

The first step in obtaining the efficient frontier of default-free bonds is to transform the yield curve to a risk-yield axis. As indicated earlier, we can obtain risk measures for default-free bonds simply from historical yield observations for each maturity. This transformation can be accomplished by substituting each maturity's relative risk index for its maturity. As an example, we examine the yield curve which existed in January 1964. Table 4 lists purchase yields and relative risk indices for each of the 10 maturity government bonds. As a reminder, the risk measures were computed using

---

[3]A par bond is one which is currently selling at a price where yield and coupon are identical. That is, a par bond with a 6 percent yield produces a $6 cash flow per $100 of valuation.

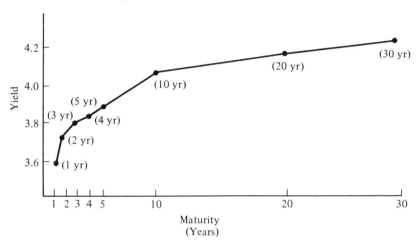

Figure 4. The Yield Curve—January 1, 1964*

*Data from Table 4.

monthly price change information from the previous five-year period (1958-1963). The risk index for the one-month bond is taken to be zero since we assume a one-month investment period. The yield curve and its transformation to a risk-yield axis are graphed in Figures 4 and 5, respectively.

If the investor holds no specific expectations for yield changes during the next month, purchase yield is the appropriate measure for expected annual rate of return. Without systematic expectations for yield changes,

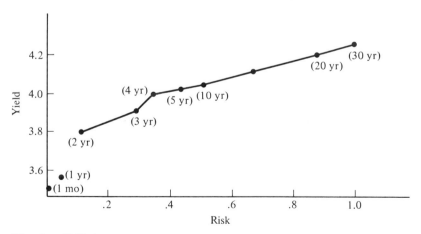

Figure 5. The Yield-Risk Curve—January 1, 1964*

*Data from Table 4.

TABLE 4   Yields and Risk Indices for January 1, 1964

Maturity	Yield*	Risk Index
1 month	3.54%	o
3 months	3.58	0.0560
1 year	3.80	0.1545
2 years	3.94	0.3068
3 years	4.00	0.3779
4 years	4.05	0.4691
5 years	4.08	0.5682
10 years	4.13	0.6638
20 years	4.17	0.8865
30 years	4.21%	1.0

*Par bonds.

the expected value of the capital gain (or loss) component of return is zero for every maturity bond. Note that this assumption is not equivalent to a zero expected yield change. While yields might always be expected to change, we are considering the case where the investor has no forecast for such changes. In this situation, purchase yields and risk indices are sufficient information for identifying the set of optimal portfolio combinations. As demonstrated earlier, the near-perfect positive correlation between price changes on different maturity government bonds allows one to ignore any pooling of risk effects when computing a portfolio's risk. Those combinations of risk and return attainable for a two-security portfolio are computed as a weighted average of each bond's respective values for risk and return. The risk and return combinations for such portfolios will plot on the line segment connecting the two bonds' risk and return. Therefore, the efficient frontier is simply the upper boundary of this set of connecting line

Figure 6. The Efficient Frontier—January 1, 1964*

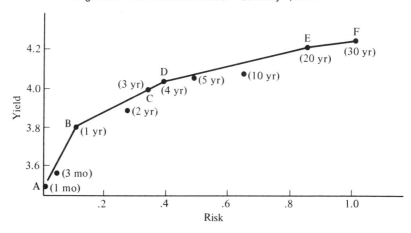

*Data from Table 4.

segments. The broken line $\overline{AB}$ . . . $\overline{F}$ in Figure 6 is just such a frontier for January 1964. Note that several different maturity bonds never appear in efficient portfolios since they fail to offer a high enough return to compensate investors for their risk exposure.

Incorporating Yield Forecasts (Price Changes) into the Efficient Frontier

The procedure for obtaining an efficient frontier is slightly more complicated when investors have specific nonzero expectations for yield changes during the investment period. In this situation, the capital gain component of return has a nonzero expected value. We recognize two types of specific interest rate forecasts. First, one might expect a general disturbance to the bond market that would cause rates to increase or decrease along the entire term structure in a manner consistent with historical yield volatility. That is, the expected yield changes are consistent with the observed patterns of yield volatility to decrease monotonically with maturity (Table 2). Such expectations might be attributable to a general tightening of monetary policy and credit availability. A second type of yield forecast would allow for yield expectations that are not consistent with the long-run tendency of yield volatility to decrease with maturity. Such expectations might result from supply and demand pressures expected to operate within a maturity range on the yield curve (segmentation effects). In either case, generating the efficient frontier requires only one additional piece of information for each bond—the vector of expected price changes during the investment period. The risk index continues to serve as a reasonable measure of each bond's relative risk. Since the risk index measures the dispersion in a given bond's *unexpected* price change, its magnitude should be independent of the *expected* price change.

When the investor anticipates a general disturbance to the bond market that will affect rates along the entire term structure, he need only forecast the expected yield change for a single maturity bond. This forecast can then be employed to obtain both expected price change and expected returns on each maturity bond. We are able to obtain the entire vector of expected price changes from a single yield forecast since our relative risk index ranks a bond on the basis of its long-run price responsiveness; therefore, if we expect a $1 increase in price on a bond with an index of 0.2, we would expect a $2 increase in the price of a bond with an index of 0.4. Note that the linearity of the expected price change–risk relationship results from the particular nature of the yield forecasts.

We again employ the actual yield and risk measures for January 1964, in order to demonstrate the method for generating an efficient frontier. Assume a 5-basis-point (0.05 percent) decrease in the one-year yield is forecast for the next month. From an initial rate of 3.80 percent this yield change would lead to a 0.05 percent increase in price. We obtain this value from standard yield tables. The predicted price change for a given maturity bond can then be obtained by multiplying the predicted price change on the one-year bond by the ratio of the bond's risk index to that of the one-year bond. As an example, the predicted price change for the 10-year bond is computed as

$$\Delta p_{10} = 0.05\% \left(\frac{0.6638}{0.1545} \right) = 0.215\%. \tag{9}$$

The vector of each bond's expected price change is given in Table 5. Each bond's expected annual rate of return over the holding period is obtained by summing its yield to maturity and its expected annual rate of price change. The latter is simply the predicted monthly change (percent) multiplied by 12.

TABLE 5   The Forecasted Price Change for Each Maturity Bond When a 5-Basis-Point Fall in the One-year Yield Is Expected

Maturity	Forecasted Price Change (in basis points)
1 month	0
3 months	+ 1.8
1 year	+ 5.0
2 years	+ 9.9
3 years	+ 12.1
4 years	+ 15.2
5 years	+ 18.4
10 years	+ 21.5
20 years	+ 28.7
30 years	+ 32.4

Note: The fact tht a 5-basis-point yield change leads to a 5-basis-point price change on the one-year bond is coincidental.

We are able to generate an efficient frontier quite easily even when one expects segmentation changes in interest rates. Again, one need only modify the vector of expected returns since the risk indices serve as a reasonable approximation for the risk of unexpected price changes. Instead of a forecast for one bond's expected change in yield, we require a forecast of each maturity's expected change in yield during the investment period. As in the previous example, a forecast for a given bond's yield change allows one to compute expected price change. The expected return vector is obtained by summing each bond's yield and its annual rate of price change. Graphically, this procedure is portrayed in Figure 7. The efficient frontier is obtained as before.

Efficient Portfolios of Municipal and Corporate Bonds

The application of portfolio analysis to the municipal and corporate bond markets indicates an added dimension over the government's market. One must account for the existence of two different types of risks.

Figure 7. Generating the Efficient Frontier When the Investor Holds a
Specific Forecast of Interest Rate Movements

$$\begin{bmatrix} \text{Current} \\ \text{Yields} \end{bmatrix} + \begin{bmatrix} \text{Forecasted} \\ \text{Yields} \end{bmatrix} = \begin{bmatrix} \text{Forecasted} \\ \text{Price Changes} \end{bmatrix}$$

$$\begin{bmatrix} \text{Current} \\ \text{Yields} \end{bmatrix} + \begin{bmatrix} \text{Forecasted} \\ \text{Price Changes} \end{bmatrix} = \begin{bmatrix} \text{Expected} \\ \text{Returns} \end{bmatrix}$$

As in the government bond market, interest rate risk results from uncertainty as to future yield changes. The method of quantifying this component of risk for municipal and corporate bonds is identical to that employed in the government market. Namely, to develop relative risk indices from historical observations on interest rate movements. Quantifying default risk is difficult for two reasons: defaults occur so rarely that one is unable to obtain statistically stable estimates of such probabilities, and default probabilities might change rapidly in response to macroeconomic phenomena.

The practice of "rating" municipal and corporate bonds is designed to supply investors with a rough approximation of the bond's relative exposure to default. In the municipal market, bonds are typically rated on two criteria: the repayment potential of the issuing agent, and the type of revenue available for repayment purposes. Rating agencies express the repayment potential of a municipal bond issue on the following scale: AA, A, BAA, etc.; where AA is the least risky issue. In rating a municipal issue, a major indication of repayment potential is the ratio of interest commitments to the total tax revenue. A municipality with a relatively small portion of its total revenue promised for debt payments would typically receive a high rating based on the sources of revenue available for interest payments. A general obligation or "GO" rating indicates that all sources of the revenue are available for repayment purposes, while a "revenue" or "REV" rated bond must rely only on the revenue generated from a particular source for repayment. Obviously, the GO rating indicates a smaller default probability than a REV bond.

The importance of quantifying both default and interest rate risk can be demonstrated quite simply. Suppose one were to generate two portfolios with equal interest rate risks but with a significant disparity in bond ratings. If the portfolio with the higher yield is heavily weighted in low-rated bonds, one would be unable to ascertain which portfolio is preferable since the higher-risk portfolio should offer a higher expected return. Therefore, any valid portfolio selection model must consider both interest rate and default risks.

For a government bond, actual return and yield to maturity will differ only if market rates of interest change during the investment period. If one anticipates no specific change in rates, yield to maturity can serve as a reasonable estimate of expected return. (This point has been developed earlier in Chapter 3.) On the other hand, the return from a municipal bond can differ from its yield even during a period in which the market interest rate on similar securities remained unchanged. If the probability of default were to increase, the market would force a lower price and, therefore, a higher yield to maturity. In such a situation the required increase in yield would exceed the increase in expected return since the former includes a default premium. Therefore, yield to maturity overestimates the expected return when the bond is subject to default risk. For this reason we are unable to employ yields in order to measure the additional "excess return" accompanying the added default risk.

We can obtain relative risk indices for municipal bonds by employing the identical procedure used for the government security market. Therefore, the specific numerical results are not presented in this book. From historical yield observations on various maturity, prime-grade (highest rated) municipal bonds we generate a series of prices and price changes. We obtain the relative risk indices by forming the ratio of each maturity bond's standard deviation in price to that of the longest maturity bond. This series of risk indices by maturity will also serve as a measure of the relative interest rate risk for bonds having different default ratings.

Selected References:

Yawitz, Jess; Hempel, George; and Marshall, William. "Average Maturity as a Risk Proxy in Investment Decisions." *Journal of Finance* 30:2, May 1975.

_____, "Measuring Interest Rate Risk in Government Bond Portfolios." *Journal of Portfolio Management,* April 1976.

———, "A Risk-Return Approach to the Selection of Optimal Government Bond Portfolios," *Financial Management* (forthcoming).

Yawitz, Jess. "The Relative Importance of Duration and Yield Volatility on Bond Price Volatility." *Journal of Money, Credit, and Banking,* February 1977.

Index

Capital (cont.)

See also Funds

Capital (reserve) decisions to analyze asset, liability and, 38-46

example of savings and loan associations, 45-46

illustrative two-asset (or two-liability) portfolio, 39-40

portfolio selection models of Markowitz and Sharpe, 42-45

schematic depiction of Markowitz calculation (figure), 43

standard deviation in return for two-asset portfolio (table), 41

Capital (reserve) management, described, 26-27

Capital notes, defined, 115

Captive sales finance companies, 212

Casualty insurance, 167

Certificates of deposit

large, 98

small-denomination, 97-98

Closed-end investment companies, 194-95

Commercial banking system, supervision of principal relationship (figure), 72

Commercial banks

applying wealth-maximization mode of banking decisions of, 84-88

alternative decisions (table), 85

assumptions (table), 84

capital of, 114-20

after-tax earnings on capital for all insured (1959-1975; figure), 93

capital accounts of insured commercial banks (table), 117

conventional capital ratios for insured (1935-1975; figure), 95

growth in assets, deposits and capital (1950-1975; table), 118

cash assets and U.S. government securities to total depostis (1923-1975; figure), 94

changes in (1930s), 62-63

under FDIC, 78-79

financial management of, 82-124

bank decisions in differing environments, 89-96

incremental nature of management decisions, 88-89

Commercial banks (cont.)

financial management of (cont.)

regulatory characteristics affecting financial decisions, 82-83

in formative years (1781-1860), 49-51

future of, 219

effects of future changes, 224

growth of

1960s, 67

1975, 68

Hunt Commission and, 222-23

investments by, 107-14

annual maturity distribution of a 7-year spaced portfolio (figure), 111

earnings effect of a municipal bond switch (table), 113

illustrative barbell portfolio (figure), 111

linear programming and wealth-maximization in, 120-23

number and deposits of all (December 1974; table), 77

percentages of assets and liabilities of different-sized (end of 1974; table), 91

policies consistent with wealth-maximization in, 96-120

attracting funds, 96-99

capital, *see* Commercial banks — capital of

investments, *see* Commercial banks — investments by

lending, 102-7

liquidity, 99-102

in postwar years (1946-1960), 64-65

principal assets and liabilities of all (table), 90

rates of return on total assets of (1951-1975; figure), 151

revenues, expenses and earnings as percentages of assets for all (1959-1975; figure), 92

time and savings accounts in (1971-1974; table), 154

Commercial finance companies, 213

Common equity, as bank capital, 116

Common stock

as bank capital, 116

defined, 33